T0348098

'A pleasure to read a psychoanalyst who is also an artist exploring creativity in therapy, art, music, her own life and development. More therapists than realized are artists and nourish profound interweaving between disciplines. This book is an explicit portrayal of such a journey, an exploration and affirmation of the vicissitudes and rewards of creative life and work.'—**Michael Eigen, Ph.D.**, National Psychological Association for Psychoanalysis

'This remarkable book about creativity, the artistic process, and the psychoanalytic treatment of creative individuals is the only one that I know of written by an artist who is also a psychoanalyst capable of explaining complex psychoanalytic concepts in terms understandable to the general public. From this dual perspective, Dr. Safán-Gerard is able to truly understand the dilemmas confronting those of us who struggle with artistic expression and to provide a skilful melding of research, clinical material and personal vignettes. In an incisive and insightful way, she covers such issues as the role of destructiveness and reparation in the creative process, the ability to hold onto the anxiety provoking experience of "not knowing", the essential dialogue with the artistic object, the alternation of spontaneous, "chaotic" periods of expression with reflective control, the development of passion and absorption, and the origins of creative block. For all of these situations, Dr. Safán-Gerard provides a cogent and coherent psychoanalytic framework from which to understand our creative patients and the artist within ourselves.'—**Beverly Feinstein, M.D., Ph.D.**, UCLA Clinical Faculty, Past President of Southern California Psychiatric Society, Past President of New Center for Psychoanalysis; Artist

'Much has been written by psychoanalysts about painting and creativity, and some writing has come from painters about psychoanalysis; but it is indeed rare for someone who is both painter and psychoanalyst to write with dexterity and authority in both fields. Here Desy Safán-Gerard accomplishes that and all that might be required to come from such a synthetic project. Aesthetics is about beauty from everyday materials, and this book wants to understand the balance between craft, accident, order and inspiration. It is a remarkable exploration of the resonance and harmonies in making a life and making things. Art is perhaps a technology of the emotions, of our experience with each other, and our world. But Desy Safán-Gerard also has the other string to her bow, another 'technology'-that of psychoanalysis. This book, a long reflection on her life's journey, welds together these two profound approaches to understanding the human gift for creativity as it is pitted in combat against all the opposing forces of chaos. Generously illustrated with her painting, the book is her personal landscape of talent, achievements, erudition and straight human passion.'—**Robert. D. Hinshelwood**, Fellow, British Psychoanalytical Society; former Director, Cassel Hospital; Emeritus Professor, University of Essex

'The author closes this marvellous collection of papers with comments on her work 'translating' a model's movements on to paper/canvas in response to a piece of music:

"There is a special thrill when I feel that the audience is caught up with what I am doing. We are all experiencing the same response to the emergence of beauty through the music, the model and the coloured lines on the wet paper. It is magic again! The same magic of a psychoanalytic session when an interpretation hits the mark, the patient feels understood in a profound way and the analyst is moved by the depth of feelings experienced in response to the patient." (p. 221)

Here, as quite often in her book, Desy Safán-Gerard echoes Marion Milner as she shows us her paintings taking off 'in their own direction', underlining the role of accident, and of dream; and stressing the influence of Milner's *On Not Being Able to Paint*, a seminal text on the creative process foregrounding the role of mistakes, accidents, creative destructiveness, fears of madness and, above all, championing the role of the unconscious in all creative life. I think Milner would have been gratified by the homage paid her in chapter 14 on 'Destructiveness and reparation: a retrospective' and, also, her implicit influence in 'From Mistake to Mistake: the Creative Process in Four Large Paintings' with its important aim of 'debunk[ing] the negative connotations attached to mistakes.' Here, as elsewhere in Safán-Gerard's book, the reader is well-served by the accompanying illustrations, colour plates of the works in question.

In honouring Marion Milner, Desy Safán-Gerard highlights her own strengths in this fascinating compilation of many of her most striking and innovative papers and lectures over a 40-year long and distinguished career as artist, musician and psychoanalyst in the United States, Europe and South America. One of the great pleasures of the book is her generous sharing of her polymathic talents, in themselves sufficient to attract a diverse audience to *Chaos and Control* – a text relevant to analysts/therapists, artists and all who are engaged with creative work or working with creative people. (As a psychotherapist who works with people with writers' block I have found it of the most illuminating help, focusing as it does on the creative process and on the particular needs of creative patients in treatment).'—**Emma Letley**, psychoanalytic psychotherapist, biographer of Marion Milner

'Desy Safán-Gerard's work is highly complex and operates in a variety of levels anticipating complex reactions. Her primary medium is light and not volume; her paintings appear to emanate an internal light that suffuses pictorial space and imagery. There is in all of her work a well-earned sense of effortlessness. Images simply appear, often in powerful, rudimentary forms. These images probe the psyche in profound ways, mirroring conscious and unconscious experience for us.

Safán-Gerard's paintings bring a special dimension to the worlds of fantasy and form. The territory her work engages is of great interest at the present time to young artists working at the edge of possibility. In a similar way, the work of Roberto Matta, another Chilean, is now receiving considerable attention for the plasticity of its visual elements and the manner in which he develops its psychology.

I have always liked the idea that painting is about the conversion of human experience into the experience of the paint. As you view the work of Desy Safán-Gerard you will find yourself converting paint back into a profoundly human experience.'—**Roland Reiss**, Benezet Professor of the Arts and Humanities, Emeritus, Claremont Graduate University

'The reader rides waves of creative ideas in this book, rising and falling along with several artists including the author. The valuable explanation and exploration of what must be undertaken to bring something, or someone, separate from oneself, into being applies to artistic creative effort and to psychoanalysis. This fascinating and inspiring work will help artists to engage in psychoanalysis, and psychoanalysts to better understand artists. As a bonus, the plates alone are worth the price of the book.'—**Leigh Tobias**, Ph.D., FIPA, Training and Supervising Analyst and President, Psychoanalytic Center of California

'Desy Safán-Gerard has gifted us with an important book. It invokes, stimulates, and provokes many dimensions and levels of response for the participating reader of her words and observer of her photographed art. Fitting Susan Langer's definition of art as a creation with evocative power, the book is itself a work of art.

A central theme is the need to be able to destroy, even ruthlessly eliminate, some of the work, making space in the resulting chaos for new creativity. Is that utter destructiveness always necessary? Dr. Safán-Gerard's friend, the composer Lucky Choi, also notes the difficult task of setting aside a "child" whose creation turned out to be a dead end, but also notes that "the work may be saved and modified for another piece, some day." I am reminded of Jeffrey Kahane's scholarly discussion of Beethoven's 9th Symphony before conducing it with the Los Angeles Chamber Orchestra and Los Angeles Master Chorale. The beautiful *Ode to Joy* theme appeared in different contexts in more than one earlier work, before the "saved child" comes forth, in full glory, in the last movement of the 9th.

Another stimulated and fruitful path of thought for this reader, a developmentally-based psychologist with much family therapy clinical experience: Is the intense painful conflict between the adolescents and their parents, observed in so many families (but not universally), producing the chaotic interpersonal environment necessary to give the parents and child space to allow the child to discover and establish his or her own identity? Perhaps this also gives the parents an opportunity to re-evaluate their own parental patterns. I am reminded of Irving Torgoff's helpful research distinguishing between achievement-inducing and independence-granting parental styles. Safán-Gerard quotes Sigmund Freud's advice to Joan Rivière in response to one of her ideas. His advice is also relevant to the parental style of independence-granting: "Write it down…make something of it…outside of you, that is: give it an existence outside of you." Dr. Safán-Gerard's frequent examples of attending to how the paints flow, how relationships between created objects or colors please or frustrate, how even accidents point to new paths, shows her sensitivity to the artworks' existence outside of herself.

There are many other significant paths of self-enriching explorations this reader was stimulated to follow when reading Desy Safán-Gerard's book. I can only urge others to seek out the rich, personal voyage that reading this book will encourage them to take.'—**Zanwil Sperber, Ph.D.**, Clinical Professor of Psychology, University of California, Retired; Chief Psychologist, Department of Psychiatry, Cedars-Sinai Medical Center, Los Angeles, Retired.

CHAOS AND CONTROL

CHAOS AND CONTROL
A Psychoanalytic Perspective on
Unfolding Creative Minds

Desy Safán-Gerard

Routledge
Taylor & Francis Group

LONDON AND NEW YORK

First published 2018
by Routledge
4 Park Square, Milton Park, Abingdon, Oxon OX14 4RN
605 Third Avenue, New York, NY 10017

First issued in paperback 2023

Routledge is an imprint of the Taylor & Francis Group, an informa business

© 2018 Desy Safán-Gerard

The right of Desy Safán-Gerard to be identified as author of this work has been asserted by her in accordance with sections 77 and 78 of the Copyright, Designs and Patents Act 1988.

All rights reserved. No part of this book may be reprinted or reproduced or utilised in any form or by any electronic, mechanical, or other means, now known or hereafter invented, including photocopying and recording, or in any information storage or retrieval system, without permission in writing from the publishers.

Trademark notice: Product or corporate names may be trademarks or registered trademarks, and are used only for identification and explanation without intent to infringe.

British Library Cataloguing-in-Publication Data
A catalogue record for this book is available from the British Library

Library of Congress Cataloging-in-Publication Data
A catalog record has been requested for this book

ISBN: 978-1-03-257041-9 (pbk)
ISBN: 978-1-78220-294-3 (hbk)

DOI: 10.4324/9780429452895

Typeset in Palatino LT Std
by Medlar Publishing Solutions Pvt Ltd, India

Publisher's Note
The publisher has gone to great lengths to ensure the quality of this reprint but points out that some imperfections in the original copies may be apparent.

CONTENTS

ix

PART II: MY OWN DEVELOPMENT

DEDICATION

This book is dedicated to Harold B. Gerard my husband and colleague of thirty-four years, a renowned professor of social psychology at the University of California (UCLA) in Los Angeles, and well-known researcher.

A brilliant and inquisitive mind, Hal entered psychoanalytic training at age fifty-seven and became a practicing psychoanalyst within a few years. Continuing his active teaching and research career at UCLA, his last groundbreaking research study dealt with the determinants of unconscious phantasy.

While missing him throughout my work on this book, I believe he would have been eager to share this experience with me. Once more, I would have been the happy recipient of his wisdom.

PREFACE TO "CHAOS AND CONTROL"

The present book presents an unusual, in fact, extraordinary and profound self-reflection of a painter whose reproductions from her beautiful work are included in this volume, and the penetrating analysis of the vicissitudes of creativity as a fundamental psychological process of the artist, by a distinguished psychoanalyst. Both of these perspectives are represented by the same person, the author, Desy Safán-Gerard, a committed, successful painter and psychoanalyst. In a deeply honest, clear and convincing narrative Safán-Gerard describes the vicissitudes of the creative process, its obstacles, uncertainties, and provocative assertion, failure and success, and the moments of triumphant emergence of the artistic product.

"Chaos and Control" starts out stressing the importance of destructiveness at the origin of the artistic creation. The creative artist experiences the initial need to express a passionate conviction, an internal reality often difficult to clarify to herself, in an act of faith, by means of an expressive form that conveys its intentionality to the viewer, the recipient in the external world. The artist's talent resides in the dominion of the technical elements of his or her particular art. Her major risk is that the very special talent of the artist, the perfection of her technical skills, not only conveys the deep reality of her internal experience, but also may constrict the free expression of that reality. The destructive "sweeping clean" of the perceptive field of the nascent work of art, the equivalence of the artist's necessary attitude with that of the psychoanalyst entering a session "without memory or desire," creates an open space for the unexpected and unimaginable. It implies the destructiveness of a "negative availability."

And then comes the "accident." The author describes the importance of tolerating the casual, unexpected, by chance perceived configuration in nature or in the material as it is employed in the artist's work, an external, capricious form or accident, an external configuration that stimulates the crystallization of the essential emotional fantasy world of the artist in a creative transformation of this "accident" into the kernel of the new work. The ambiguity of the accident becomes the certainty of the structure of the artistic product.

In her creative work, the artist struggles with her own, internal, unconscious conflicts, and attempts to reach a synthesis in the universal war between the forces of love and hatred, between Eros and destructiveness, the ultimate source of the pressure for a creative solution in the work of art. Desy Safán-Gerard illustrates the conflict between her emotional impulses and her efforts at a rational organization of their presentation in the dialectic between background color and linear design. From a broader perspective, one may differentiate the specific content of the work of art from the particular style or formal elements that express this content. Both form and content convey conscious and unconscious communications that link the personal meanings and conflicts of the artist with the universal meanings and conflicts that the successful work of art conveys to the recipient.

The creative artist learns about herself, as the deeper, unconscious meanings of the work of art are revealed in the process and the resulting product of the artistic creation. The author conveys the ongoing oscillations between "knowing" and "not knowing" as the work evolves through the successive phases of perception, elaboration, expression, and evaluation. Artistic creativity, Desy Safán-Gerard convincingly argues, is a dangerous process for the artist. It confronts her with omnipotent fantasies and "impasses," as such fantasies are dismantled in the unavoidable crises of the elaboration of the artistic work. The artist is faced with her own destructiveness, narcissistic fantasies and aspiration. In overcoming these painful experiences, the activation of paranoid-schizoid fantasies is worked through, and the integrative processes of the depressive position, the reparative function of the artistic creation may take over. The tolerance of making mistakes, of "fusion and confusion" in the repetitive, ruthless demolition and reconstruction of the work reflect the artist's trusting the creative effects of her unconscious guiding forces.

Throughout comparative analyses of the psychological processes involved in artistic creativity and in psychoanalytic explanation, the author demonstrates striking parallelism of these domains of exploring the human mind. She illustrates the creative implication of regressive processes, on the one hand, in the relationship of artist and viewer, and, on the other, in the psychoanalytic relationship between patient and analyst.

This book should be of greatest interest to lovers of art as well as to all psychoanalytically oriented mental health professionals. It opens new views to the understanding of artistic creativity, and to potential sources of its inhibition.

Otto Kernberg, MD

ACKNOWLEDGEMENTS

This book has been enriched by the many questions and suggestions from colleagues, artists, friends, and family, who responded so generously to my developing chapters.

Special thanks go to colleagues Gene Lichtenstein for his initial focusing guidance, and Morris Eagle for his valuable input on chapter six. Thank you to the most inspiring supervisors during my psychoanalytic training: Dr Albert Mason in Los Angeles and Dr Michael Feldman, who supervised me via telephone from London.

My enormous gratitude goes to my gifted composer-friends Jane Brockman and Lucky Choi, as they were the most passionately engaged in the writing of this book. I would like to mention the help of my artist friends Ruth Weisberg; Marion Milner's biographer, Emma Letley; and a most inspiring artist and author, Meg Harris Williams.

I thank my daughter, Denise, her husband Randy; my son, Mauricio and his wife Vivian; my three granddaughters, Lauren, Jessica, and Hannah; and my step-daughter, Sarah, for their never ending support, encouragement, and love.

Against his wishes, I need to acknowledge the special involvement of Dr Henri Hodara, for his valuable and critical comments on many of the chapters. I also shouldn't forget to mention Susan Hodara, author and art writer, whose amazing writing skills encouraged my own.

But most of all, this book would not have been possible without the steady help and sustenance from my able assistant, Cindy Cronk Vukovic. Computer-savvy and an artist herself, she has worked on the book relentlessly from the beginning. I cannot imagine a better collaborator for this project.

Thanks to the Staatsbibliothek zu Berlin and Art Resource, NY, for the image of Beethoven's musical sketch for his "Fidelio" opera, second act of the vocal quartet No. 15 *Er sterbe*, 1805. Photo Credit: bpk Bildagentur/Staatsbibliothek zu Berlin, Stiftung Preussischer Kulturbesitz, Berlin, Germany/Art Resource, NY. I need to offer a special thank you to Dr Alan Gosman, associate chair of the Department of Music at the University of Arkansas, for his generous assistance in helping me locate the Beethoven sketch used in chapter one. He in turn was greatly helped by Julia Ronge from the Beethoven-Haus in Bonn, Germany. Dr Gosman is the coauthor of a most beautiful and magical critical edition of *Beethoven's "Eroica" Sketchbook*.

I also thank the Estate of Norman Mailer for use of excerpts from *Selected Letters of Norman Mailer*, Copyright © 1953 by Norman Mailer, currently collected in *SELECTED LETTERS*. Copyright © 2014 by the Estate of Norman Mailer, used by permission of The Wylie Agency LLC.

Special thanks go to the Matisse family for the use of the twenty-two photographs in process of *Large Reclining Nude*. © 2017 Succession H. Matisse/Artists Rights Society (ARS), New York; as well as the Baltimore Museum of Art for the photographs of *Large Reclining Nude* by Henri Matisse in process, states 1–22, May 3–October 30, 1935—Dr Claribel and Etta Cone Papers, Archives and Manuscripts Collections, The Baltimore Museum of Art (CP30.6.1–22).

ABOUT THE AUTHOR

Desy Safán-Gerard is both a psychoanalyst and a painter. Born in Chile, she attended the University of Chile in Santiago where she earned a degree in psychology. Early in her career she created a research program at the Faculty of Music of the University of Chile. In that capacity, she developed tests of musical talent as well as helping students with their performance anxiety and relationships with family and faculty.

She won a Fulbright scholarship to carry on graduate studies in psychology at the University of California, Berkeley. Her main interest in and love of music led her to a Master's thesis on the "Personality correlates of musical taste". After earning a Ph.D. in clinical psychology from the University of California, Los Angeles, she taught and carried out research on creativity at the California Institute of the Arts (CAL ARTS) in Los Angeles. She subsequently pursued psychoanalytic training at the Psychoanalytic Center of California (PCC), where she is currently a supervising and training analyst.

Parallel commitments to art and psychoanalysis have been the focus of Dr Safán-Gerard's life. Her psychoanalytic practice has centred on working with creative patients from a variety of fields. She has published papers in several journals such as *Psychoanalytic Review*, *International Journal of Group Psychotherapy*, and *Journal of Melanie Klein and*

Object Relations, and given talks at many psychoanalytic conferences in the United States and abroad. Some of the chapters of this book are a direct reflection of these conference presentations and publications.

Ever since she began painting, her dual life as psychoanalyst and artist has been anchored in her love of music. She has translated music into the visual realm with performances whereby a nude model moves to the music of contemporary composers while she paints with both hands. Her performances have been staged in both Paris and Los Angeles.

Safán-Gerard has shown her artwork in Los Angeles, Santiago, Stuttgart, New York, Paris and at the Museum of Latin American Art (MOLAA) in Long Beach, CA, where two of her paintings are part of their permanent collection. Describing her work, she has written, "By engaging in constant experimentation, I create a play of destructive and loving forces that permeate all of my paintings."

INTRODUCTION

What do I say to patients trying to create? Suspend your judgement. Let yourself draw from yourself, no matter how crazy, unconnected, or disjointed. Don't judge, just do. You are simply a helper in something that does not belong to you, an adjunct in a process that has a life of its own. Let IT be the one to guide you!

Only then can you marvel at what happens and now you can enhance that marvellous beginning with more, and more, and more of the same. Don't stop to judge, not yet. Let it run by itself some more. This is not you, not yet. It is something foreign that came out of you and needs to be tended to; more tending, more development without thinking of you, but all the time responding to IT. Let it govern what you do and just follow, follow, follow, without concern for yourself, without stopping to judge and analyse. That will happen later, much later.

My main objective for this book is to liberate creativity, more so than sharing the notions acquired over the years of trying to understand it or my own path. Both art and psychoanalysis are ways to tap into and support the richness of one's inner life. In over thirty years as a practising psychologist and psychoanalyst, I have worked with creative patients both individually and in groups where my idiosyncratic ideas on the treatment of the creative patient first surfaced and developed.

This book is divided into two parts. Part One describes the difference between talent and creativity, the common biases and pitfalls in the analysis and therapy of creative people, the nature of creative blocks, passion and its absence, and the problem of being able to exercise one's freedom. Other themes in the first part of this book are the special needs of creative patients and the common problems and solutions arising in their therapy.

Part Two describes the history of my own creative path and process. "The evolution of a painting" represents an instance of self-exploration where I kept a diary of dreams and thoughts during the four months it took to complete a large abstract painting. "Love and hate in the creative process" resulted from my diary of ongoing reactions as a series of paintings developed. The role of chaos and subsequent control, the special significance of mistakes to develop one's work, and the importance of music and painting in my life are all autobiographical accounts of my relationship to art and psychoanalysis.

It is my hope that this book will inspire therapists and analysts working with creative patients, creative readers in all fields, artists considering an analysis, and those who hesitate in considering themselves creative.

PART I

THEORIES, CONDITIONS, AND OBSTACLES

CHAPTER ONE

Chaos and control in the creative process

A book on creativity should pay special tribute to the life force that lies at the root of any creative act. Thus the reader may be surprised that this first chapter begins with the seminal role of destructiveness in creativity, a recurring theme in the various chapters of this book.

The tumult and chaos of one of Beethoven's surviving sketches plunges us into an empathic turmoil. Trying to sort through the messy surface, erasures and frantically crossed out notes one cannot avoid feeling the composer's anguish and frustration as he struggled in his search, not knowing yet what he was looking for. This is one of Beethoven's surviving sketches from the finale of his only opera *Fidelio* (Figure 1.1), for which he wrote four overtures, before settling on the last one. These sketches, most beautiful on their own, constitute the basis for an understanding of his creative process and its ongoing destructiveness, an understanding that can be extended beyond Beethoven to represent the basis of the creative process in most fields.

At a certain stage during creative work destruction becomes as necessary as the ensuing reconstruction and control of its elements. From my photographic documentation of abstract paintings in progress, I have often been struck by the alternation of chaos and control.

Figure 1.1. Beethoven's musical sketch for the sixth and three following measures before the trumpet signal in his *Fidelio* Opera, second act of the vocal quartet No. 15 *Er sterbe*, 1805. Photo credit: bpk Bildagentur/ Staatsbibliothek zu Berlin, Stiftung Preussischer Kulturbesitz, Berlin, Germany/Art Resource, NY.

The destruction of the painting structure represented by a chaotic image is typically followed by an organised image indicating that its elements are now under control. The destruction the artist engages in is a response to something not working out in the work when things seem to go awry. Such destruction restores the dialogue with the work in progress whereby the artist regains control. This sense of control arises once the artist is satisfied with the changes made and the dialogue with the work is restored.

Composer Lucky Choi says, "Destruction of my 'child' does not always come easy. There is often no alternative when I instinctively know when I have reached a dead end or I have gone down the wrong path. I somehow sense that I have lost communications with the work's voice. What doesn't work for this work may be saved and modified for another piece some day." In a similar vein, gifted composer Jane

Brockman writes, "I am struck by the efficiency of Nature's cycles. This is true of composing also. Nothing is wasted. Vast quantities of musical detritus must be jettisoned to nourish the life of a new work."

An exception can be made of Maurice Ravel's *La Valse*, originally conceived as a ballet. Several times throughout the piece he engages in the destruction and reconstruction of its main theme. The audience's pleasure is in their participation in Ravel's cycles of creation and destruction with the waltz ending in a total collapse, but still under the composer's control. As Jane Brockman suggests, "Perhaps we so enjoy it because we have all witnessed the creative cycle in nature where new life arises and is nurtured by the decomposition and destruction of old life".

Destruction of work in progress may have different sources. Sometimes the artist is unhappy about a painting in progress and, in anger or hate towards what is in it, ruthlessly destroys parts of it or the whole painting. Much anguish is stirred up when destroying a painting in what may have represented hours of loving involvement with it. After such destruction, a leap of faith moves the artist to engage in a renewed effort to create something of value again. At other times, out of an ongoing dialogue with work in progress, artists believe they are merely "responding" to the painting that seems to be asking them to do something different. There are many feelings involved in these chaotic situations, and I write about my own attempts to bring them under control in Chapter Thirteen, "Love and hate in the creative process," Chapter Fourteen, "Destructiveness and reparation: A retrospective," and Chapter Fifteen, "From mistake to mistake: The creative process in four large paintings".

The role of destruction in creativity was introduced to psychoanalysis in 1912 by Viennese psychoanalyst Sabina Spielrein, an early participant of the psychoanalytic movement, whose visionary contribution has long been forgotten. Her theoretical paper entitled "Destructiveness as the cause of coming into being" not only discusses Jung, Freud, and the ideas of other early psychoanalysts, but also Nietzsche, Wagner, as well as Christian, Jewish and Asian mythology. She was invited to become part of Freud's Vienna group of disciples after presenting this paper at one of their Wednesday meetings. According to Spielrein, we all have the desire to maintain our present condition, as well as the desire for transformation. The artist enjoys his "sublimated product" when he creates the "typical" instead of the "individual". She concludes her paper claiming that "the purely personal can never be understood by others" (p. 164).

While experimenting with free drawings, British analyst and artist Marion Milner (discussed further in Chapter Ten) found that in the drawings that were satisfying to her "there had been this experiencing of a dialogue relationship between thought and the bit of the external world represented by the marks made on the paper" (1950, pp. 115–116). According to Milner, a dialogue between the artist and the work is essential to creativity. If the artist experiences the painting as a mere extension of herself, such dialogue with the work is not possible. We could then call the artistic process "narcissistic", because the work is done "to" the painting, and not "with" the painting. If, instead, the painting becomes "the other"—having desires and demands of its own—there can be a transcendence of the preoccupation with the self. We can then engage in a true creative act, experiencing ourselves at the service of the work. It is at this point that the communication between the artist and the work begins—the artwork now has a life of its own and the creator can interact with it. This is also the case with writers who enter into a dialogue with their characters, but at times even experience their characters as taking over their creation.

The painting having a life of its own can involve not only the artist, but also the model. Writer James Lord (1965) posed eighteen times for a portrait made by his friend Alberto Giacometti and wrote a portrait of the artist at work:

> An exceptional intimacy developed in the almost supernatural atmosphere of give and take that is inherent in the acts of posing and painting. The reciprocity at times seems almost unbearable. There is an identification between the model and the artist via the painting that gradually seems to become an independent, autonomous entity served by them both, each in his own way and oddly enough, equally. (Lord, 1965, p. 23)

James Lord recounts that, while sitting for Giacometti's portrait, he would ask him to take a break for lunch. Giacometti would refuse—he didn't want to stop at a time when the portrait was not going well. Two hours later, a quite hungry James Lord would ask again to take a break to have something to eat, but Giacometti would again refuse, claiming they shouldn't stop now that the painting was going well!

Regarding writing, Joan Rivière, an early contributor to psychoanalysis, described how Freud exhorted her to write about a psychoanalytic idea that had occurred to her and he said:

"Write it, write it, put it down in black and white ... Get it out, produce it, make something of it—outside you, that is; give it an existence independently of you" (Rivière, 1958, p. 146). This is not unlike what happens in painting. There is a need to put on the painting all we have, to see it, to discover it, to find out what it is, to do something with it, to give it life. Much of what is put on the canvas at these times is voluntary, but some elements are experienced as accidental and reacted to as "messy" or "bad" (Ehrenzweig, 1967; Safán-Gerard, 1982). These are generally projections of split-off parts of the self that find their way into the work. Hopefully, in the course of creative work, these bad and messy accidents can become understood, appreciated, and integrated into the work (this is further elaborated in Chapter Three, "The role of the accident" and Chapter Fifteen, "From mistake to mistake").

During the act of destruction of aspects of the work, the artist is concerned that there might not be anything worthwhile left after the attack. In his account, writer James Lord was dismayed at Giacometti's continual destruction of the work in search of some elusive quality. He had to learn to trust Giacometti's judgement that such destruction was necessary (Lord, 1965). Analyst Hanna Segal quoted the painter Elstir, in Marcel Proust, who said, "it is only by renouncing that one can recreate what one loves" (Segal, 1981, p. 190). Like Beethoven and Giacometti, the artist has the courage to destroy because he trusts that he can ultimately make it right, and that the work will survive. At these moments, all the artist has is the courage to destroy in hopes that the creation survives. The sense of otherness of what is created goes together with our realisation that it will survive our destructive attacks (Winnicott, 1971). The move from chaos to control that underlies the creation of art is not limited to the artistic form, be it music, painting, or other. It is also intrinsic to psychoanalysis. Chaos and control comprise the essence of creativity in both.

The artist needs to work through the elicited chaos in the work so that he can eventually achieve a measure of control. This is the aim of artistic creation. Likewise, the psychoanalyst has to respond to, sort out, and offer some understanding about the chaotic memories and feelings the patient may be experiencing. While the focus is on the patient, the creativity of the analyst is at stake because she has to respond to the content of the session and the feelings and expectations of the patient. While noticing her own feelings in response to the session in progress, she offers the patient an interpretation with care and concern. Such is the outcome of the creative work of the analyst. Art and psychoanalysis: two paths to creativity through destruction that engage the richness and wisdom of one's inner life.

CHAPTER TWO

Talent and creativity

Quite often in my career as a psychoanalyst and visual artist, I had felt alone in the pursuit of understanding the creative process, its dysfunctions, and in finding ways to help creative patients in their quests for internal freedom. I had heard about Dr Jerome Oremland's work on creativity and was honoured to be the discussant on his talk entitled "Talent and creativity" at the Los Angeles Institute of Psychoanalytic Studies (LAISPS) on March 29, 1981. Finally, I was in good company, enjoying his lecture in spite of his classical orientation. My psychoanalytic training had not yet begun, but I was already gravitating towards the progressive ideas of Melanie Klein and Wilfred Bion.

In my discussion, I was somewhat critical of the way Dr Oremland dealt with a couple of cases. To my surprise, in his response, he agreed with my criticism, stating that he had seen these patients over twenty years earlier and that he would not deal with them the same way now. He harboured no resentment about this and he later invited me to lecture on creativity in San Francisco, which led to a consolidation of our friendship. Having lost contact for several years, I had the pleasure of visiting Jerome in Sausalito, California in 2014. After a delightful lunch by the water, he invited me to his home to see again his impressive collection of Renaissance and Contemporary art. In our conversation, I mentioned the present book project, for which I was compiling my writings on creativity. He expressed great interest and was full of encouragement noting that, finally, the author of such a book would be an analyst *and* an artist.

Sadly, Dr Oremland died on February 19, 2016, so I was unable to gain his insight and commentary. With immense gratitude for his encouragement, support, and friendship, as well as his contribution to our understanding of creativity, I dedicate this chapter to his memory.

Prototypical studies on creativity since Freud have been based on the content of the artwork, rather than the process of making it, which has given these studies a psychopathological flavour. This was later modified by Mary Gedo, viewing "art as autobiography" (1980), by John Gedo, recognising "creativity as an alternative to loving" (1983), and by Jerome Oremland describing "creativity as meta-autobiography" (2014). Their contributions to the understanding of the creative process are unparalleled.

I have recently reread John Gedo's *Portraits of the Artist: Psychoanalysis of Creativity and its Vicissitudes* (1983). According to his own experience, the key to the psychology of men of genius is the underestimation that typifies their formative years. This leads to their "demonic efforts to create and to their fragile sense of worth" (p. 99). Concerning women artists, his impression was that "in our society, parents tend to be less tolerant of the eccentricities of their gifted daughters than of their gifted sons" (p. 99). I believe that this was true in my case. My mother revealed to me her embarrassment when I, at age three or four, would read out loud the advertisements posted in buses we were riding. She was afraid, she told me, that other passengers would think that her daughter was a freak. Later, in my adolescence, she was very critical of my hours of listening to contemporary music and told doctors that she was convinced that the dissonant music was the source of my chronic migraines.

Dr Gedo's chapter five is particularly interesting; he describes in detail the work with a male homosexual patient who believed he had made a grave error in giving up his musical ambitions. Dr Gedo felt free from the constraints of being an analyst and suggested to the patient that it might not be too late. He writes, "Consequently, at an appropriate moment, I told him that he would forever be tortured by these doubts and regrets unless he obtained a reliable estimate, even at this late date, of the actual extent of his musical talent". Challenged by this idea, the patient eventually resumed piano practice and submitted himself to a series of auditions before judges of progressively greater stature. Their verdicts were entirely consistent: the patient possessed "musicality" of the highest order, but his piano technique was too deficient to be remedied without years of concentrated effort. In other words, the patient was essentially correct in judging that he had missed his "true vocation" (p. 76). I was personally touched by this story, as I still regret not pursuing music as my primary occupation (more on this in Chapter Nine).

Dr Gedo ends his account of the treatment of this patient, "Although the analysis had proceeded reasonably well to his point, the patient had overcome neither his dissatisfaction with his wife nor his occasional homosexual activities—the latter becoming increasingly concentrated during periods when our work was for some reason temporarily interrupted. We were therefore completely unprepared for one of the consequences of his new routine of several hours of piano practice: never again did he feel the need for sexual relations with men!" (p. 76).

Biases of the analyst

Jerome Oremland reminds us that Greenacre (1957), Erikson (1959), Kris (1952) and others have concluded that creative people possess a special kind of mental functioning that is not necessarily neurotic and/or narcissistic. This shift in emphasis is not typically reflected in the work of clinicians. Today, artists are still perceived as "difficult", narcissistic patients who elicit strong countertransference reactions in the analyst.

First, as Dr Oremland suggests, the creative patient is usually not involved with the analyst in the intense way other patients are involved. The analyst is only one person among many in a patient's life, and certainly less important to the patient than his own artistic work. This is often difficult for the analyst to handle. The patient will tend to be perceived as distant and self-preoccupied, and the analyst might interpret accordingly.

Also, the analyst may envy the patient's creativity as many analysts, at some point in their careers, experience a strong desire to produce something out of themselves, rather than always being in the helping role. My colleagues reveal that they often experience a sense of being drained, depleted of energy, with a strong need to "nourish" their own lives. If the analyst is doing creative work, he is less likely to resent the creativity of his patients. As is always the case, envy is often not perceived internally as such unless one is on the couch being analysed. This envy may be translated into a dislike for the patient, with accompanying justification. We know that analysis is most successful when the patient's envy of the analyst is recognised and interpreted. This also applies to the analyst's envy of the patient.

Another problem in therapy occurs when the analyst's lack of understanding of the patient's work results in countertransference reactions. If the analyst feels unable to aesthetically respond to the patient's work—and the patient wants to share it—she might not know if her own lack of response is due to sheer ignorance or her envy of the patient's creativity. It is indeed rare to find an analyst who is comfortable with her own ignorance in art matters. Recently, an analyst friend remarked to me, "This patient of mine has had very good reviews so the work must be good, but I don't understand it at all. All I can do well is analyse. If the patient provides me with his associations, I can work with them." On the other hand, another analyst friend, himself a respected psychoanalytic writer, would not allow a patient to bring into a session a piece of sculpture for which she had won an award. As per an analytic formula, he saw her request as "acting out", limiting himself to question and interpret her need to bring in the work. This created a sustained crisis between the two, as the patient felt betrayed. The analyst's denial of the patient's need to bring the work in may have stemmed, at least in part, from his avoiding a situation in which his lack of understanding would become evident to him and the patient. His omnipotence would have been challenged and *he* might have felt narcissistically injured. The analyst's fear of reacting to the patient's work is not mere fantasy: creative patients *are* often disappointed to find out how little their analyst knows about that which is so vital to them.

At one time, I believed that an artist's fear that his creative abilities would be in danger once he started analysis was due to his own lack of understanding of the creative process. Any tampering with the unconscious could stop its mysterious development. By talking with analysts who work with creative people, and as an artist myself, I realise now that a "prejudiced" analyst could indeed cause distress or harm.

Creativity and talent

In his paper, Dr Oremland distinguishes between creativity and talent: creativity having to do with originality and talent being a highly developed skill. Pure unadulterated creativity would be at one end of the spectrum and exceptional skill at the other. This distinction enables him to discriminate between truly creative acts and what he calls "compromised creativity", which involves the embellishment of someone else's product, or highly skilled derivative work. I am troubled by this distinction because of its implications for analysis. How many analysts have the depth of artistic knowledge to characterise a patient's work? Is the analyst in the position to decide which type of activity characterises the patient's work at any given time?

In the world of music one would be hard put to find a young composer who did not adopt the style of an older master. For example, J. S. Bach imitated the work of Buxtehude. Young Mozart emulated the work of many composers, especially Haydn. Young Beethoven was influenced by the work of Mozart and Haydn. Schubert and Schumann emulated the work of Beethoven. Brahms emulated the work of Schuman. Chopin emulated the work of John Field. Mahler, Richard Strauss and Arnold Schoenberg emulated the work of Wagner. Perhaps these composers were able to reach mastery precisely because they began by imitating great masters who came before them.

Every creative person has periods of untethered creativity and other periods of difficulty that lead to compromised, derivative work. However, we may find out years later that even those moments of cutting loose and going to the edge were influenced by cultural forces operating from within. One wonders then, is there anything truly original?

The only answer we can give is "yes". The imponderables—the way the colour is applied, the line work, the empty spaces, the shading, and the proportions—these elements are unique to the artist. However, we are immersed in the cultural pool we live in. We know that every discovery in art, as in science, is built on earlier discoveries and turns out to be a synthesis of elements that already exist. We are all trapped by the myth that there is true creativity that comes from nowhere. Recognised artists often hide the sources of their inspiration, since, if they were to reveal them, their work would be seen as derivative—the greatest sin of all!

The confusion in psychoanalysis regarding the origins and psychodynamics of creativity stems from the fact that most psychoanalytic studies of creativity are of artistic content rather than of the artist's process. Mary Gedo's (1980) view of art as biography supports this idea. Other pioneers in the study of the creative process are Gilbert Rose's (1980) psychoanalytic dissections of the aesthetic experience, John Gedo's (1983) view of creativity as an alternative to loving, and

Dr Oremland's ideas regarding art as a form of object relatedness (Oremland, 1981, 1984, 1997).

We need to free ourselves from regarding interpersonal relatedness as the highest order of functioning. Impersonal and personal object relationships are more enmeshed with each other than portrayed in traditional psychoanalytic theory. Some years ago, while working with artists in a group, I was struck by their ability to apply what they were learning from their own creative process to the world of close relationships.

There is a constant pull we all feel towards the familiar, those things or people that are known. The "new" creates discomfort and anxiety. In any given piece of work we experience this oscillation between the new, or what Dr Oremland calls true creativity, and the familiar, akin to what he calls embellishment. Some years ago, after listening to Schoenberg, Stockhausen, and Alban Berg in a class on contemporary music, our lecturer would play a bit of Mozart at the end. He jokingly called this "detoxification time" as if the "new" had become toxic or too anxiety-producing and we needed to be grounded by the familiar before leaving class.

Working on a painting, I move very clearly back and forth on this continuum of the new and the familiar. Sometimes when I'm not sure where I'm going, I will focus on a small segment, getting lost in it, embellishing it, detailing it as though it had nothing to do with the rest. At a certain point, my need for the familiar seems satisfied and I can look at the whole again to see what the "worked" part does to the rest of the painting. Sometimes my small segment doesn't fit at all and I might end up having to destroy it—two hours of work! But thinking that way would get me into trouble. My time is not important, the painting is! And the two hours of work were necessary to allow me to get back to the "new" with my anxiety level considerably reduced.

Another example: I used to work with watercolours and although they dry faster than oils and acrylics, they did not dry fast enough for my impatience. Unfinished pieces with problems I could not resolve were kept in a pile in my studio. Sometime later I went through the pile and noticed a little painting that seemed too familiar to me, even boring. I had worked it like a tapestry so there was detail all over. At the time, I was also working on large-size paper or canvas with bold, wide, sweeping brushstrokes, wet on wet. This little unfinished painting felt so tied, finicky, almost like a prison, and I was tempted to throw it away, but in my quest to challenge myself to work things out in spite of the difficulties, I didn't. I very seldom throw away anything. I could not change this particular painting. It demanded detailed work and it had to be finished in the spirit with which it had begun. One day, I picked it up and, almost with gratitude, finished it just the way I had to. I am sure that my change from boredom and annoyance to liking and excitement had to do with the fact that the new work I was doing at that time was becoming toxic in the sense of Schoenberg or Berg—too new, too ungrounded. Perhaps then going back to this familiar painting represented a relief.

These personal examples have their counterpart in the research on architects, writers, and painters by Barron, McKinnon and others at UC Berkeley in the 1960s. Their research showed that tolerance for ambiguity is a feature that characterised creative people in all fields. If ambiguity and the new produce anxiety in most people, the greater tolerance of these conditions by creative people may mean either that they tolerate anxiety better or perhaps they have come to accept and deal with it in ways other than making negative inferences about the work or themselves. The anxious, less creative person may conclude that there is something wrong with himself, or that he is not good at the task at hand, whereas the artist will reduce anxiety by seeking the familiar without negative inferences. Experimental research on familiarity and liking shows that familiar visual figures have an anxiety reducing potential. Under a condition of high anxiety, subjects relate more to familiar stimuli rather than to that which is unfamiliar.

Clinical material

Any interpretation that attacks the creative act, however derivative the art might be, will have a negative effect on all creative activity. If it is hard for the analyst to discriminate between derivative and authentic creativity, it is even harder for the patient, who will start questioning *all* of his motives. Dr Oremland wonders, "It is the link to the unique rather than the usual that makes creativity suspect; Is it originality or is it insanity? This doubt may be shared by artists as they struggle with the sense of aloneness of true exploration" (Oremland, 1984, p. 254).

Dr Oremland's main point through the discussion of his cases is that talent may defend against creativity. He also talks about the crucial importance of how these abilities are first greeted. A painter friend of mine told me recently that he was neglected as a young boy. Unlike many potential artists who are discouraged by parents or teachers, no one ever bothered to tell him he could not paint, so he did! In this case the patient didn't have to fight or overcome the opinions or judgements of others.

Dr Oremland had a musician patient who complained that his head was "filled with the tunes of others," which he saw as a case of compromised creativity. Even though we artists experience the muse and the ideas as coming from somewhere else, they are in part the product of what we have taken in, and that is no minor achievement. However, being exposed to a lot of music does not necessarily make a musician, just as being in contact with nature does not inspire many people to paint. Creative people have a capacity to *use* the object: take it in, digest it, and incorporate it. A major accomplishment for that musician was, in fact, filling himself with the tunes of others. To interpret that as compromised creativity might have had a paralysing effect.

In the case of the poet, another patient of Dr Oremland's, it was the full mourning for a mother with whom there was an intense hostile bond that allowed her to start writing again. Like the musician, she was dealing with the experience of need/anger/destructiveness towards the primary object. In both instances, spontaneous creative action emerged only out of the full experience. I am impressed anew each time at the paralysing effect of an emotion not fully experienced. The paradox is that the more the patient wants to create and move out of this state, the less he can. The more he gives in to what *is*—the figure—the more movement. This moment "happens" spontaneously from nowhere, like the musician's first original tunes coming to him or the unselfconscious writing of the poet. For music, poetry, and ideas to emerge, one has to leave the door open. This indicates that perceptual openness works like long-term memory—you ask yourself a question to be answered later. The answer comes very much like the tunes to the musician or the poetry to the poet.

Some people have the capacity to take in, but they require what they take in to stay there, locked in, filling up emptiness. The creative person takes it in, but lets it out in an unselfconscious way. Gifted psychoanalyst Donald Winnicott (1971) wrote about a "transitional space" where this can happen: the space that is neither inside nor outside us. Staying in that space longer and more fully constitutes the aim of every creative person. It is a selfless state, and yet in it one has the best possible sense of oneself. The practice of psychotherapy or analysis can have that quality, especially when one works with creative people who are not fearful of losing their boundaries in the process. The analyst can help the patient remain in this transitional space by encouraging him or her to slow down their thinking.

I was impressed with the beautiful account of the few interactions Dr Oremland had with a woman painter. He told her that he thought her symptoms (puckered mouth and indistinct speech) represented a fear of speaking for herself. As in the other two cases, I see the fear of speaking for herself as also having to do with the awareness of her own infantile needs, anger, and destructiveness. This case is a marvellous example of psychoanalytic psychotherapy working most parsimoniously. An apparently superficial interpretation revealed the acute sensitivity of Dr Oremland to his patient's situation. Also, he made full use of his power as an authority figure to permit her to separate from the old man in himself and have her own life. When the patient said later, "I am very grateful to you. I have thought of calling you several times but there really was no reason to," she was actually saying that there was no reason to connect and live through someone else.

In her book, *On Not Being Able to Paint*, Marion Milner points out that reversals are the earmark of the creative process. She is referring to perceptual experiments on figure-ground reversals whereby the subject focuses on an image that contains another image underneath it. The second image only becomes apparent when the subject relaxes his attention on the first one. I have used actual instances of perceptual figure-ground reversals in my teaching about the creative process to illustrate the kind of full immersion in the figure that is required in order for a reversal to take place. Frustrated students have told me that, as they decide to give up the task, the flip occurs and they realise that there is no volition involved—just a state of relaxed attention.

Dr Oremland also discussed a thirteen-year-old musician whose real dedication to the cello he questioned, since the boy longed to be with friends and to be normal. The boy's concern with the cello was in conflict with his need for a normal childhood with friends. Dr Oremland claims that it was easy for him to recognise that the cello represented hanging on to his mother, control of the big instrument of his father, but most of all a male companion he could control rather than fear. The patient appeared to have accepted his analyst's interpretation as reality. He later became a teacher and helped young students. His obvious sensitivity to young adolescents, especially to those not accepted by peers, makes me think that he had also identified with the analyst, who had helped him in a similarly sensitive way. The boy's primary interest was to teach and help children, not necessarily in music. Could it be that he came to regard the cello and the music the way Dr Oremland interpreted it during the analysis? What would have happened if, instead of pointing out to his neurotic over-determined interest in the cello, the analyst had validated the conflicts between playing the cello and his need to be with peers? What if the analyst never questioned his interest in the cello and concentrated solely on what the patient was bringing into the therapy situation? Perhaps the patient would have decided to become a teacher anyway, but then we would know that it was *his* decision, not the analyst's.

I have had artist patients who have told me how their analysts actively discouraged them from pursuing their craft, suggesting that their ambitions were "unrealistic". Most analysts are subtler than that, of course, but in many ways convey their suspiciousness of artistic involvement and point to loneliness and isolation as a necessary price. I strongly feel that if an interest is not genuine and backed by creative potential, it will drop out of the patient's life as he becomes aware of his ongoing experiences. There is no telling either for the patient or the analyst what's in the background waiting to be revealed. The cellist, whom Dr Oremland regarded as neither talented nor creative, may have identified with the analyst and his values, and thus relegated other possibilities to the background. The only reason that leads me to believe that Dr Oremland may have been right is that a true artist would have fought, sooner or later becoming one of those "difficult patients" who might even drop out of therapy.

A songwriter patient of mine consulted me because of his conflict between the relationship to his music and to his five-year-long relationship with a woman. He was not sure if his two-year long creative block was due to the fact that he could not hold two relationships at the same time. He also did not want to blame the woman for what might be strictly his difficulty. This is not an unusual case. Artists are often torn between an interpersonal relationship and the relationship to their work in a way similar to a married person trying to sustain an affair. The difference is that the artist does not know for sure which one is the "spouse"—the solid one—and which one is the affair. They often complain about their inability to maintain both or to give the best of themselves to each. Dr Oremland believes that a person who cannot accept ambivalence as part of a relationship cannot truly love, while a person who has trouble accepting change in the self or in the work at hand is unable to create. He points out that if we accurately understand the true structure of the complaint about an artist's difficulty with his or her art, therapy can also help with these. I agree that in the psychoanalytic literature there is precious little attention paid to work and to the understanding of dysfunctional work.

The therapy of the creative person

Psychotherapy and analysis make use of the transference—the patient's reactions to the analyst happening right there in the office. The hope is that understanding of the transference will help clarify the patient's distortions and misperceptions of significant others. This is always important. Perhaps Dr Oremland's (1997) most significant contribution is his view of the analyst as patron who shields, supports and most importantly never competes with the art. He concludes that, "the patron is the unsung hero in creativity" (p. 128).

I fully agree that the analyst has to identify with the artist's ambitions. We can characterise an ideal analyst as one who is able to tolerate ambiguity, a quality of the creative person. There are three factors that can greatly improve the patient's capacity to tolerate ambiguity and change. The analyst can model such tolerance by not allowing herself or the patient to prematurely jump to conclusions. In other words, the analyst can encourage the examination of *all* the aspects of a problem without necessarily reaching a conclusion. And the analyst can encourage the patient to become comfortable leaving the door open to new information or interpretation. For example, my songwriter patient wanted to understand certain feelings about me and his reactions to something I had said in the previous session. At the time, I noticed his discomfort with not reaching a clear understanding. I suggested that we leave it alone, like an unfinished song that will be picked up later. This was an experience he could relate to—he had known how to wait at times and it had served him well. It was a little messy, but it was all right to leave it open and unfinished.

In a session with another patient, a writer, he complained at some point that he was annoyed at not being able to follow what I was saying and asked me to repeat. I suggested that instead of trying to be a good listener, he should follow the distracting thought and we followed it all the way, fantasies and all. It was certainly much more important for him to go into this self-discovery than to be on the receiving end of my wisdom. His problems with his writing were clearly related to his need to control the outcome, not allowing in the distracting material. He has observed that the less he has tried to control the outcome, the more interesting the material becomes—something he is learning right in the therapy hour. In these two cases, the problem has to do with excessive control, and the therapeutic process can be used to admit increasing doses of chaos into the patient's thinking. In other cases, the problem is not lack of free expression, but the inability to exercise judgement of what is produced. The patient goes from one thing to the other without understanding how they might connect. In this instance, once again, the therapist has to help the patient slow down the process to understand the implications of what he is saying.

Dr Oremland suggests that individuals with unusual abilities present a considerable diagnostic problem. Attempting to differentiate between true creativity and talent does not seem as useful to me as it is to determine whether the patient's thinking suffers from excessive control or a lack of discrimination and judgement. The analyst can see evidence of these dysfunctional cognitive styles in the way the patient thinks in the therapy hour. The patient can be coached into experimenting with different ways of dealing with her own material in the session. For me, this kind of intervention is as valuable as an interpretation. Patients learn that anxiety is a natural reaction to unresolved, messy chaos. And if they begin to allow themselves to stay in that chaos a little longer each time, they will have their eyes open to the conflicts that are going on. An interpretation, even if ripe, can be filed away as insight and leave the patient unprepared to face the next bit of chaos in her life or work. Instead of being the source of insight, I see the analyst as the reassuring presence of someone who intensely values what the patient is after, and who will help the patient think more freely and fully. The solutions will be applicable not only to life problems, but also artistic problems.

Dr Oremland raises some important issues, which can be translated into the analyst's work. For example, more analysts should be fearful of destroying the creativity in their patients. Wouldn't it be nice to know that analysts are aware of the power they have regarding their patients' creativity? Valuing and expressing creativity in their own lives will give analysts the ability to generously foster it in their patients.

CHAPTER THREE

The role of the accident in the creative act

W hen the artist gets deeply involved with the work in progress things inevitably happen that seem out of his control. At times, these "accidents" in the work are welcome and at other times they act back on the person as though they were projections of unwanted parts of the self that have come to haunt him. In other words, the accident may be perceived by the artist as an opportunity to take the work beyond convention or personal limitations or it may be perceived as a disruption that interrupts the work in progress. These different perceptions and reactions to the accident occur not only in art, but also in other life pursuits as well as in psychotherapy. Accidents can be experienced as challenges, opportunities for unforeseen change for the better, or as disruptions and interruptions—annoying events that block us from what we intended to do. The accident seems to require a temporary surrender of a sense of control and a relaxing of our sense of direction, which tends to induce anxiety.

I would like to examine more closely what happens between the person and the work in the face of an accident, but will first examine how artists in the past dealt with them. Has the generally positive attitude that most contemporary artists seem to have towards accidents always existed? Art historian H. W. Janson has surveyed the history of the accident in art and I will be drawing freely on his investigation (Janson, 1973, p. 340).

An observation of images made by chance in rocks, clouds or blots is perhaps as old as mankind itself and the art of the Old Stone Age shows evidence of this. However, thoughts about this awareness are not recorded before classical antiquity. For a long time, these accidental images were explained by attributing a hidden purpose to chance, which was perceived as an agency of the divine, a view that is still popular even today. During the Renaissance, these accidental images were acknowledged as rudimentary and ambiguous and were made explicit by the beholder's imagination. Psychologists draw inferences about a person's state of mind by examining how he or she perceives ambiguous figures. The view of the accident as an agent of the supernatural or as an ambiguous stimulus that stirs up one's imagination are both linked with past and present ideas concerning the nature of creativity and are responsible for many of the myths that people hold today.

Rocks, blots and clouds were the primary focus of attention in Classical antiquity. In Pliny's *Natural History* there is a story of a painting of a dog by a Hellenistic painter Protogenes, where the artist was trying to represent foam at the mouth of a dog unsuccessfully. He hurled a sponge at his panel in a rage and the foam "was wondrously made" with Fortuna intervening, which surpasses any human intention.

Cicero believed perfection has never been achieved by accident. We can see the germ of the controversy between magic and scientific thinking had begun then. Accounts rationally explaining happenings by chance complement the classical preferences that dominated Roman art of the late Republic and Augustan era. In contrast, the story of the sponge-throwing painter already reflected an admiration for spontaneity. An almost romantic attitude seemed to have existed in Hellenistic art in which "Fortuna" appeared to favour only the artists of importance (Janson, p. 341).

Aristotle noted images in clouds also, but they were not given the importance of the incredible images made by nature or Fortuna in the rocks and blots. In fact, the ancient painters seem to have been apathetic to clouds—the skies in ancient landscapes rarely depicted them, certainly not because of any lack of skill to represent them. The most widespread chance images were accounted for in the Middle Ages. Blocks of marble, stones and gems that were cut revealed chance images, which were almost perfect paintings (1973, p. 343).

During the Renaissance, Leone Battista Alberti wrote a treatise *De statua* around 1430 where he theorised about the beginnings of sculpture. Alberti believed that certain shapes in tree trunks and clumps of earth were observed and could be made to resemble a natural shape by adding and taking away, which eventually led to artists perfecting their own skills to do this. Janson identifies this as "the earliest statement of the idea that what sets the artist apart from the laymen is not his natural skill but his ability to discover images in random shapes, i.e., his visual imagination, which in turn gives rise to the desire to make these images more explicit by adding to or taking away".

Around 1480, Leonardo da Vinci, suggested that painters look for landscapes and figural compositions in nature by observing patterns found in stained walls, multicoloured stones, clouds, and clumps of earth. These images were not objectively present—the artist must project the image into the material using their imagination. Leonardo developed his chance-image theory from identifying past observations in sculpture and applying them to his present painting. By this time, there seemed to have been a new awareness of the unstable and subjective character of chance images—the images were now in clouds rather than in trees or rocks. In sixteenth-century paintings, clouds were depicted in a variety of ways and were an accepted pictorial device for representing incorporeal beings: Raphael introduced cloud angels in his work, Correggio depicted Jupiter as a cloud, and El Greco painted the human soul as a cloud-like shape (p. 346).

So far, these accidents have one characteristic in common, they are found among the chance shapes of the outside world. They are not created, but are discovered, leaving the distinctiveness of the natural object unaffected. British landscape painter and drawing teacher Alexander Cozens revived Leonardo's idea at the end of the eighteenth century, when he published an illustrated treatise entitled *A New Method of Assisting the Invention in Drawing Original Compositions of Landscape*. He suggested making large ink blots to serve as a source of compositional ideas and recommended making many blots using crumpled paper that would be flattened again. The artist would then choose the most suggestive sheet of blots, place a piece of transparent paper over it, and selectively trace over it. Cozens cautioned the artist to avoid embellishing it, but to finish the drawing with ink wash. This method allowed artists to create chance images in the studio without having to look for them in nature.

The purpose of Cozens' blotscapes was to "free the artist from involuntary servitude to conventional schemes of landscape composition by making him relinquish deliberate control of his movements as much as possible in the beginning; the selective tracing of the blots is intended to redress the balance" (Janson, 1973, p. 350). Cozens wanted to free the artist from convention, but was also allowing sufficient control in the selective tracing to balance excesses.

One of the negative legacies of this search for freedom is in the relatively minor role that purposeful activity has today. There is as much value in the generation of new ideas as in good editing, otherwise the work becomes self-indulgent. If the artist devalues purposeful activity, he will tend to avoid or shy away from the necessary editing.

Cozens' ideas about accidents are somewhat similar to those found in Eastern civilisations. At the end of the Tang dynasty in the eighth century, there were Chinese painters using methods similar to Cozens' inkblots. Their style, called i-p'in (untrammeled) is known from literary accounts such as the one about Wang Mo. Before he would start a new painting, he would drink enough wine to become drunk, and then splatter ink. He would then use his feet and hands to smear it, while also employing a brush. He would follow the shapes and make them into mountains, rocks, clouds, and water.

Descriptions of these Chinese painters' methods influenced future artists in both China and Japan, emphasising individual expression and discovery in the use of ink and other mediums. Landscapes were often described as "made by Heaven" or "brought forth with the suddenness of Creation" instead of being man-made. Janson believes this "aesthetic ideal must have led the Chinese to the discovery that certain kinds of veined marble could be sliced in such a way that the surface suggested the mountain ranges and mist-shrouded valleys characteristic of Sung landscapes" (1973, p. 353). They framed these marble slabs like paintings and supplied some evocative inscription. Some of them must have reached the West with the expansion of Chinese trade in the eighteenth century, which would have influenced Cozens' teachings.

Although Cozens' accidents were regarded by his contemporaries as chaotic and were often mocked, they had a lasting influence on the great Romantic landscape painters Constable and Turner of the early nineteenth century. Cozens' "method" likely laid the foundation for the Rorschach ink-blot test along with a parlour game that became popular in England around the same time, while the German physician and poet Justinus Kerner produced Klecksographien, ink blots on folded paper, modified slightly, with descriptive poems written about them in his *Hadesbuch*, published in 1890. Hermann Rorschach most likely knew of Kerner's Klecksographien and used the same technique for his tests, but with oral interpretations to infer characteristics of the person projecting images onto them.

The Romantics' approach to aesthetics favoured spontaneity, sacrificing control, while also putting forth the idea that painting was less art than music. Arguing in favour of this view, Whistler began to call his paintings "harmonies", "nocturnes", or "symphonies" to emphasise his belief that descriptive values in painting are as unimportant as they are in music. His attitude was far more extreme than Cozens' in defending and advocating for the accident. At this point, however, we begin to approach a different situation where accident and intention become inseparable. There is no way to tell how much Whistler used accidents, because representation, the aim of art since the beginning of time, began to give way to a new primary reality and interest, that of the brushstroke itself.

Impressionism, Cubism and abstract art disregarded the idea of "images made by chance", but even under the discipline of an abstract style, the artist's imagination remains principally iconic, finding images where none were intended. An example of this is found in Picasso's story about fellow Cubist, Georges Braque, which he related to Françoise Gilot. During his period of Analytical Cubism, Picasso discovered an unintended squirrel in Braque's painting. Braque tried to paint it out, but Picasso insisted he could still see it, suggesting that even through an abstract lens the imagination endures.

Accidents and chance made a comeback as Dada and Surrealism "acclaimed chance as the basis of aesthetic experience" (Janson, 1973, p. 352). Marcel Duchamp was the most prominent and influential member whose work championed this model. The Dadaists liked to describe their use of accidents as "'chance meetings'—unexpected juxtapositions of objects which by their very incongruity would have a liberating effect on the imagination" (1973, p. 352). In their search for freedom, they were against all conscious discipline. For them, the creative act was to be totally spontaneous, a belief that creates problems of its own for the creator. To this, Surrealism added Sigmund Freud's theoretical framework for its view on the unconscious. Surrealist painters returned to the use of accidents that would reveal the unconscious in iconic representation, and again sought likeness, which was also sought by other artists of the time not directly involved in the movement. The outcome was a renewed mindfulness of the connection between accidents and inspiration.

I have chosen this topic because I think the experience of the accident and its resolution is what makes creative activity a growth experience. I am also using the creative act as a paradigm for many work or life situations that confront us with the unexpected. Therefore, learning about the vicissitudes of the creative act and in particular the vicissitudes of the accidental can have implications for a variety of situations one would not call artistic. One could say that these situations demand an artistic solution or an artistic attitude.

We might then ask ourselves the question: what does the artist do when faced with an accident in his work? I think it would be fair to say that, first of all, he gets anxious and/or annoyed. For a while he may stop working or he may leave the work in anger. Then, he may look at how it happened and what happened to the work. His anxiety has to lower before he can look at the "mistake". Then, if we are talking about a painter, he may begin to work in another area of the painting, acting as if nothing really happened, but knowing that something did. What is he doing? He has gone to a more familiar area of the work where he is doing a little editing or perfecting. He is trying to lower his anxiety level enough so that he can go back to the troubled accident area and look at it again, anew. He may do this shift from the familiar to the accidental several times, each time just looking again at what he did. Each time there is less judging of what he did as an isolated accident, and more as a given that can be worked into the painting.

While working on the familiar, the accident is relegated to the background—when working with the accident, it becomes the foreground. Each part of the painting is at times foreground and at times background. Once the anxiety about it is reduced, the accident becomes just one other part that has to be worked in. Eventually, the painting is seen as a totality, as a new Gestalt where the parts are to work together. Usually the artist takes some steps back at this point, squinting his eyes in order to blur the details so that he can see the total picture. This requires that he go back to work on a part of it that has to change to become part of the totality.

It is painful to be suddenly aware that one must kill a part of what one has created to give a full life to a piece. It is a daring moment indeed, but how can one justify the hours spent in developing something if it is not to be used? How does one come to terms with the loss? The only way to understand this is by acknowledging that, at some point in the creative process, our waste of time and effort—our involvement—is immaterial. The work is emerging as separate from us and we will do to it what it needs. From being lovers with the work, we become mommies and daddies. This idea that the work begins to emerge as something separate from us is very important. It requires an internal recognition and acceptance that we are separate from the other, and the work is like "the other". The joy, the delight with what is happening between us gives way to an altruistic attitude, a true concern with what is happening to it. To me, the ego merely becomes background, while the painting becomes "figure", center stage.

A well-known Chilean writer friend of mine, Fernando Alegría, told me how an accident was responsible for the final version of a novel that he had been working on for months. He used to teach at Stanford, would write systematically every morning, and go to the campus only in the afternoons. He went to the dentist and while he was sitting in the chair, the dentist captivated him with a story that would be perfect for his novel, only that he would have to throw away two hundred pages of it that now would not make sense. He struggled with this dilemma while driving home. By the time he arrived home, he went straight into his study, found those two hundred pages, and threw them away immediately. It seems, he told me, that this is not an uncommon event for him. Someone that has not yet been able to give a work in progress "a life of its own" might find this story painful, as though he, his sense of self, his pride, would also be thrown into the waste basket, especially if he had not yet written the material that was to replace those two hundred pages. As a good writer, Fernando was indeed brave.

What can one learn from the artist and his way of assimilating the accident? First of all, we don't assimilate everything at once. We have to take an experience in parts and only then integrate them in a way that is enriching and meaningful. As with digestion, the experience has to be broken into parts, and there is a timing that is dictated by our bodily processes, not by our will. When we face an experience we cannot assimilate, the impasse feels like indigestion: we will try to get rid of it through any means available. Sometimes we get rid of it by putting it inside of somebody else. The other person is perceived as though he had the thing we wanted to get rid of. Babies do this when they put their hatred inside the parent and then react as though the parent was a monster out to get them. Patients do that with us many times as part of the transference. Spouses do that with each other in what becomes a dance macabre. An unwanted accident can at times be the result of an unwitting projecting or putting into the work an experience we cannot digest, or, we might say, an unwanted part of the self. These accidents are the pictorial equivalent of a slip of the tongue. Our unconscious is revealed. From the work, it does to us what it did inside of us. Therefore, our first inclination is to eliminate it by washing over it, covering it up with paint. The artist is able to contain this impulse by distancing himself from the accident. He may work on other areas of the painting, thus lowering his anxiety enough to be able to look at it again. In the process, the accident may become integrated into the painting and reintrojected back into the self, thus enlarging and enriching the self. As Ehrenzweig says it so well, "Taking back from the work on a conscious level what has been projected into it on an unconscious level is perhaps the most fruitful and painful result of creativity" (1967, p. 57).

Of course we do not need a major accident to reach this feat of integration. We could say that there is an ongoing stream of minor accidents in our interaction with the work. The artist has an idea and the materials provide a resisting medium with mutual impact between idea and medium. The creative act would not occur if there were not a true conversation between the artist and his work. The artist has a passive but acute watchfulness for subtle variations in the medium's response and what he does in each successive brushstroke is contingent upon how the canvas responded to his last brushstroke.

A desire to control what happens on the canvas with a disregard for what the canvas says about it may be efficient but sterile. If the artist fails to relate to the work itself, the creative process goes stale. This will certainly become apparent to the viewer, who will not be touched or moved by it. There is no growth for the artist, or for the viewer, as a result of pseudo-creativity.

In our work with patients, we expect them to learn from their experience. This involves having experiences and being able to think about them and assimilate them. Otherwise, all the experiences that are unpredictable and unwanted would be gotten rid of either by denial or by projection, putting them into someone else. I compare the experience of the patient unable to think with that of the artist unable to create. As we have seen, the artist works on the different parts of the painting before he connects them and deals with the whole. If an art teacher were to suggest to a student that he look at the whole picture before he has assimilated the parts, the student would react as though caught in the middle of an undigested meal. There would be an impasse with the teacher, who is no longer trusted, and the student might begin to doubt his talent.

Patients dealing with experiences they cannot truly think about express distress and feel as stuck as the artist confronted with an accident. Rather than suggesting to a patient to look at the whole picture or think about the whole situation, the therapist may suggest that he deal with each part of the experience separately with the less distressing, more familiar one first. Once the person's anxiety level lowers, he will go back to talking and thinking about the experience that had earlier felt foreign and unthinkable, and make it his own.

This can be illustrated with an excerpt of a therapy session. Sally, a twenty-two-year-old woman I have been seeing for two years, begins talking about her sprained knee. She is quite distressed and talks about feeling confused and overwhelmed. She wonders if the physical therapist she is seeing is really helping her and she is very angry with him. In treatment he asks her to report to him when the leg starts hurting as he applies different weights to a pulley.

Sally: I think he is hurting me. It is hard for me to know what I feel with the leg, it seems to hurt all the time and I don't know if I am misguiding him … but he ought to know. I don't know if I want to go back there. I don't know if he is really helping me.

Therapist: You would want him to know what is going on with your leg. You get angry with him for not knowing, and with yourself for not guiding him.

Sally: I am making it worse by not following his advice and staying off my feet. I went shopping yesterday because I was feeling better, but I am overdoing it. I shopped for seven hours (starts crying). I don't know … I am so confused. Everything goes wrong!

Therapist: (After a while) Tell me about the shopping.

Sally: Seven hours! Of course I cannot expect to get better. I am always overdoing it (continues to cry).

Therapist: There must be something good about the shopping. You would not do it just to spoil your treatment.

Sally: I really enjoy finding the right things for my apartment, left a lamp on hold, which will be perfect. And with clothes, too. Remember when I started therapy how I talked about hating to make decisions? And the problems with what my mother likes and what I like? Now I feel very confident about my taste and how I put things together. I don't get overwhelmed in a department store anymore; I know how to find what I want.

Therapist: The contrast is very clear: in bed, unable to move with your leg up and helpless; in a store feeling in charge, competent, creating something new ...

Sally: I hate being stuck in bed and needing help and no one there to bring me a cup of tea ... I guess when I go shopping I forget everything about being in need or getting angry that no one is there. I can do what I want to do by myself and it makes me feel good ... to the point where I forget about taking care of myself ... [After a silence] ... I have two exams coming up this week. I will stay in bed all during the week studying ... at least I'll have a sense of purpose and that'll help me not to focus so much on my feeling needy. I still have a lot of problems with that and that's why I can't afford to get sick ... [pause] ... I'll continue with the physical therapist. It's not his fault really if I can't tell him what I feel. [smiles] Poor guy! I was so angry with him.

As you can see, I have her talk about her shopping experience at the time of impasse. Talking about the shopping breaks up the situation and helps Sally focus on that experience only—supposedly a good experience—rather than being overwhelmed by the whole picture. It also distances her enough from the distress so that she can begin to look at what she does. She discovers that, in the shopping, she has a sense of mastery she misses when she's helpless in bed, with no one there. She finds out why she shops with a vengeance—to avoid the painful feelings of need and anger if she were at home and resting.

Now that her anxiety is lower she can begin to talk about what she's going to do. Projective identification in which the physical therapist is perceived as harming her is also resolved as she comes to understand at the end that this is not so, and that she was projecting her anger onto him. That understanding means that she has been able to assimilate her own anger at her helplessness. In other words, she takes in her projection.

Whether accidents are found in nature, purposefully created, or the result of an unconscious projecting into the work, they are an opportunity for liberating ourselves from cultural conventions or from our own limitations. As Leonardo pointed out, ambiguity in the images forces us to project something into them. The ambiguity in an image gives us a chance to find out about ourselves, whereas less ambiguous images do not allow us such discovery. Clear, unequivocal images give us a reassuring sense of the stability of the world around us—we are able to relax and we don't need to think. Ambiguity, on the other hand, while offering hope for self-discovery, has a price—anxiety. We are forced to give up our omnipotence and to recognise that we don't know. Ambiguity forces us to think or do something different!

Throughout history, artists have cherished the ambiguous and the accidental as an opportunity to free the imagination and the self from internal limitations. Freud attempted to reach a similar goal with his use of free association; the relinquishing of conscious control could allow the primary process to emerge and reveal the inner workings of the mind. I think the artist, the therapist and the patient are all dealing with what emerges as a result of accidents, purposeful or not. We all have to be able to withstand the anxiety of an exploration where parameters are often unclear, where feelings are often confusing, and where there is no clear outcome. Yet, we all stay in it because the promise of freedom and higher integration is also there and continues to tantalise.

CHAPTER FOUR

The psychodynamics of creative blocks

At the beginning of a new project, whether a painting, a short story, or a new music score, there is an excitement, but also great trepidation. Through experience, one knows that they will have to come to several painful impasses during the work, yet one does not understand enough about the nature of these impasses to trust they will be overcome. Because of this, one goes into a new project with a mixture of excitement and fear. I would like to examine here what actually happens inside one's head, or in one's mind, at these critical points. I will approach this problem from two different vantage points: the emergence of feelings of discomfort, irritability, and helplessness, reminiscent of similar feelings experienced during infancy; and the experience of a sense of loss accompanied by depression.

Somewhere along the way, in spite of some anxiety, the artist has started this new work with a sense of his own power, but he now seems to lose his sense of direction. He may need to make a decision and does not know exactly which way he ought to proceed. Along with his sense of direction, he loses his ideal of himself as being capable of controlling, directing, "running the show", and also his ideal image of the work—which is not turning out the way he envisioned it. Before he can proceed, he has to come to terms with and accept this loss. If the loss is of an ideal self that *knows* what to do, he will have to relive again and again these feelings of helplessness, discomfort, incompetence, and ignorance. This is not merely a psychological shift from an omnipotent adult to a helpless child, but a fall from an all-knowing state to a messy, incompetent and ignorant child. If he loses the ideal image of his work, he will have to face the fact that it is not what he envisioned—he will have to develop it in a direction that is more in line with where *it* seems to be going by putting himself at its service.

Submitting to the requirements of the work means getting oneself out of the way of all the expectations one has invested in it and seeing what it needs. If the work is to have a life of its own, the artist has to *help* develop that life rather than assume the role of a powerful "creator", having all the say in how its life is to be shaped. Paradoxically, while giving up the sense of his own importance, the artist enlarges the scope of the work, which in the end produces more satisfaction. In the process, he will get a chance at being surprised by what happens between himself and the canvas, the page, the piece of clay. What goes on between the artist and the work in progress is like a communication between two people where there is no hidden agenda, but a mutual responsiveness to what the other is saying. It is only then that the creative process is alive. The surprise and awe at what might then happen compensates for the anxiety over one's lack of control during the process. It is that surprise and awe at something we did not intend that actually nourishes us and restores our strength to continue working.

I have referred to impasses that are not merely current editions of similar impasses or crises I have gone through in previous work, but to some impasses or crises we have gone through at different stages in our early development. It is not the scope of this chapter to review what these are to understand that, ideally, we have to learn to resolve these impasses if we are to mature properly and lead full and real lives. This is not to say that we have to resolve certain issues in our lives in order to become good artists—this is a thorny issue that we could not even begin to explore here. Yet, I am assuming that if the major crises in life have not been somewhat resolved, this will have a negative effect both in the development of the artist's talent, and in his capacity to overcome the many impasses that arise in the creative process. However, at these early stages of development, one has to arrive at a kind of resignation, since our infantile needs and wishes cannot be completely satisfied. I will clarify these ideas later by examples showing the behavioural and mental manifestations of incomplete accommodation to early losses.

What about the unpleasant feelings stirred up during a creative project? Underlying both sets of feelings (helplessness and depression) is our need of something, ultimately someone, and the awareness of such need. My main thesis here is that one protects both sets of infantile feelings by inhibiting or repressing the awareness of need. If there is no need for someone, there is no helplessness, and we can continue to pretend we are in control. Helplessness is to be avoided because it implies the fact that one might need something from someone. If we do not need anyone and do not have anyone, nothing can be lost—the possibility of a loss is ever present when we have someone.

In light of defences against dependency, what are the chances of overcoming impasses that stir our dependency again and again? We both relive and experience our helplessness and our feelings of lost ideals, or we have to abandon the task (at least temporarily). In the first instance we will be continuing the work with more humility (perhaps as to its goals or our own) until it catches fire, surprising us with an unintended event; this also helps us get over our previous infantile struggle. If we do not want to go through our painful feelings, we can either abandon the project (deciding it is not worth the effort), or we can pursue it, but this time armoured with a delusional system.

In the latter instance, we deny our helplessness in the face of the problem, we deny we are losing ground, and we forge ahead nevertheless as though we still *know* what the work needs. We will probably enter into a power struggle with the matter at hand—an uncomfortable situation that has to be ended by suppressing the incipient awareness that the work needs something different. The work will be brought to a premature closure that no doubt will hurt it. In this case, the person distorts outer reality, or his view of himself as "creator". As we can imagine, the solution has a dear price for the work, but also for the artist: confusion, a fragility of the self, the sense of not having a core, the fear of something not being true, or the fear of being found out.

Why are we so fearful of reliving infantile needs and fears? What makes them so deserving of repression? Attached to the unpleasant feelings are other more frightening ones that would get awakened as well. The feelings of helplessness of the infant stir powerful feelings of envy of the mother and those that, like her, are perceived as having what one wants. The envy involves a wish to hurt and destroy the loved one, which the infant does in fantasy. For the child, there is no distinction between a wish to hurt and actual destruction: the child has to bear the consequences of having destroyed the mother. The situation is more complicated because once the infant destroys her—or those like her later on in life—he will be fearful of being destroyed by her or the now loved one. Therefore, the awareness of need brings with it powerful anxieties related either to the destruction of the loved one, or in retaliation, the destruction of oneself. The infant is aware of his dependency on the mother and others for survival. How terrifying to be afraid that the person we need the most might get hurt or hurt us—even destroy us? So saying that we have to become aware of our need in order to create is suggesting no simple task. The awareness of need evokes much anger, envy, and paranoia; we have that infantile part of ourselves reacting in our unconscious just as we did when we were young infants. We still resort to infantile solutions divorced from awareness and pain to avoid such anxieties.

Let me digress for a moment to talk about what happens in the therapy situation where we replay these early solutions during the analysis, especially when the analyst has been or is going to be absent. We have a chance then to re-experience these early feelings and make conscious what is now unconscious. Another opportunity for a replay is in creative work—although in this latter case we are at a great disadvantage by not having the needed *other* observing and communicating to us what he sees us doing, again and again. One could say that creative work puts us in touch with these early feelings, anxieties, and the early strategies to deal with pain just as analysis does. Both the work in front of us and the analyst behind us can surprise us. In the creative act, however, we are left alone during the struggle with these feelings, whereas the analyst's understanding is essential at these times to be able to look at, tease apart and understand the source of our pain and confusion. No wonder many have said that it takes great courage to create; one goes through early feelings again and again without a helping hand. I do not think the artist gets any more understanding of the conflicts involved as a result of this exposure, but he gets at least an enlarged capacity to tolerate distress without having to run away from it or having to cover it up by delusions. In fact, one of the consistent findings in research with creative people is their greater capacity to tolerate ambiguity and chaos. A test of creativity based on these findings predicts quite accurately that a person with this increased capacity will be more creative in a number of fields, not only the so-called creative ones.

We have talked several times about strategies to deal with the pain of dependency and to suppress the awareness of need. What are some of these strategies? What are the solutions the infant and, later on, the artist finds to get rid of the host of feelings we have been talking about? One solution or "cure" to the anxiety aroused by an awareness of dependency is that of fusion with the other, a fantasy that the mother and you are one. Another cure is dissociating oneself from the infantile part of the personality that *needs*.

These fantasies occur in our unconscious mind and we can only infer their existence through some behaviours and feelings that are conscious. In the unconscious fantasy of being fused with the mother one resolves the problem of dependency altogether: anger, destruction, and fear of retaliation. One does not need the mother or anyone, one *is* the person needed. This pretension or delusion can be kept alive, but one lives in a world of unreality. One forgets events having to do with what goes on with relationships, anything that might remind us we are separate and possibly alone. One loses a sense of time, nothing matters that much so that things don't get accomplished and one does not understand why others are constantly angry with us. This person lives in a world without conflicts, without mental pain, but a world with no roots, no clear identity, no consuming passion except maybe the wanting to blend with someone else who becomes idealised. This disposing of the infantile part of the personality as if garbage, on the other hand, does away with the infant that is needy, messy, and lacks control. In doing so, however, one does away with the capacity to enjoy life, to be spontaneous, curious, which are all essential in creating. If the dissociation is very successful, we have a person whose life runs like a computer, but where there is a chronic depression and longing for a larger meaning in life. If the dissociation is less acute, the person finds himself in fear of doing "stupid" things he cannot control where he loses face. The infantile part seems to resist this constant pushing him away and appears "through the back door", so to speak, every time it has a chance. The person does not mind when the infantile self provides the excitement and passion for things or people, but he will mind a great deal when the child makes a mistake and the adult loses face—in this case he will berate himself without mercy. One can well imagine how both these strategies of dealing with need and dependency affect creativity.

Let us briefly look at how a patient may portray these conflicts in the consultation room. A twenty-two-year-old woman comes to the session and complains she is forgetting everything. She had also forgotten her first appointment after my return from vacation. She looks and acts in a dissociated manner, usually referred to as "spacy". She complains and worries she might be getting a heart attack. Here we begin to see how her solution to the need and pain of my absence is to forget me and her need of me. Her chest pain seems to be that of the infantile part of herself that has been squeezed out of existence in her effort to forget me, this new mommy, and the part of herself that needs me. She then describes a situation at home where her sister and parents were angry with her. She had completely forgotten to give them a message from her sister, who had asked her to tell their parents she would not be sleeping at home because she did not want them to worry about her whereabouts.

Aside from the jealousy with her sister and her connection with the parents, one can see how, in order to maintain the denial of her own dependency on her parents and on me, my patient has to forget a message where there is concern and care for the other person's welfare. She then forgets the session with me. One could say that the poor memory is motivated by her desire to forget her own dependency and the complicated feelings associated with it. As I have said, delusions such as this will stand in the way for creativity to emerge and flourish.

In order to create, we need contact with what is happening and we cannot get such contact when we shut off a part of the mind. This shutting off not only affects our awareness of need, which is the true engine or motivation for any creative pursuit, but also mental functions such as perception and memory.

One can draw this conclusion: if one pursues a creative activity, one needs to develop the courage to limit this protecting of oneself against psychic pain. The denial of psychic pain increases the paralysing effect of the impasses we referred to earlier; it increases confusion, the fear of not having talent, the sense of unreality or falsehood of the self as we present it to others, and the constant fear of being found out. Delusional systems erected as a protection against pain (i.e., believing we *are* the person we need or we already *have* what we need) stand in the way of us having contact with our internal world and we need to have some access to this internal world. They in turn limit what we can see or use in the external world.

The artist has to tolerate loss both in his life and in his work. In order to go through and suffer the loss, he has to be aware of his wishes and needs. If such awareness is distorted or denied, there is no chance to experience and mourn a loss, since, in line with the delusion, nothing has been lost! The pain of one's neediness and the pain of loss are being avoided, but there is much pain to be had in the person's life and work.

The nature of the impasse

In what follows, I would like first to illustrate these ideas with excerpts of sessions of two patients who are not dealing with what we call creative blocks as such, but with life situations and their responses to them. This seeming exploration in trivia may appear unrelated to creativity; I hope nevertheless to show how maladaptive responses in everyday life are bound to affect the creative work we do.

Judith, a woman in her early thirties, complains of a recurrence of psychosomatic symptoms she had when she began therapy: stomach pains, allergies, the feeling she is coming down with a cold. Her wedding day is approaching. Last Saturday, she tells me, she had a splitting headache that began while she was buying lingerie. She hates spending money on such things, she says, and talks about how much healthier cotton underwear is.

> Nothing seemed to fit. I would have walked out if it weren't for my friend who kept bringing me other things to try on. I also had to buy cosmetics—I had run out of most things. I hate to spend any time putting on make-up. If I can't do everything in five minutes I won't bother.

I remark, "Trying on all those sexy clothes may have stirred up some feelings ..." (Silence). "Mother had these awful-looking cotton slips and underwear but my sister Mary ..." Judith began to talk at length about her older sister (four years her senior), who was so beautiful, had flawless skin, green eyes, blond curly hair, and spent hours taking long baths and putting on make-up. In other sessions, Judith had talked about Mary having such big breasts and how she had wanted to have breasts like hers. "She walked around in those see-through negligees [and laughingly adds] but all she got was father's crude remarks and a couple of obscene phone calls." She seems to enjoy this memory. I said, "It must have been painful for you to compare yourself to her. You laugh when you remember there were some crude comments from your father and a couple of obscene phone calls. These memories seem to be a 'cure' for that pain." Judith continues, "Her skin was so flawless while I *still* get zits! Sometimes I think I'll never get through puberty. [After a long silence] Actually, I asked her a few times to teach me how to put on make-up but she never did." I say:

> You wanted your sister's good attributes very badly and the comparison must have hurt. You found a solution to cover up that pain by devaluing her fancy underwear and make-up as superficial things representing the wrong values. But that was a phony solution, one to avoid the pain of the discrepancy between you, the little one, and your well-developed, beautiful sister. You never truly resigned yourself to the fact that you were not going to have green eyes, curly hair, and big breasts. If you had, you might have come to appreciate what you *do* have and enjoy making the best of it: finding the best clothes for your figure, the most flattering cosmetics, and so on.

Judith is right when she says she is still in puberty. Puberty is a tumultuous age where one does not know what kind of man or woman one will become. Just as Judith (as a baby) envied her mommy, she also envied her sister, friends and anyone who seemed to have what she would have liked for herself. She gets around that painful resignation by devaluing all she does not have. However, confronted in the dressing room by her image in the mirror, she gets flooded with early feelings of envy and rage and the wish to destroy what others have, namely her sister, and her mother before that. The headaches may be replacing the guilt over those attacks on them. After a long silence, Judith adds, "And then I went to this party [a shower in her honour] and I could not enjoy myself."

When she is the one to receive or to have the good things in life as her mother or sister did, she identifies with them in a destroyed form. Having unconsciously attacked them in the past and having denied them their sexuality, their beauty, and their womanhood, she cannot now enjoy it herself. In addition to the early unconscious fantasies brought up by the lingerie, she has difficulties in adjusting to a new type of resignation: that of losing her youthfulness. She says, "Standing there in front of the mirror I thought my thighs looked like those of an older woman. I wanted to get out of there fast. I could not stand it." One can see denial and avoidance operating again.

How do avoidance strategies affect Judith's work and creativity? She started working in a small, fast-growing company about a year ago. She was delighted at the opportunity to learn on the job, working with a couple of young, bright, first-rate professionals in her field. They needed someone who would get involved, learn their procedures and, in time, become well trained in their field. This suited Judith's wish to develop a successful career while working. She assimilated complex ideas and procedures without having had earlier training. The partners are surprised at how fast she becomes knowledgeable and ask more and more of her, taking her to important meetings, and asking her to make decisions on her own. This satisfies Judith's wishes to erase the discrepancies between them and her (as she did earlier in life), and it satisfies her desire to be considered an equal. Yet, she is constantly afraid of being exposed in her ignorance, of being caught not knowing something or being found out. It is hard for her to accept her subordinate position with respect to her bosses and to acknowledge that she needs them. When she asks questions and receives quick answers she does not understand, she acts as though she does and struggles on her own to find the answers. The demands she puts on herself show up in various physical symptoms of stress and anxiety in particular. She is slowly coming to understand how she avoids an awareness of her position as the little one in the company, the little one who was recently asked to write a report about a meeting she was sent to that her partners could not attend. She writes very well and has always been commended for her clear ideas, but she has always been terrified in front of the blank page. This time was no exception: her relative ignorance could become apparent, as the ignorant little one would have been revealed. It is worth noting that her mother was well versed in languages and that Judith's difficulties with English composition and early interest in science and disinterest in literature had to do with her feeling that she could never equal her mother's command of languages. She procrastinated and procrastinated with this report to the point where she had to give excuse after excuse and began to fear being fired from the job. Her anxiety was mounting.

We examined the full extent of her wish to be equal to the partners and how, having idealised them as perfect, she also strived for perfection; this is understood in relation to her earlier attempts to be equal to her mother. Only then is she able to write the report, amazed at how easy it is after she manages to torture herself for weeks. She becomes aware once more how being the little one puts her in touch, not only with her dependency, but also with powerful feelings of envy and hatred, and how much she fears destroying those she needs. As we have explained before, she is, in fact, destroying them in unconscious fantasy. The conscious awareness of this infantile envy and of her destructive wishes can now be mitigated by her more mature appreciation and gratitude for what her bosses are giving her and recognition of how much they have helped her. As she finds it easier to assume her position of the junior one vis-a-vis them, her work is proceeding with much less conflict.

Let us now look at excerpts of a couple of sessions with another patient. Eleanor, an artist in her late forties, starts this session by putting down everything, everybody, and herself. Sarcastically she remarks, "Well, this session was the only thing for me to look forward to today." She implies that this is still another unfulfilled expectation. She talks at some length about a trip she had planned with Sue, an older friend, and describes an unpleasant interaction with her about the trip. The conversation with her friend is left unfinished and she comments:

"It's not going to work." I comment that she again seems to be doing something about which she has no conviction: "I don't hear you say to Sue or to me what you *would* like." Annoyed, she says: "I'll go, I am committed!" There seems to be a refusal even to think about what she would like to happen and I say:

> Eleanor, if you don't allow yourself to want all the good things from Sue or me you can never hope to get a little of the good things. I agree with you that you are in for a disappointment because you, as many people, want *everything*. You would probably like me to give you advice, direction, wisdom, that I cuddle you or embrace you and comfort you and you will never get all that, especially in one session. But, if you demand all 100 per cent you cannot be aware of the little bit of good you *are* getting, like my complete, undivided attention, my care in trying to understand you, and my compassion. That may be 10 per cent or less of what you might like, but it might make you feel good about me and about you, about the work we are doing together. You seem to be so afraid of pain that you don't even want to dream of something good for fear of spoiling it or destroying it. Then you start protecting yourself by predicting a bad outcome and what do you get? A sense that you already *knew* it wouldn't work out. But this is no consolation for the little Eleanor within you, who is kept starved—only a consolation

for this other part of you that wants power, control and wants to know ahead of time what is going to happen.

In the following session, Eleanor brings a long-awaited letter from a man with whom she has had a long on-again, off-again relationship. She had been quite concerned that after she had been unpleasant with him the last time they were together, he would not want to continue seeing her. At the end of a lengthy and revealing letter, he invites her to spend a weekend with him. Sarcastically she says: "I thought of showing this letter to Dr X [this other psychologist she had seen a few times]. I don't know why I brought it when I know I won't be getting any reaction from you." I tell her, "You seem to want to have reactions so that you can react to them, not to the letter. I wonder what *your* reaction to the letter is." Eleanor agrees and—tearful now—she admits to having no reactions. She talks about having walked aimlessly in Beverly Hills for a couple of hours looking for clothes, not knowing what to buy and adds, "I keep looking for myself, it seems, but I find nothing. I feel so lost." After a while I say, "Your sense of self is connected with your own reactions and your own reactions are, in turn, connected with your deepest wishes. You don't want to have any such wishes: it's so dangerous, disappointing, etc., and then the you, the real you, is nowhere to be found." She starts putting down the letter, "As soon as I saw it I didn't want it. I didn't even want to open it." She had been wanting this letter, the connection with him, his responding to her and the sense of his care for her, but she finds this too risky to admit to herself and very quickly there is a protective part of her that says "I don't care". She continues: "We are worlds apart—he is finding pleasure where I can't." And I reply, "I think you are both after the same things, but he is taking some risk and you are not, and the comparison hurts. You present the whole thing as an impossible situation so you won't have to risk anything. You want the whole thing or nothing." I remind her of our last session:

> You can want the whole thing, but then you have to settle for something like 10 per cent or less in that direction. You have this pride and you want equality at all cost and don't like the idea of settling for anything less than the whole thing. If it is less than everything, it is all "bad", like me. You were not sure how much I would be able to help you with the letter, therefore you treat me as though I am already the "bad" therapist who won't help, whereas there is someone good, or more ideal, somewhere else. The problem is that

once you decide I am not good enough, you are in trouble because the hope of getting a bit of good from me disappears and leads you to despair, which is even more painful. So what do you gain? Better grab a hold of the 10 per cent, don't you think?

How do Eleanor's reactions affect her creative work? Her reactions to me and to that long-awaited letter are the same as her reactions to people helping her exhibit her work. She recounts the several opportunities where she could have shown her paintings, but for one reason or another, she rejected them, one after another. Accepting an offer would have meant accepting the loss of the perfect relationship, the whole thing. There were other artists she would have to show with, other artists who would have shown before or after her. Any comparison would have been evidence to her that she didn't have an exclusive relationship with the dealer, with the teacher, with the potential buyers. She has never accepted the loss of an exclusive relationship to her parents: mother or father. She takes the most immediate pleasure of being the one that says "no", the one doing the rejecting. In this way, she can deny and devalue the offer while also turning the tables to project the little Eleanor into the other person, who would then have to be the rejected one, not her. But the pleasures are short lived, as they leave Eleanor with a sense of her own incapacity to make use of opportunities.

In one of the sessions discussing this, she seems to have gained an awareness of how self-defeating these responses have been and is appropriately sad. But very quickly the sadness of the loss gives way to anger and hatred towards a friend who makes good use of opportunities. She cannot tolerate her awareness of loss and depression; the hatred towards the little Eleanor, who needs something from others and has to accept loss, who is turned outward once more in an envious attack on a friend who is idealised as getting all the good things, or having qualities she does not possess.

We can see how the chances to develop our work are intimately tied up with our personality development and with the resolution of early conflicts. Whatever is not true or real in the personality seems to become amplified in one's creative work.

Failed creativity

Let us turn our attention now to a couple of cases of failed creativity to see how these issues of need, loss and acceptance of the loss play their part in the actual vicissitudes of a creative project. Karen is working on a book, on and off for two years, on a subject she knows well, since the action takes place within a field with which she has intimate familiarity. It is a light-hearted tongue-in-cheek exposure of the corruption in that business and its effect on the public. With some variations, she is the main character in the story, and at this point in her treatment, she is not at all happy with the results. The book is episodic, lacks unity, and she fears editors won't like it. She is right: editors do not like her dialogue and sense of timing, and suggest she needs a stronger story that can keep the reader's attention throughout the book. She tries to generate ideas that tie the elements together, and begins by attempting to take the lead from a successful writer in her family, but the effort goes nowhere. Karen sets up luncheon meetings with people who are familiar with some events in their workaday world that might become the connecting threads of her book. These events are woven here and there in the different chapters and, like the solution of the writer, force her to change quite a number of the smaller vignettes. The editors find the stories not original enough to make a bestseller, but she is determined to write a bestseller.

Karen complains to me that the character of the heroine herself is not developed enough, but continues to try to satisfy the editor and publisher's requirements. Her distress turns into open hostility when one of them suggests that she ought to play down the vignettes and give more strength to the story. She complains to me: "But this is not *my* book! I would have to completely forget what I want!" Disgusted, she follows the suggestion of one publisher and shelves the book for a while—maybe she will be able to use portions of it here and there in another project. By now, she has begun to write another book related to a personal crisis of hers. The publishers express deep interest in this new book that promises to be scandalous and juicy, describing the details of the break of a relationship between two prominent people. This project has another host of difficulties, as she struggles with the problem of truly understanding what is going on between them and not exposing too much of what does not belong to her.

Let us examine the obstacles to the first book. To start with, she is in grave danger of losing the connection with herself or "getting off the track" by her wish for the book to be a bestseller. In her case, it is not just a wish, but also a demand she imposes on herself. This will make her extremely vulnerable to other people's ideas, especially those of successful writers who have written bestsellers, publishers who publish bestsellers, and successful people in other fields who present her with ideas. She is no longer trusting that she can come up with something, but she has to *take* from someone bigger and more competent. She begins to feel the insecurity of a child and anger at all these people who are withholding from her, including me, her therapist. My interpretations—which suggest that her demand for a bestseller is premature and does not let her grow along with the book—are turned against me. She claims I don't understand her—she would not settle for something mediocre. Besides, she is used to having money and now needs that income. She does not want to consider such a possibility and makes me into the inadequate one who settles for mediocrity and cannot afford grown-up luxuries. She turns the tables, having me play the child part of herself who feels inadequate and lacks what grown-ups seem to have. She sees my interpretation as stemming from my envy at her success, not as a wish to help her understand the nature of her unrealistic, omnipotent demands, which she is not likely to fulfil.

At the point where Karen complains to me about her heroine not being developed as a character, she is closer to finding something of value for herself that, if pursued, could enrich the character. This would make her confront and eventually accept aspects of herself—her infantile hostilities and fears that are dissociated and put into me and others. She engages in an instant cure of these feelings by her grandiose fantasies of incorporation of other people's ideas and by leaping forward to fantasise about having a bestseller. She now reads bestsellers to understand what the key is in them. She thinks if she could figure out the ingredients of a bestseller, she would have no problem.

Let us look at another example of this same issue with another patient. After struggling for a couple of years, David, a young comedy writer, gets some good television assignments and is recognised as one of the new writing talents. On the basis of a collaboration with an older writer on a movie script, he is offered a movie—his first one alone. The subject matter has to do with a situation he is familiar with from his childhood and he is truly delighted. This movie is going to *make* him big—he will not have to apply for jobs ever again—they will seek him out. In the future it will be entirely up to him to choose a project or not and his financial problems will be over, forever.

The producers give him the main idea for the movie and he is asked to turn in the first forty pages in a couple of months. After a month's work David realises that he cannot write the story the way it was suggested.

The approach is too sleek: it presents things in a black and white way he detests—he would like more subtleties in the character development, no good guys and bad guys. After all, this is the problem he used to have with his ex-partner: he was quick in creating certain effects, great for storyline, but his treatment hit the audience over the head. He wants to show that he has a better way of doing things and this is his chance. He struggles with an idea that is quite a departure from what the producers had suggested to him and he has to ask for an extension. His anxiety mounts as he imagines they won't like his development of their story. He fantasises arguments where he defends his position and wins—they are amazed at his talent and give him a carte blanche to pursue his ideas. He is not happy with the forty pages and says to me, "It's not really an example of the whole thing because I don't know yet how the whole thing works out. I hope they understand that."

David finds out, through the assignment, that the producers hated his treatment. The assistant producer lets David know they are very angry at his changes and that they want to meet with him. David is devastated. When he finally meets with them, he barely defends his idea and follows every suggestion they make. In the ensuing session he comments:

> I was meek; I felt I had nothing, not one idea to contribute. They had it all: power, ideas, everything, and I agreed to everything they suggested. I was scared—I didn't want them to fire me from the project—it meant too much to me. Yet I can't stand myself. I kissed ass all the way.

As in Karen's case, this project is invested with all the power to make him big. Even though he wants a more complex treatment than the producers suggest, he cannot live up to the requirements of the new version of the project. This new development requires time, but he is not willing to admit that he needs time to figure it out. After all, if the movie script is supposed to *make* him, he should be able to figure it out right away. He gets caught up in his own omnipotent fantasies and, as is always the case, he only has to hear that they are angry with him to have all those fantasies collapse. He becomes a frightened child ready to agree to anything. In a strange way, his negotiating with the producers mirrors what he hates about the script: the good guys know everything, and the bad guys know nothing. Had he been more accepting of the infantile part of his personality, and able to learn from someone with more experience, he could have been a better advocate for himself, defending the notion he had earlier presented to me:

> They should not judge me on the basis of these forty pages, since they are not an example of the ensuing pages; they are rather an example of the way I am struggling with this new idea. I would like them to bear with me to see the outcome of this treatment. I believe in what I am doing ...

Again, as in Karen's case, he begins to frantically follow every piece of advice he gets and everything seems to lead to a dead end. His anxiety mounts. He begins to suffer stomach pains and is unable to eat or sleep. In a fit of despair, he tells the assistant producer he has decided to abandon the script and is willing to refund the money that has been advanced to him. It is no consolation that he is one of several writers hired for the project, the others quit or were fired. By this time, he is dimly aware that his unwillingness to make contact and accept the infantile part of himself has a great deal to do with his inability to tackle this script at this time.

It is hard to assess to what extent the editors' suggestions for Karen's book or David's script are an improvement on their ideas. Many would agree that a good storyline makes a book more readable than would a set of vignettes, however interesting, or that viewers of a movie will get confused without a clear sense of purpose. The artist needs to be accepting and loyal to where he *is* at that point in time, even though this may mean the work not succeeding in generating a desired response. Karen's state of mind was not integrated, and she cannot possibly write an integrated book unless it is not *her* book. The one option in the direction of literary integration is, as she discovers herself, to find out what is not right with her heroine. Even with that, she might not have a best-selling novel. The important thing is that her chance of maturing as a writer parallels her chance of growing up as a person, and she is not taking that risk. She wants an instant, magical solution for her heroine and for the novel as a whole. Such a solution does not grow out of quick, magical cures. The artist is forced to take account of what is truly happening to him.

One may ask, "What about the productivity of great artists whose pathology is well documented?" This is not the place to explore the relationship between creativity and madness, a complex one for sure. It seems to me that even in the most pathological cases, great art results from moments of integration and not from those where the pathology is flagrant. Van Gogh, for example, who is often cited as an example of a crazy artist, spent long periods of time when he was unable to paint at all.

How can the artist benefit from the help of others? An artist will truly enrich his perception of his work and make possible its further growth if he is not blinded by defensive manoeuvres. He can stretch his capabilities and follow a lead, but only if this lead is "received with the conviction that it is right—this is right, this is what I needed". In this case, the lead is a pointer in the right direction, but a direction that is already possible within the artist's conception of the work. Karen and David lack conviction of their own when they follow other people's suggestions. They cannot discriminate between what fits and what does not. They follow suggestions blindly, not for what they are, but because they see them coming from someone powerful, someone who knows, someone who has what they feel is missing in themselves. Their only conviction is that they have nothing; and the only way of getting what they want is to take, rob and dispossess others whom they perceive have the goodies. This is clearly not a conscious conviction, but an expression of unconscious fantasies that grip them. The result, as we have seen, is a dead end and leaves them empty. Furthermore, it leads them to confusion and mistrust about their own talent. Karen and David cannot find anything of value in what they are doing because they are not operating from their own need—to find, to reveal, to make fit. If they were, they would be empowered by that need.

Here again, we come to an important paradox in creation: if we pursue the work with full contact with that part of our personality that needs, that wants, and that is hungry, we will nourish ourselves from what we find. Only to the extent that we are in contact with this need can we engage in a fulfilling give and take with what we have in front of us. If, on the other hand, we are under the spell of an unconscious fantasy of having all that is needed—either having gotten what we need from someone, or about to get it—there will not be anything to guide us in the search. It is our need, our hunger, and our desire that guide and energise us in the pursuit of that which will be satisfying. It is only then, as I say, that we are "on track". Questions about having or not having a core self do not arise when we are operating from something that feels like a core. The smugness resulting from the fantasy that we already have what we need results in a pursuit without conviction and a goal-oriented relationship with the matter at hand that cannot enrich us or satisfy us.

The self-defeating nature of omnipotent fantasies also applies to the relationship with the work itself. The artist cannot only use the suggestions of others, but can also go on his own after material that he can use. The search is difficult, however, if he feels he has to have all of the knowledge inside him (another instance of omnipotence); and in this case, an omnipotent demand on himself. The attitude towards his surroundings will be very different if he is in the grip of omnipotent fantasies of having it, or if he is aware of an absence. In the first case, as he is not searching, he may miss many opportunities to enrich his work. In the second, his need can guide him as he scans his environment for possibilities. It is only in the latter case that serendipity is welcomed and properly used.

This brings us back to the beginning. Impasses in the work put us in touch with the more infantile, helpless, incompetent and needy part of ourselves and with the absence of that which will give us help, knowledge, and competence. We are faced with our aloneness, separation, and having to seek help from others—in short, our dependency. Again and again we relive the loss of union with mother, the illusion of oneness with her, and all the losses thereafter. The loss of direction in the work makes all the earlier losses reverberate in unison, and we have to resign ourselves to being the child once more without attempting to escape. Each time we succeed, we grow a bit more loving and tolerant; and the work, also, has a chance of growing better, stronger, and richer.

CHAPTER FIVE

On *not knowing*: discerning the mental and emotional requirements of creative work

Creative activity is work. Like any work it involves difficulties and obstacles. This chapter describes some of the difficulties and obstacles of creative work that are sometimes obscure and difficult to observe. This is not surprising, since creative work is not physical; it occurs mainly "in the mind". I will primarily draw ideas from Wilfred Bion, who, as a psychoanalyst, was exceptionally talented at dealing with very difficult aspects of the mind. He was also a talented painter and perhaps his insights regarding *not knowing* came not only from his readings of Freud and others but also from the obstacles he may have encountered in his creative work as a painter and the solutions he found to cope with these obstacles.

In a letter to his brother in 1817, the poet John Keats used the term "negative capability" to indicate the state of mind of someone who can remain in uncertainties, mysteries, doubts, without reaching after fact or knowledge (Keats, 1899). Bion (1970) expanded Keats's definition to include the state of mind necessary for psychoanalytic work and life itself. As used by Bion, "negative capability", a necessary ingredient in all forms of creativity, is a state of openness of mind where one does not know what the work needs or what one wants for it. It is relevant in many creative situations including the non-artistic, such as those in industrial and business practices.

The importance of Bion's theory of thinking lies in how he managed to connect emotions and cognition. He was as concerned with exploring how emotions become meaningful as he was with a model of how the capacity to think develops (Thorner, 1991). The clinical application of Bion's negative capability is rooted in Freud's insistence that the analyst cultivates a state of suspended attention, so central to his method. This state is often abandoned under the pressures of anxiety in both analyst and patient, who may want things to resolve quickly. According to Freud, the analyst needs to give equal notice to everything and this was a counterpart to the demand made on the patient to communicate everything without selection. The analyst should withhold all conscious influences from his capacity to attend, and give himself over completely to his "unconscious memory". Bion exhorted analysts to simply listen and not bother about keeping anything in mind. Freud (1912b) had suggested that during an analysis, both analyst and patient should give equal notice to everything and communicate everything without selection. Analysts often have to attend to the unconnected element the patient brings up, often presented in chaotic disorder. Bion claims that the analyst should resist the urge to order the elements in his or her mind, or arrange them according to cause and effect. The analyst should simply allow himself or herself an emotional experience in response to the patient's material, and refrain from being the "manager" of the session. In Bion's view, negative capability is at work when the analyst behaves without irritably reaching after facts and reason until an underlined pattern evolves. Just like in analysis, during creative work a pattern evolves when the artist allows the work time to develop.

Negative capability is necessary both in art and psychoanalysis. As an artist and practising psychoanalyst, I am often confronted with the question of how the analytic work resembles the artist's work. In what follows, I hope the relationship between the two becomes clear, as I see no difference between the creativity of an artist and that of an analyst at work.

Both Freud and Bion have agreed that the analytic attitude requires the analyst to wait. As poet T. S. Eliot remarked, "the faith and the love and the hope are all in the waiting" (Eliot, 1943); waiting without expectation or inclination, according to Freud; waiting without memory or desire, according to Bion. This waiting constitutes the essence of negative capability with its suspension of goals, aims, even the determination of the analyst to understand.

Bion has helped analysts reach an awareness of their role in receiving or deflecting the patients' projections, inviting them to focus on the relationship rather than the objects in them. In his view, analysis becomes a two-way street rather than the work of one person trying to help another. This is because the analyst's waiting encourages the patient to also wait rather than to try to explain and make sense of things or events prematurely. This is a point I stress when writing about the treatment of the creative patient. I need to encourage such patient to wait, allowing various thoughts and feelings to surface before responding to an interpretation (see Chapter Four, "The psychodynamics of creative blocks").

For Bion (1959), there is no fundamental difference between conscience and unconscious. In fact, he conceives a state of mind that is conscious and unconscious at the same time. He argues that, in order to comprehend an emotional element, it is necessary to "see" the conscious and the unconscious part in a "binocular way". Elaborating on this idea Sandler (2011) argues that "binocular vision" helps the analyst tolerate paradoxes without having to rush into an attempt at solving them. One can see how Bion's binocular vision and Keat's "negative capability" are related and why Bion has adopted the latter. They both imply a capacity to enlarge the scope of attention to the matter at hand, to tolerate uncertainty and not knowing. Bion even suggests that the analyst should ignore coherence. The analyst must come to accept and confront the incoherence and incomprehension of what is presented to him. Beyond bringing about insight, negative capabilities expand the function of interpretation (Mawson, 2015) and allow the analyst to engage in the creative work of the artist.

One can very well extrapolate these notions and apply them to the artist at work. In an early and related paper, four stages of the creative process that take place in every interaction with the work were delineated: perception, elaboration, expression, and evaluation (Safán-Gerard, 1978). The functions of each of these stages were described in order to understand the various sources of blocks to creativity. Because of their close relationship to negative capability, we may focus here specifically on the first two of these stages, *perception* and *elaboration*, because of their importance in not knowing. During *perception*, we take in what is in front of us. This is no simple matter, since, at times, due to defences against various anxieties stimulated by what we just did, the "taking in" doesn't take place. The necessary openness to experience, a requirement both in art and in psychoanalysis, is not a given. The artist, the analyst, and the patient may be unable to listen or see the "new" and continue to rely on the "old" (what they already know), preventing development. In the *elaboration* phase, what is taken in is brought into contact with other internal experiences where it can interact with them. This new element brought in may lead to internal links, which, in turn, may lead to conflict between them and various anxieties. If one defends against such anxieties, the new thing inside remains as a foreign body, encapsulated and prevented from exchanges with the parts of the self that might be reacting to it. If, on the other hand, the new thing we have taken in is allowed to impact us, there might be strain or internal turmoil but, if tolerated, it can lead to a response (often a surprising one) in the *expression* phase of the creative act. We could say that it is at this time when the internal turmoil is accepted and tolerated that the artist becomes free to create.

Another factor to consider when facing the requirements of creative work is that of the links or connections between parts of the self, since the nature and number of these links may contribute to the richness of the work. The complexity of the links involved will depend on how many parts of the self are available and how much conflict is stimulated. Projections of parts of the self into others are inevitable. This does not necessarily imply a restriction in creativity when such projections are reversible. If projections are fixed and irreversible, there will be less conflict stirred up, but the work will suffer. This is the case when we consider self-righteousness (for example, Safán-Gerard, 2002). A self-righteous person tends to project an unwanted part of the self and becomes morally indignant when facing this part of the self in others. Having eliminated conflict and having assumed a completely moral stance, the person is less likely to welcome new material for fear that it might stimulate internal conflict. And when this new material is allowed in, the resulting links are only between accepted parts of the self. The work then becomes sterile and again, creativity suffers. What is common in all four stages is the person's internal freedom to examine and interact with new material and the willingness to experience the anxiety or distress evoked in the process.

Back to Bion, we might want to examine the anxieties that interfere with *not knowing*. For the most part, they are the result of all our preconceptions of "good work"; from our reading from theorists, academia, critics, the art market, and even the media that interferes with our simply noticing what is in front of us. These are the confining boundaries we create ourselves. They explain the importance of the writers' cliché, when talking about creativity, to emphasise the need for "thinking outside the box". In these moments, the creator's image of a critic evaluating the work is so pervasive that anguish is exacerbated, even immobilising the creator. This is well illustrated in Chapter Thirteen, "Love and hate in the creative process".

The openness that *not knowing* requires allows new ideas into one's world—objects that need to be considered, evaluated, or simply thought of. With each new idea that surfaces while working one is burdened with thinking in order to discern, evaluate, and make choices. One of the main consequences is that thinking is at times quite painful and the creator has to develop a capacity to endure such pain. Even in a good relationship with the work, there is pain to be endured. Artists who, for some reason, have abandoned creative work complain about how much they miss it, but reveal that they are also relieved of the struggle that such work had demanded.

Sometimes creators believe and trust that certain elements in their work reveal their most precious identity. The narcissism implied in this belief dominates and narrows down any new development and growth in the work. Not willing to part with their perceived identities, the work suffers as no growth is then possible. Only clichés seem to be expressed when the creator appears to copy him or herself. Without risk-taking there can be no creative breakthrough, which is what artists strive for. Not to suggest that there is no value in exploring one's rich and pregnant ideas, as there is much to gain in taking the work further, particularly when *not knowing* where it will end up. All levels of *not knowing* are operating then, as different parts or details in the work seem to continue their development on their own and the creator is simply required to follow. The artist always has the ultimate power and/or responsibility to make choices. In a happy moment, the artist is not in conflict with the work, but seems to be engaged in a dance with it. Such moments are what creators live for and where the passion of creative work lies! The important thing is, as Ralph Waldo Emerson wrote in *The Conduct of Life* (1860) that, with respect to work, one should maintain concentration and avoid dissipation. Like Rodin in Paris, Emerson extoled the value of work. As he so eloquently put it, "You must elect your work; you shall take what your brain can, and drop all the rest. Only so, can that amount of vital force accumulate, which can mark the step from knowing to doing. No matter how much faculty of idle seeing a man has, the step from knowing to doing is rarely taken" (1860). It is in the risk of *doing* that creators' anxieties have to be tolerated.

We have been exploring the positive consequences of not knowing. Is there such a thing as knowing? How can one know how to start a new work? How can we know when a piece of creative work is finished? Perhaps at a certain point the work in progress does not need anything from us anymore. An impaired capacity to recognise that work in progress has ended and that working should stop can result in a case of failed creativity. It may seem contradictory that we need to be *not knowing* during work in progress, but at some point the *not knowing* state also has to be relinquished. There is pain in this relinquishing because it represents the end of the relationship between artist and work, like the end of a dance between lovers.

The parallel question to the creativity of the analyst is in his or her failed capacity to recognise the emotional cues of the patient just as the artist may miss recognising an unexpected new element in the work, Silence is then needed during the session to allow the patient to process the interpretation. In the case of a painter, one could appreciate that finishing a painting entails much conflict. "Is my work with this piece over? Is it finished? Does it need something else?" Just like the analyst with a patient, the creator may need to allow time to digest the latest intervention and what it has done to the work. Did it fit? Did it add or detract from the work? In this regard, a glimpse into my own difficulties while painting is documented in Chapter Thirteen, "Love and hate in the creative process", where I write about my feelings in response to these struggles.

CHAPTER SIX

Why bother? From indifference to passion

arly in the history of psychiatry, madness, in league with passion, was exiled from its vocabulary. One was not mad, but suffered from nerves. Madness was also banished from professional jargon. It disappeared from the classification of disorders as a shameful reference, concerned as psychiatry was with having a scientific bearing. Madness and possession were not scientific notions. André Green's *On Private Madness* published in 1985 represents an exception. During the Middle Ages and the Renaissance, madness was embellished with an aura that made a mystery of it (in the religious sense of the term) and something on the order of the divine or the demoniac showed through it. For the mystics, there could be no happy passion except the *way of the cross*.

By the beginning of the nineteenth century, the concept of nature began its task of undermining God and religious passion. With the emergence of modern science in the following century, rationalism chased passion from philosophy. Psychiatry was born of this mutation. In psychiatry, the *I* wishes to be objective—that is to say, without passion.

Today there is little discussion of passion in psychiatry or psychology, and practically none in psychoanalysis. If psychoanalytic thought had not deemed it necessary to attach particular interest to the psychoses early on, it is probably because in psychoanalysis it is implicit that all delusions are the fruit of repressed sexual passion. However, in apparent contradiction to an earlier view, Freud wrote in *Civilization and its Discontents* (1930a) that Eros is our brightest best hope against the ravages of Thanatos. On the other hand, for Freud, the state of being in love or of amorous passion represents a short psychosis, a view that has been held by many analysts after him. For Green (1985) all the vicissitudes of Eros are believed to be tainted with a potential madness.

Whereas passion and madness appear to be banished in Freud's meta-psychological writings, in his case histories amorous passion reappears within the transference—that is, the feelings that get transferred between the patient and the analyst. However, Freud was more at ease with the analysis of infantile sexuality (which belonged to a repressed past and with daydreams connected to it), rather than with the reality of love and hate in the consulting room. His noted patient Dora was capable of anything because her feelings of love for Freud pushed her not only to transfer them, but also to act them out in acts of vengeance. According to Green, to approach unconscious meaning by means of dreams, as Freud did, was to introduce a mediating distance from a potentially dangerous situation. Freud's defensive feelings in response to Dora drove him to give a watered-down version of passion. Perhaps the frequent requests today for re-analysis arise from the lack of attention given to dangerous passions and its relation to the psychotic part of the personality. Green is probably referring to the irrational rages a patient can display towards the analyst or the acting out in the session of an erotic transference. It seems essential to re-establish madness in the place where it has to be recognised: at the heart of human desire, something Freud seldom experienced in the consulting room. In *On Private Madness*, Green states: "To take the full force of transference passion is doubtless exhausting but it is the price to be paid by the analyst if the analysis is to succeed" (1985, p. 241).

Passion, as I understand it, is not synonymous with affect. Affect is a quality of aliveness and responsiveness that does not necessarily engage an object and it may be temporary. Passion is an aliveness in response and in relation to an object and has a sustained quality. This distinction will become clearer as we discuss the precursors of passion. My intended focus is on the overcoming of indifference. I want to restrict the meaning of passion to that of direct and sustained interest in an object outside the self. Passion is the opposite of living one's life by "marking time" (Winnicott, 1975).

Precursors of passion

Some patients seem to have problems attending, noticing, and linking. Taylor (2006) considers attending, noticing and linking to be functions of consciousness. I see them also as precursors of passion. These difficulties in attending, noticing and linking are associated with a profoundly passive position at some deep or early level of the personality. Patients experiencing these difficulties are not able to be independent initiators of action. Their lack of response seems to have arisen in infancy or childhood because of some emotional failing in the primary object. They have had to disengage an infantile part of the personality and resort to other routes to deal with potentially intolerable or impossible states of mind.

Passion is a necessary ingredient in creativity. How can the analyst help in the development and growth of passion? The development of the patient's potential passion depends on the analyst's sensitivity and alertness to the smallest signs of attention, noticing and linking in the patient; in doing so, the analyst champions and supports these developments. In fact, the analyst needs to be attentive to what is incipient, rather than pointing to what is already obvious. In *Attention and Interpretation* (1970), Bion adopted the term pre-monition in describing forewarnings of emotions about to develop. For him, the analyst needs to be an advance scout of attention whose function is to recognise what is anticipatory.

Taylor offers an account of the treatment of a very damaged patient who lived as a homeless man whom he only saw every other week for some years. Initially (and continuing for the next three years) the patient sat on a chair far from the analyst, was unable to keep eye contact, and the interactions were stilted. Taylor was responsive to any signs of attention, noticing, and linking. Eventually, eye contact was sustained and the patient began to notice objects in the office. Taylor supported these signs by responding immediately to their appearance. Such signs of attention begin to appear in the patient in the later stages of an analysis and especially during termination. This is important because passion cannot occur without them. Patients begin to notice paintings and objects in the consulting room they had been oblivious to for a very long time. These precursors of passion are signs of mental health and indicate an improved capacity to relate to objects in the external world.

Interests

Neither traditional psychoanalytic theory nor psychoanalytic ego psychology account for the development and significance of having interests. In a lucid and comprehensive chapter, Morris Eagle (1982) draws from indications from several sources including physiological, experimental, anecdotal and sociological to clarify an aspect of personality central to psychoanalytic theory and to creativity (1982, p. 159). He attempts to understand those behaviours pertaining to the development of an interest in other people and objects and the psychological significance and functions of such interests. Eagle claims that interests play a central role in maintaining personality intactness and integrity, particularly in extreme circumstances. He draws on evidence from "autobiographical accounts, animal investigations, epidemiological studies, clinical impressions and studies of infant behavior" (1982, p. 160).

In psychoanalytic theory, the idea most relevant to an understanding of the development of interests is sublimation. Sublimation results from "the instinct directing itself toward an aim other than and remote from that of sexual satisfaction" (Freud, 1914c, p. 94). Interests are the creation of the rerouting of sexual goals to "higher pursuits". As Eagle explains in his paper:

> A formulation of interests in terms of the concept of sublimation does not adequately take account of their development and psychological function … Observations regarding the importance of "having something to live for" point to recent epidemiological studies supporting the informal observation that the survivor in a long relationship in which one of the partners has recently died is more susceptible to death and to illness than others of his or her age group.

However, this "something to live for" function can also be fulfilled with dedicated interests and values. There are many first-person accounts of prisoners in concentration camps that describe the role that these interests and values played in upholding psychological integrity (1982, pp. 161–163).

Back to our focus on creativity, Eagle has found that "lack of interest is a negative prognostic indicator" in a therapeutic situation, but "on the other hand, a creative talent or gift, and the intense interest that can accompany it, often can serve to sustain people with considerable pathology". Without this centre of creative interest, these people would decompensate. Of course, this does not imply that only persons with a creative talent or gift have a chance in life. Whether or not as an adult one has acquired long-lasting interests is not a casual affair or peripheral aspect of an individual's behaviour, but a central feature of personality (1982, p. 162).

Difficulties in experiencing deep interests play a prominent part in the symptomatology reported by patients today. Rather than simply circumscribed depression or anxiety, patients report experiencing meaninglessness and emptiness—including lack of meaningful interests, ideals, and values. Eagle believes that "analysts are preoccupied with narcissistic personality disorders, while political scientists, literary critics, historians and writers are writing about the 'new narcissism' as a widespread cultural phenomenon" (1982, p. 174). A critical feature is the lack of interest in others per se. Interest is dictated mainly by the aims of self-enhancement and self-aggrandisement, particularly in narcissistic patients.

Absorption dimension

The link between deep interest and passion lies in the fact that one of the manifestations of passion is the capacity to absorb oneself in something outside the self. Absorption as a dimension of personality is the object of personality research and includes a thirty-five year longitudinal study (Tellegen, 1992; Block & Kremen, 2002). According to Block and Kremen, the psychological disposition to enter into states of absorption is "characterized by openness to aesthetic experiences, breadth of interests and humor—and thus suggests that absorption is related, in both sexes, to a willingness to destructure conventional and everyday pragmatic modes of cognitive and perceptual processing" (2002, p. 257). Absorption has been linked with imagery ability, synaesthesia, fantasy proneness, daydreaming, experiential involvement and alterations in attention. It has been alternatively labelled as openness to experience.

Young women who score low in absorption seem less troubled and hostile than young men, but they nevertheless seem immature and defensive. Both young men and women who score high on the capacity for absorption appear interesting, interested and responsive to the world around them.

Passionless patients

Because passion is a necessary feature of creativity, its absence is a deterrent. Passionless patients demand much from the analyst and psychoanalytic treatment can take years with these patients. Riccardo Lombardi has written about patients who are "driven to analysis primarily by an inability to feel alive" (Lombardi, 2006, p. 1). His patient Antonio only felt alive when he gambled. From the start of the analysis the patient tended to keep silent and not respond to any attempts to stimulate his participation. When asked directly, he claimed he felt nothing and thought nothing. However, Lombardi observed Antonio's "extraordinary ability to convey violent hatred", which his analyst found very hard to contain (2006, p. 2). He noticed that he himself tended to become absent from emotional feeling, which probably was Antonio's solution for managing his hatred, absenting himself mentally. Regarding Antonio's silence and unresponsiveness, his analyst continued to pursue him, "The fact that I did not give in to the blandishments of absence and silence was, I believe, an important element in catalyzing development" (2006, p. 2).

When Lombardi's comments were aimed at the feelings between patient and analyst, they were met with rigidity or they were totally rejected. His patient's reaction seemed more constructive when the analyst spoke of hatred in general and of his propensity to ignore it. In other words, Lombardi was spurring Antonio to observe his way of relating to hatred rather than to emphasise his hatred of him. The two of them were observing a third object, the patient's hatred, rather than their relationship to each other. The analyst felt that it didn't matter what they spoke about. "The essential thing was keeping the dialogue going thus keeping open a channel of communication which would make it possible to develop a relationship and to evolve a way of thinking based on reality (common sense)" (2006, p. 3). Antonio was by no means indifferent to his analyst's contribution, as he persisted in pretending. His inclination towards silence and paralysis clearly returned with the approach of the first long interruption of analysis.

Insisting that the patient continue to express what was happening to him in the here and now of the experience meant for Lombardi "facing my own violent participation in his hatred, which I felt quite tangibly in the form of strong physical sensations, culminating in intense and inexplicable nausea" (p. 3). Perhaps while Antonio became mentally absent, his violent feelings were projected onto his analyst. Lombardi writes, "I neither considered nor interpreted his hatred as directed principally at me, but instead understood it as a signal of his approach to sharing an area which until that moment had been dissociated and acted out" (p. 3). We could even say that the analyst's nausea was perhaps his way of sharing the patient's hatred. Lombardi believed that the experience of hatred in the session represented some "progress towards the world of emotions, and not an attack upon the analytic relationship". Lombardi felt his patient could not relate in the "you and me" fashion of the transference, but that he needed to experience his hatred as something that he and his patient could observe together. Encouraging Antonio "to be present and to register the experience of temporal limits determined by the approach of a separation was particularly useful". This was confirmed by the patient's acceptance of a third weekly session (p. 3).

What we observe in Lombardi's patient is that a joint interest between analyst and patient as something outside the self precedes the focus and interest in the "you and me" of the transference—that is, the relationship with the analyst. Even though in Lombardi's patient the concern was the hatred arising from him, the patient, both analyst and patient were observing it as something external to himself. The emphasis here is on an experience where the patient perhaps follows closely the analyst's interest with an eventual sharing of experience. Only from this kind of sharing can there be an interest in attending, noticing and linking the "you and me" of the transference. Perhaps the patient projects his own interest in the analyst, who is then perceived as having an interest in him.

We may want to go back to Taylor's (2006) homeless patient and his countertransference—that is, his emotional response to the patient. At the beginning of the sessions he found himself attending closely, but then his attention drifted off. The lack of reciprocity in the interchange made Taylor feel "why bother" and tempted him to give up trying to keep the contact alive. He writes that, at times, he felt intellectually "not up to it". The compound feelings of connection and loss of the connection evoked had an effect that the analyst compared to an emotional roller coaster. Another British analyst, Edna O'Shaughnessy (1999) has written about the earliest ruptures in the relationship between self and object. It can be very difficult for a mother to know how to interest an infant who seems not to have developed the "approach responses". In a similar way, it must be very difficult for the infant when the mother doesn't have the maternal equivalence of the sucking motion to approach the infant, her ability to wait quietly *and with interest* while the infant's interest is deployed somewhere else.

Linking is a particular kind of emotionally dynamic relationship between people in which they are "affected by each other". In the interactions between people, we expect a kind of reciprocity of the interchange. After some years, Taylor realised that his patient was noticing a painting in the consulting room. This was a new development and marked a shift in the direction of contact with the external world. It also became clear to Taylor that, even with such a small sign of relatedness, the patient was quite aware of impending vacations and breaks in the treatment and this suggests that underneath the apparent indifference there were strong feelings towards the analyst.

Another problem for the analyst regarding passionless patients is the relationship with a narcissistic patient (even though in this case it is hard to talk about an absence of passion). As we will see with my patient Robert, they can be quite emotional, which can be confused with passion because of its intensity. Narcissism in adults is an instance of an absence of passion in relation to other people. It is rare that these people develop a true passion other than towards the self or activities that enhance the self. In view of this feature of narcissism, we can see how difficult it is for an analyst to establish a relationship with such a patient. It took several years for Robert, a patient of mine who didn't want to use the couch, to make eye contact with me. Sitting across the room, he talked and talked, interestingly, about his many experiences and observations. It was hard for me to put a word in edgewise as he would stop me and continue his talking. He did this sometimes by saying angrily, "Wait a minute. I am not finished!" He used humour effectively and seemed to use me simply as an audience that he entertained. I had to cope with my frustration by humouring him back about his paying me money to simply use me as an audience. I remember saying to him (when I finally could!) that I felt like a mother with a bottle of milk trying to find his mouth to feed him. This amused him a great deal, as he felt successful in thwarting my efforts. Eventually, after several years of this, he began to ask me to repeat my interpretations, confessing that he didn't pay attention to what I said. He said he really wanted to hear what I had to say and would close his eyes to help himself concentrate. Sometimes he even asked me to say it twice. It was clear how hard it was for him to listen and how hard he was trying now. He began to make reference to my interpretations in the following sessions, giving evidence of how he was finally using me, and how he was using his high intelligence to learn about himself.

For a long time, the sessions focused on his problems at work and on his difficulties in keeping his temper. This had been the cause of his being held back from a position of responsibility, even though his performance was outstanding. I thought it would be helpful to give him an opportunity to discover his incipient skills relating to others in a therapy group I was leading. He was able to do this in spite of the fact that several times he was so enraged with someone in the group that he stormed out of the room. As of late, his work situation has improved a great deal. He has been able to control his temper there, in the group, and in our sessions and he appears far less self-righteous. We spend time discussing the problems in his relationship with his girlfriend of several years, linking this to the relationship with me. He still has difficulties controlling his temper with her, but now they just recognise they had another fight and they don't keep breaking up with the ensuing anguish in both of them.

Fostering passion

Is it possible to engage with passion in an activity without a secure base to come back to? Studies on attachment show that the toddler will engage in exploratory activities and in play when the mother or the caretaker is close by and that the toddler will interrupt his play to go back to the mother for some kind of emotional refuelling. Other people functioning as caretakers may fulfil that role with adults. The notion that there is somebody there in the background may allow an artist, for example, to engage in hours of art making. A colleague was telling me of a very productive six weeks of writing in an isolated place some years ago. If he hadn't known he would be joining his wife (who was then across the country), he would never have been able to immerse himself in his work the way he did.

After my husband died, I felt reluctant to work on a paper the whole afternoon without a prospect of seeing anyone the whole day. I would make plans to have dinner with a friend that evening. With that idea in mind I could go to the computer and work steadily for two or three hours. I knew I would be seeing her and that I had some precious time to work before I did. I remember the pleasure of many hours in my studio or at the computer when I knew that my husband was nearby reading or writing. This is reminiscent of Winnicott's (1965) statement regarding the capacity to be alone in the presence of another. We may want to see the capacity to be alone as a sign of maturity, ignoring that, perhaps no matter how old and mature we have become, we still need the connection to a significant other.

A paper on passion became interesting to me because some years ago I had noticed that my passion for painting and writing had diminished and wanted to understand why. Of course I had blamed it on the three years of mourning my husband and thought that I would recover my passion some day when the mourning was over, if that were possible. But, I came to think that I still needed the presence of another. A few years ago, one lonely Sunday, I forced myself to my studio. With the help of one of Shostakovich's chamber pieces, a piano quintet that a dear friend gave to me, I was able to work steadily for several hours. I emotionally refuelled by appreciating the love of my composer friend who gave me the Shostakovich CD and the music itself, a different kind of presence.

We seem to find various ways to bolster our passion by having a background object to support us. In my case, my first art teacher worked with the radio on and it had to be a station where there were interviews and talking. If the radio was not on, he could not paint. A writer I know does his best work at Starbucks (much like Sartre writing at Les Deux Magots), where the people around him become the background object. I have written the first draft of my best papers on airplane flights. I experience great comfort in being surrounded by other passengers and in being catered to.

From a developmental point of view, these strategies to find emotional refuelling may be indicative of an immature ego, where the internalisation of a good parental couple has not taken hold in one's internal world. This goes along with the notion that the capacities to be alone and to work alone are signs of mental health, a notion that tallies with the American culture, where independence and self-reliance are highly valued. One could alternatively argue that the more internalised the parental couple, the more the person is able to supply the background object needed for refuelling. Early on, Fairbairn (1952) wrote about a mature dependency rather than independency. For him, the idea of independence is fostered by a schizoid fantasy of not needing anyone. Along the same lines, Sidney Blatt (1996) has written about the necessity for a healthy integration between autonomy, self-definition, and relatedness.

I hope that by now we have come to an understanding of how difficult it is for analysts to keep the patient's passion alive and how working with such patients demands much of them. As we have seen, the analyst may need to respond to the slightest sign of noticing, attending, and linking, as well as supporting and encouraging the slightest sign of relatedness. In the case of a narcissistic patient, the analyst must be alert to and support any sign of interest in something or someone outside of the patient himself, even if it is photographing a sunset. My patient Robert came to take delight in photographing participants in a Halloween Festival, indicating an incipient and positive interest in others.

These accounts might help the reader understand how challenging and (at times) ungratifying the work of the analyst can be and why analysis can last years. Of course our analytic work can also be enormously enriching and fulfilling. As part of my interest in art and psychoanalysis I have come to recognise that a good interpretation has an aesthetic quality. On the contrary, the absence of passion can make an analytic interpretation meaningless.

In his paper "On narcissism", Freud (1914) maintains that, in healthy development, one moves from narcissism to object love and writes that in the final analysis "one must love in order not to fall ill". As gifted analyst Morris Eagle notes, if one is to thrive psychologically one must move from self-absorption to absorption (a form of passion) in objects outside oneself (Eagle, 2015). Regarding this chapter, I hope that my love and admiration for the colleagues and patients described has become as apparent as the appreciation of my love for analytic work. Again, art and psychoanalysis are two paths to the discovery and recognition of oneself.

CHAPTER SEVEN

Is creativity dangerous?

People visiting my studio who like my paintings often ask if I teach art. I have always replied that I don't—I am stingy with my limited time to paint. But, a year ago it occurred to me that I might help people engage in creative work as an alternative (or complementary) way to do analysis. It would not be art therapy because I would not interpret the content of what they did, but instead, I would focus exclusively on the process. This group work would give me an opportunity to debunk certain long-held beliefs about creativity, talent, originality, the role of the accident, premature closure leading to mistakes, and the importance of destructiveness.

For a year I led a small group of people who responded to an announcement entitled "Expanding the limits" that I sent to colleagues, former patients and friends who expressed an interest in the arts. These were not artists or people who had special artistic inclinations; they had or were still in analysis and had become intrigued with the idea of a different way of freeing themselves from paralysing constraints in several aspects of their lives. The group would give me an opportunity to put into action my own beliefs about the creative process developed from painting for over thirty years, from writing papers on creativity and for working with creative people in my practice. My very first paper, "Creativity as communication", appeared in *Psychology Today* in 1978. Some years later, I went on to document the evolution of a single painting and kept track of my conscious thoughts as I worked on the painting, keeping a journal of dreams that related to it (see Chapter Twelve). My beliefs have also stemmed from my writings about artists such as Max Beckmann, Picasso, and Lucian Freud, along with aspects of my own work. I gave a major retrospective paper accompanied by 112 slides that I prepared for the International Psychoanalytic Association (IPA) Congress in Santiago, Chile, in 1999, and again in Paris in 2000, where I gave it in French—the most gratifying experience I have ever had (see Chapter Fourteen).

My role in the art experience group I created was to mind the members as they worked and to mind the work itself. I moved from one participant to the other, as they worked on their artworks at a large table in my studio. I commented on what I saw, what seemed different, promising, worth developing, while also letting them work by themselves. I provided them with materials and let them choose the size of paper or canvas they felt like working with, a very telling indicator of where they were at the time and how much freedom they were willing to tackle. Most importantly, I didn't let them give up. I encouraged them to continue to look for something of value in what they did and to forget factors such as balance and harmony, which are so emphasised in painting classes.

Before they started painting, I had the group sit in my studio on the same couches where my group therapy patients sit (incidentally, they have preferred to meet in my studio, rather than in my office downstairs). I would hand each of them a small pad of paper and have them write a sentence on top, covering what they wrote by folding the paper, and then writing the last word again on the next open line. They passed these notepads to the next person, who would then improvise a sentence beginning with that single word. We would later read the crazy outcome they had improvised. Apparently, this is a well-known game in the United States, but I first learned about it in Chile years ago. My hope with this exercise was to loosen up their thoughts so that they would bring this "loosened-up mind" to the table where they painted. I also had them listen to music and was careful of which music I selected. For example, I would have them listen to portions of the second movements of Beethoven's Razumovsky string quartets, opus 59 (No. 7 in F major, No. 8 in E minor, and No. 9 in C major). I felt that their immersion in this beautifully painful and sensitive music would allow them to have access to their inner emotional life that could be brought to bear later on when they made their paper selection. The slow music had begun to quiet down the manic feelings they came in with, which were usually caused by fighting traffic, finding parking, and their anxiety about painting something worthwhile. Listening to Beethoven in this way was a revelation for most of them. I also had them listening to one or two slow movements from Shostakovich's quartets. They became curious about the music, but that curiosity was put aside (or, I believe, transformed) when they approached the big table around which they worked. They seldom talked while painting at the table, but slowly became curious about the others and what they were doing. After a while, I would ask them to stop and reveal how they felt about what they had done so far and they expressed quite freely their doubts or misgivings. The others would come in and talk about their own reactions: what they liked, what was upsetting to them, and so on. An ambience of collaboration and real interest about the other members' work developed. At times, one of them would express disgust at her evolving work or one aspect of it and others chimed in expressing, instead, positive feelings towards it. I would then ask them to be specific about what pleased them or didn't. Their camaraderie was touching. How, for example, they would encourage the one who was so disparaging of her own work by pointing to the interesting and beautiful elements that they could see in it. The member involved would then be charged with new energy and ideas to pursue the work.

It has been gratifying to find out that at least half of them have pursued art as a career, joining studios where an artist mentor has helped them to further develop their art. Three of them have already had exhibits of their work in prestigious galleries in Los Angeles. This was an unintended outcome of this art experience group, more impressive than merely my original aim of expanding the limits of freedom.

Reflecting on what I have learned with this group, with all of my work before this group, and with myself while painting, I have to conclude that creativity *is* dangerous. That is why so many gifted people give up halfway. Creativity is dangerous, not only because, just like in analysis, one gets in touch with unwanted aspects of oneself, but also because it makes one primarily aware of one's destructiveness. As a new member of the group tried to continue painting, she stopped and, turning to me, said in exasperation: "Here is where I quit!" She had attempted to paint many times in her life, taking various art classes, but would come to this stumbling block. This time around, I was watching her and her painting. I asked her to show me the smallest area that she liked, encouraged her to develop that area, and to forget the whole painting as well as the notions of balance and harmony expected from finished work. During the next hour, she expanded her work from that very small area, eventually covering two-thirds of the painting in complete abandonment. And, working in layers, she stayed with that painting for three consecutive sessions. The judgement of balance and harmony she was used to became not only appropriate, but also necessary in the last layer. As expected, the workings of her unconscious and conscious mind had been at play and could proceed smoothly from free expression to judgement and back to free expression in a constant flow.

It is paradoxical that the move away from narcissism that is necessary when one paints is at the same time the most acute expression of the self. I presented this notion to Neville Symington during a conference at the Los Angeles Institute and Society for Psychoanalytic Studies (LAISPS). He agreed that art-making represents such a paradox. Artists are aware of this paradox when they distance themselves from the work to be able to see it as a separate object and to be able to do the editing the work requires. As they pay close attention to this separate object in front of them, what develops comes to represent the essence of who they are. No wonder it is dangerous! While they pay attention to *it*, they see themselves in the mirror and many times don't like what they see. This is better observed when there is a slowing down in the process and people get a chance to move around to see what other people are doing—something I have encouraged the members to do.

They would then go back to their own work, appreciating its uniqueness. However, they may have liked what they saw in others' work and decided to incorporate it into their own work. "Time to steal!" I have said to them. This is so frequently frowned upon in art schools as they mainly value true originality. So, I encouraged shameless stealing from here and there while voicing their stealing as they realised that their work would be enriched in the process. They not only came to appreciate the work of others in the group, but also their own work.

Composer John Corigliano wrote his own notes in the programme about his Symphony No. 1 when the Los Angeles Philharmonic performed it for the first time in January of 1993 with David Zinman conducting. It was an account of all the stealing he had done while working on it—an appropriation that resulted in a most original work.

People are afraid of making mistakes and art-making is no exception. It was immensely freeing to the group members to be encouraged to make mistakes and to learn how to profit from them, rather than quickly dispose of them. After all, we go from mistake to mistake, from destruction and reparation many times over in the course of a single painting. The best aspects of an art piece are frequently the results of a mistake that forced the artist to develop the work further. One of the group members looked at what she had done and exclaimed, "I wrecked it! I always wreck everything! I shouldn't have come today!" And, discouraged, she added, "I better leave early." The idea that she could build something new on top of the wreckage had never occurred to her. She has since been able to appreciate the wreckage as the fertile ground of new work, ending up liking what she did with it. She learned to look at her own destructiveness in a totally different way, making peace with it. Of course, I don't underestimate the role I play in helping people like her accept destructiveness as a necessary ingredient in the cycles of destructiveness and reparation. I am the new mother who is not afraid of their destructive impulses and I am there and steady, minding them and minding their work, while the others (the siblings) are there learning too. As Sabina Spielrein wrote in "Destruction as the cause of coming into being" (1912), destructiveness represents an essential aspect of creativity.

I also encouraged them to stay in the "not knowing place" Bion wrote about (1967). That was the most refreshing aspect of the first art class with Keith Finch I joined in Los Angeles many years ago. Nobody in that class knew what they were doing and were not afraid of admitting it! What a relief from the clinical training in psychology at UCLA, where omnipotence was rampant among professors and students alike.

A few years ago, I gave a workshop at the New Center of Psychoanalysis (NCP) in Los Angeles entitled "Creativity: From the art studio to the consulting room". Colleagues attending this workshop were expressing the same concerns as the members in my art experience group. As I mentioned at the beginning, I wrote a blurb about the art experience group "Expanding the limits", because overcoming the fear of creative work is tantamount to a substantial increase in the capacity to withstand doubt and uncertainty. This capacity translates into a new freedom. And isn't this pursuit of freedom also the goal of psychoanalysis?

Freedom to think, freedom to speak one's mind, freedom to feel, freedom to confront oneself? In the case of creativity, we have to add the freedom to plumb oneself.

An art dealer from Germany visited my studio and I showed him some of the work by the art experience group members. He could not believe that it was not the work of mature artists or graduate students in an art department. It is clear to me, I told him, that the reason their work looks so good is that they are overcoming the dangers of creative work and plunging into the joys of creativity. One of the most gratifying aspects of this work, however, is that, in moving away from narcissism, the group members developed a true appreciation for each other and for each other's work. They really looked at each other's work! And one of them, the most recalcitrant, would bring a camera to take photos of the other members' works in progress. He said to one of them, "You work in layers. Hold on! I want to keep track of the layers before you continue."

CHAPTER EIGHT

Art and madness

It is with delight and trepidation that I embark on this dialogue about the Prinzhorn Collection, which was featured in the documentary film *Between Madness and Art: The Prinzhorn Collection* by Christian Beetz, as well as in the book *Beyond Reason: Art and Psychosis: Works from the Prinzhorn Collection* (Brand-Claussen, Jádi, & Douglas, 1996). The documentary is a complex assortment of historical data and a biographical account of Hans Prinzhorn's life. It also includes footage of a few institutionalised artists talking about their work, footage on the advent of Nazism, and the infamous "Entartete Kunst" (Degenerate Art) exhibition in Munich in 1937, when art from the Prinzhorn Collection was appropriated and shown side by side with the work of artists of the time. There is also some footage on Grafeneck, one of the four extermination camps where many of these schizophrenic artists died. The documentary leads to important questions about the nature of individual self-expression, the boundaries between artistic creativity and mental disturbance, the relationship between art and psychosis, and the nature of creativity itself. These questions have concerned art historians since the collection was uncovered in 1963.

In *The Artistry of the Mentally Ill* (*Bildnerei der Geisteskranken*) (1922), Prinzhorn attempted to develop an aesthetic theory that claimed schizophrenic artists possessed an "essential insight" that led to an art based on the artists' deepest emotions. Ernst Kris criticised Prinzhorn's aesthetic theory in his book *Psychoanalytic Explorations in Art* (1936). He believed these forms were not primal manifestations of universal formative forces, but a psycho-dynamically organised attempt at self-rescue on the part of the floundering ego. The main question one is left with after watching this film is whether schizophrenic art is an expression of the patient's impulse to create or is it an attempt to reconstruct an ego that is in shambles because of the psychosis. Grebbing's incredible calendars shown in the film are an example of the latter—he desperately tried to bring order into his chaotic world and he did this for more than four decades. If we agree with Kris that the psychotic's creativity is an attempt at self-rescue, does this mean that psychotic art is a valid art form? I propose that, even if a painting's aim is a reconstruction of the self, psychotic art has the same validity as non-psychotic "sane" art. In all forms of artistic creation, the person (artist or not) manifests externally what is going on in his or her internal world. There might be cases where the aim can be both an expression of the internal world and a reconstruction of a psychotic process. I reiterate that, however it comes about, we can consider psychotic art a valid art form.

As far as the boundaries between artistic creativity and mental disturbance go, I would like to take this opportunity to debunk certain mystiques about psychotic art. There is an aura of demonic possession about it, a superstitious feeling. The fear of psychosis reveals the fear of our own unconscious. We all have secret places that break open when (and if) we become psychotic. If one loses the boundary between dream and reality, one innocently paints the dream, which seems to be reality. The content of this art is often conventional and the subject matter banal, but the ideas about its aim can be unrealistic, like saving the world or being the bridge between France and Germany. There is the fear of crossing the boundary and of losing contact with reality. Because of this fear, the average person is afraid to give in to fantasy. Sane artists take that risk but still hold on to reality, although we are all familiar with artists like van Gogh (the proverbial mad artist), who lived and painted in spite of his psychosis. The sane artist has access to his dream and when he paints he knows it is his dream. However, the permeability and flexibility of the mental structure of artists put them at risk of a psychotic collapse or the ongoing experience of psychotic states. Many well-known artists, past and present, have had long periods of inactivity when a psychotic state is in the ascendance.

Some people believed the art produced by these patients was the result of demonic possession, rather than divine inspiration. Psychotic art is the result of a dream that spills into reality. August Natterer, a patient who believed he was a descendent of Napoleon IV, wanted to bridge a gap between Germany and France. He was so compelling that it took a while for people to realise that his letters were representing his dream world and not reality. He worked for twenty-six years on an imaginary family tree supporting his fantasy. Vera Schmidt, the patient who had been subjected to electroshock therapy, was saving the world with her drawings. She believed that her simple lines had a beneficial influence in the world.

Hans Prinzhorn's book *The Artistry of the Mentally Ill* (1922) had an enormous impact on the Expressionist and Surrealist movements of Europe in the early twentieth century. The Expressionist movement, characterised by heightened symbolic colours and exaggerated imagery, developed in different countries in Europe around 1905 and was influenced by outsider art (art produced by people without any formal training or connections to the art world and often considered anti-cultural). The German Expressionists tended to dwell in the darker, sinister aspect of the human psyche (examples include the works of Max Beckmann and Otto Dix). Rouault represented an isolated expressionism in Paris, while Egon Schiele and Oscar Kokoschka created their work in Austria.

Influenced by Freud, the Surrealists became fascinated by primitive art, children's art, the art of the insane, and outsider art. They developed a strong interest in getting in touch with their unconscious and tried to get to it by painting with their eyes closed or by automatic writing. This is all explicated in André Breton's first *Surrealist Manifesto* (published in 1924) in which Breton states that whether faced with the products of hypnotic trance, psychotic delirium, free association, or surrealist automatism their common source is the unconscious. Breton thought that their results were amazing proof of the fluency of what Freud called "primary process". The formula of pure psychic automatism was officially unveiled in the manifesto as the cornerstone of the Surrealist theory of creativity.

Pursuing the widespread interest in primitive art, Paul Klee believed that we ought to take the art of children and the mad seriously and began collecting children's drawings and outsider art. He produced the largest body of analytical work, over 4,000 pages of notes on his observations (now preserved in the archives of the Klee Foundation in Bern,

Switzerland), which has had a tremendous influence on aspiring artists of every school. He believed in a hidden source of creative power, the main thesis of this chapter, and had a unique capacity to set other artists free to make their own way. In 1945, the artist Jean Dubuffet started an incredible collection of what he called "Art Brut" (raw art), a form of outsider art. In his collection (based in Lausanne, Switzerland), he found a source of inspiration for his own work. For him, these works had authenticity, originality, passion, and a frenzy that was lacking in the works of professional artists. He sought this divine madness in his own work and experimented constantly with various techniques. Prinzhorn's book even influenced the Abstract Expressionist movement, which started in the United States in New York in the 1940s.

Writing this has helped me reformulate some of the principles of the work I did with an art group in my studio. I had resisted teaching art for years until I came upon this notion of helping people in a different way than traditional art therapy. People—I consider them outsiders—came to paint in my studio once a week in order to regain creative freedom they may have had as children. I called it "the art experience group" and made the point that they were not doing this as art instruction or with the aim of becoming practising artists, but as a way to expand the limits of their freedom. This was not art therapy because I did not interpret the content of the members' creations. However, I can't deny that what we did was therapeutic insofar as any expansion in freedom is therapeutic.

In dealing with the participants, I used what I learned about the creative process during my years of painting and my observations of painters while they worked. When I began to paint almost forty years ago, I was fascinated with watching artists struggle with their work and wondered what factors helped or hindered the work's development. I became very interested in my own process and, like Klee and Dubuffet before me, I documented my work in progress in various papers accompanied with slides. In one of these papers, "The evolution of a painting" (see Chapter Twelve) I traced with images the development of its progress during the four months that it took to complete the painting. I also discussed several dreams I had during the work that related to the painting in progress. Years later, I presented a retrospective paper on the occasion of the first International Psychoanalytic Association (IPA) Congress in Santiago, Chile, in 1999, to celebrate the thirty years of having left Chile (where I was born), and thirty years of painting.

This one had 112 slides and was titled "Destruction and reparation in the creative process: A retrospective".

The artist has an acute awareness of his internal realities, the inner reality he seeks to express, and external reality. But, he needs to differentiate what is internal and what is external. A basic difference between creativity and delusional creativity is that, at times, the insane artist fails in this recognition. For example, Vera Schmidt, an artist featured in the documentary film *Between Madness and Art*, thought she could change the temperature with her colours or impact the world with her lines.

According to Hanna Segal (who applied Melanie Klein's notions to the understanding of creativity), in the impulse to create we confirm that there can't be art without aggression. Even the first step in starting artistic work contains tension and aggression. The first line drawn on the canvas or on the paper indicates that something hurtful has been inflicted and it has to be made good. The artist works through the infantile depressive position—called depressive because of the sadness at the recognition of the damage inflicted on loved ones. In Kleinian theory this means that, in his unconscious fantasy, the artist is attacking the internal parents and their babies; he then recognises this and repairs the damage. True reparation must include an acknowledgement of aggression and its effect. The artist needs to create something in his inner world corresponding to the recreation of his internal objects and world. The truth the artist is after is primarily psychic truth, a truth he ends up manifesting in the external world. This implies a resolution of the infantile depressive conflict, which suggests that the reparative attempt at this resolution has been successful. Achieving something in the external world is essential to his feeling of a completed reparation and marks his return to external reality.

In any work of art, destroying and recreating occur constantly. The resolution is completed internally, but the artist's reparative work is never completed. The artist seeks to locate his conflict and resolve it in his creation. It is a paradox that the artist's work is new, yet arises from an urge to recreate or restore. The work of art is then felt as having a life of its own, which will survive the artist.

What grips us when facing art, especially the art of the insane, is the artist's intentions. This is not a matter of intellectual comprehension. Freud was baffled by two problems: the nature of the creative impulse and the means by which the artist captures and engages his audience. According to Freud (1914b), the artist aims to awaken in us the same emotional attitude that produced in him the impetus to create. This is perhaps Freud's most original and profound statement regarding creativity. Subsequently, much has been written about the "significant form", the end result of the impulse to create.

I have learned about creativity and its inhibitions in my studio. When it comes to painting, one of the factors inhibiting creativity is a premature concern with harmony and balance, notions that are so stressed in art schools. I believe such a concern should come at the end of a long time of experimentation and of tolerating the unknown, which I see as the major factor in helping the work move forward (Safán-Gerard, 2002). This surely also applies to writing. I had to go through this period of not knowing when writing this chapter, tolerating the anxiety of not knowing if I could pull some ideas together.

This necessity to stay in this not knowing place while creating is what kept me attending an art class many years ago: nobody knew what they were doing and they were not afraid to admit it. This was in stark contrast with the omniscient attitude of psychology students at UCLA, where I was doing my clinical training. I don't believe the artists in the Prinzhorn collection cared much about knowing what they were doing—they simply followed their own impulses. As I have implied before, the difficulties with tolerating the unknown have to do with a fear of a loss of boundary between one's conscious mind and one's unconscious. The grip on reality can be lost and it can be terrifying. Many artists stop the work at this point, which can turn into a long period of time. I have seen this happen to those painting in my studio. I have found that this reaction comes about when the artist is observing the whole painting in progress and wants to find balance and harmony in it. At this juncture, I suggest to them to focus on a very small area that they like and work only around that area for a while. Paul Klee had also advised artists to be very modest and focus their attention on the smallest possible area. He must have realised how focusing on the whole painting can be detrimental to the progress of the work. Perhaps focusing on the whole unfinished painting stirs up psychotic anxieties that can't be managed. The chaos in the painting becomes the mirror image of one's internal chaos.

One's imagination allows vast problems to be solved very simply, especially by children. In the film, Vera Schmidt draws with yellow and green and says these colours represent heat and cold. Pointing to the yellow she says, "The cold went away thanks to my painting". This brought to mind something that happened with my daughter years ago. My daughter Denise and I were sitting in the waiting room of a doctor's office and I gave her paper and pencil to draw while we waited. She was only three or four years old and drew a typical figure of a circle with stick legs and next to it a square with four circles underneath. She said it was a little girl and a car. I said, "Poor little girl. She may get run over by the car." She listened and, while drawing a straight line from the girl to the edge of the paper, she commanded, "Little girl, move!" While looking at me, relieved, she said, "She moved." All she needed was a straight line to solve the problem. But the opposite, however difficult it is to create, can be true as well. Artist Alberto Giacometti asked his writer friend James Lord to pose for him for a portrait. This was no minor task because Lord would have to sit for him on several occasions. Lord agreed, but only if Giacometti allowed him to carry out a written portrait of the artist, which resulted in a marvellous little book with sixteen photographs of the work in progress and Lord's description of Giacometti at work. It turned out that Giacometti complained constantly that he should have never become a painter; that the work was going badly; that he never learned to draw properly, and so on. After a couple of hours, Lord asked Giacometti if they could stop for lunch and he replied, "No, we can't leave now because the work is going badly." He continued to complain for the next couple of hours. Lord was by now very hungry and suggested that they should stop for lunch. Giacometti replied, "No, we can't! It's going better now and we can't leave it." We can see here how both the fear of not being able to paint and the fragility of painting well can lead to the same compulsion to stay connected to the work even while ignoring physical needs.

Ever since the Surrealists and Expressionists discovered Art Brut and Prinzhorn published his book, there has been a definite movement towards including outsiders in the art world as we know it. Prinzhorn's book brought about a shift in values. The artists' essential insights of the deepest strata of the mind placed their work on equal footing with "professional art". The first exhibit of their work was the Degenerate Art exhibition in Munich in 1937. The Nazi propaganda machine appropriated some of the work from Prinzhorn's collection and exhibited it alongside the art of contemporary artists to discredit and reject modern art-making. They wanted to show that all modern art was insane and that the Jewish art dealers who were promoting this art were also insane.

The first proper exhibition of outsider art and Art Brut called "Outsiders" took place at the Hayward Gallery in London in 1978 and attracted much interest. An exhibition in the Los Angeles County Museum of Art (LACMA) of Dubuffet's work in 1962 had much impact on California artists. A selection of over two hundred drawings by fifty three artists from the Prinzhorn Collection was exhibited for the first time in 2000 at the Hammer Museum in Los Angeles, titled "The Prinzhorn collection: Traces upon the wunderblock". This exhibition marked the last time the work would be loaned before it went on permanent display in a museum dedicated to the collection at the University of Heidelberg in 2001, the realisation of the institution Prinzhorn had envisioned.

Then came another exhibit at LACMA entitled, "The spiritual in art: Abstract painting: 1890–1985" and its sequel "Parallel visions: Modern artists and outsider art, 1992–1993". In "Parallel visions", we find contemporary artists side by side with the outsider artists who inspired them—just like in the Degenerate Art exhibit.

Andy Nasisse (born in 1945), a sculptor and ceramist who exemplifies an American mainstream artist, has both documented and collected the work of numerous outsider artists. In the same spirit as Dubuffet many years before, he said that what interested him the most about outsider art is

> the sense of inspired innocence it reveals. The visionary or self-taught artist often doesn't identify what he or she makes as "art." Many are illiterate and have never been to a museum or gallery. The work they make is not conditioned by society's definitions or limitations and is consequently startling and fresh; it is made out of a vital need or compulsion and the maker's motivations are pure and intense. (Krukowski, 1991, p. 21)

Nasisse uses this benchmark for the work of all artists, insiders and outsiders.

In 1984, artist Bolek Greczynski and Dr Janos Marton, a psychologist at Creedmoor Psychiatric Center in New York, hatched the idea of setting up an art programme for hospital residents in Building 75, the Center's 40,000 square foot abandoned kitchen and dining hall (Marton, 2002). They cleaned up the space and invited patients to fill it with artwork. Over 700 patients have worked in the Museum since then. The now-called "Living Museum" is both studio and museum—an art space open to visitors and a studio that invites the constant production of new works. The artists in residence are self-taught. Creedmoor's "curator" Greczynski responded to Kurt Hollander in *Art in America*, about the programme (1993): "The Living Museum is not a reaction to or an improvement in the field of psychiatric art. The fuel for this project comes from more populist, more generous traditions. We address group consciousness, fear, collaboration and defiance. It is a laboratory in which cultural ideas and perceptions are destabilized for artists and viewers". Here we see how Greczynski and Marton value the potential for growth in the disruption the viewers can experience while looking at this art.

So what is the nature of creativity? In Prinzhorn's collection one can see that it embraces an enormous diversity of creative approaches, which makes it impossible to define overall. There are no grounds for the notion that this is an Art Brut collection, comparable with Dubuffet's collection in Lausanne. A significant part does consist of works that can be called Art Brut, but also of exploratory works in the spirit of twentieth-century art. Pure naive art is rare. Most commonly, psychotic art contains a combination of Art Brut, exploratory art, and naive art. The most important outcome that can result from seeing this collection, even if only in reproductions or in film, is the expansion of our view of what can be possible in the mind. Psychotic art becomes an opportunity to engage in a confrontation with our own unconscious. It is exciting, but also frightening. The good news is that it is the result of a creative impulse that leads to growth and development, both in the creator and in the viewer. It should be celebrated!

PART II

MY OWN DEVELOPMENT

CHAPTER NINE

Music: my first love

Early years

At the age of five or six, I learned to appreciate classical music from my father, who loved baroque and early chamber music. He had an exceptional memory for repertoire and a good ear that allowed him to recognise within a couple of bars which of the known violinists was playing. Once, while watching him shave, I marvelled at how he could also hum along by heart all of Wagner's *Overture to Tannhäuser* as it played on the radio. Recognising my love for music, my parents hired me a piano teacher, but her long fingernails made such an irritating sound when she played that I detested her lessons. Moreover, the unbearable scent of her nauseating floral perfume permeated the whole house. I managed to last a year. Unfortunately, the experience left me hating the piano and so my appreciation for piano music came much later.

As a teenager, I attended the Friday concerts at the Teatro Municipal in Santiago sitting in the cheapest galleria nosebleed benches along with music-loving college students and young musicians. At intermission we would discuss the performance, but I often disagreed with their opinions. Later, my father would compare my opinions to the concert reviews by Juan Orrego Salas, the music critic of *El Mercurio*, and would point out to my great thrill that my opinions were similar to his. After many such debates, I would anxiously wait for the Sunday paper to be vindicated by Orrego Salas' review.

Around that time, I recognised my youngest sister Doris' fascination with music, so much so that I registered her to study violin at the National Conservatory of Music at the University of Chile. After the entrance exam, a renowned violin teacher who only taught advanced students accepted her. Doris would astound me by playing parts of Bach's violin concertos by ear when she would get home from class. She learned these just by listening to the lessons of older students while waiting her turn to work with her teacher! Growing up with my father and Doris made a tremendous impact on my relationship with music.

My attempts to share my love for music with family, friends and colleagues have not always been successful and that is a constant source of pain. But I remember that in Chile, when I was about thirteen, I extended my love for music to our illiterate Mapuche-Indian maid, who would listen to the classical radio station while cleaning the house. One day, I realised that I had succeeded in a major way when, after I turned the radio on, she said, "*I don't feel like Bartok today!*"

Law school and travels

I chose law because it would give me time to study music composition. It was the only subject that didn't require attendance in class, only to examinations. During law school, I organised an a cappella choir of sixteen members at a Jewish academic organisation of college students, the IVRIA, and we did very well in our performances. As a result, my friends insisted that I enter a competition sponsored by the Jewish Federation to attend a four-month youth programme in Israel. There were three contenders and I had to learn quite a bit of Jewish history. The choir I had created was probably the main factor in my winning the scholarship, due to a very complimentary and timely newspaper interview conducted after a concert a week before the committee's decision.

Young women didn't travel alone in those days. Despite the fact that we had a few of my father's relatives in Israel who had emigrated from old Yugoslavia, my parents were reluctant to let me, an eighteen-year-old girl, go alone on such a long and complicated journey. When the Jewish Federation announced their decision it happened that my three younger sisters and I had the mumps. Our Jewish family doctor who came to see us told my parents he would get us well, and lectured that they really should not deny me the opportunity to go to Israel because, otherwise, I could get a neurosis!

It was a great experience going to Israel—living in Jerusalem, meeting my family in Haifa (and especially my cousin Shimon, a handsome soldier in the army), attending lectures, travelling with other Jewish students from Latin America, and—most of all—attending concerts of the Israel Philharmonic in Tel Aviv.

While travelling through Italy on the way back to Chile, I met a pianist on a train who was about to have his debut as conductor of a Brahms festival with the Santa Cecilia Orchestra in Rome. His all-Brahms programme included the Second Symphony, the Second Piano Concerto and the *German Requiem*, music that I knew very well. We discussed these works in great detail and compared versions by different conductors as we looked at the scores. I was in heaven! He urged me to get off in Rome with him instead of continuing south to Naples and told me he could certainly get me a fellowship with Petrassi, one of the most renowned composers in Italy at the time. It was tempting, but I decided to return to my parents, who were anxiously waiting for me and blaming each other for allowing me to travel. This encounter, however, gave me the impetus to drop out of law school and rededicate myself to music.

Juan Orrego Salas, the music critic I followed in *El Mercurio*, was the one I wanted to study with, but he had left Chile to take a teaching position at Indiana University. Eventually, I began studies with Chilean composer Leon Schidlowski while taking piano lessons with his German wife, Susan. They had just returned from Cologne, where he had studied composition with the wunderkind of avant-garde music Karlheinz Stockhausen. Impressed by my musical memory they offered to teach me pro bono.

My parents were very upset at my leaving behind a law career for a "bohemian life" and an uncertain financial future. There was truth in this as I witnessed how Leon and his family struggled. Later, I followed Leon's advice to get a different career under my belt so that I would not suffer privations like they did.

Taking a new path

Other than music, psychology was the only other field I felt I could go into. The interest originally came because of my mother's curiosity in it. While studying mathematics at the University of Chile, she took a psychopathology course at a psychiatric hospital on the famous Olivos Street (*olivos* had become synonymous with "crazy"). So, while in high school, my mother's former professor allowed me to audit his classes to which he brought the most fascinating psychiatric patients to talk and respond to our questions. I remember my amazement at seeing a manic-depressive psychotic patient three months apart in his two extreme states. This trajectory into psychology ultimately led me to my work in psychoanalysis.

From early on, Bach had been my most favourite composer. During my training in psychology, I so wanted to sing Bach's *Christmas Oratorio* with the University of Chile's choir, but the rehearsals were over and performances had already begun. Nonetheless, I persevered and was allowed to take a special exam that qualified me to sing as a second soprano in their third performance. There was nothing as spiritually uplifting as singing Bach in the midst of a choir with full orchestra and soloists! For my father, who shared with me this passion for Bach, I was able to obtain permission for him to attend our full choral and orchestral rehearsals for the remainder of the term—a real thrill for him. I was so pleased to reciprocate a bit of the immense joy that he had given me from having introduced me to the world of music.

My training in psychology ended with a thesis in which I researched the relationship between rhythm and mental health in children. The guide and adviser for my thesis was my friend Claudio Naranjo, a psychiatrist and pianist who later became a well-known spiritual guide in the U.S. and in Europe. While teaching anthropology at the Medical School of the University of Chile, Naranjo also taught a course on the psychology of art at the school of architecture of the Pontificia Universidad Católica de Chile. Shortly before he relocated to California, I inherited his teaching position, which was a great opportunity to interact with both art teachers and students, something I did years later at the California Institute of the Arts, teaching and doing research on creativity.

When I completed my training, psychology was still a new field in Chile, so jobs were scarce. Seeking another way to connect with music and continue to study composition, I submitted a proposal to the conservatory, part of the music department at the University of Chile. I offered to develop tests that would assess musical talent in new applicants and to provide psychotherapy to advanced students who were having problems performing or adjusting to academic life. I developed the tests with the help of Juan Lehman, a gifted pianist on the faculty, and provided psychotherapy to several music students, including the use of hypnosis to address performance anxiety. Most important, however, was that I also managed to study composition with Gustavo Becerra, an exceptional composer, the year before he left Chile for political reasons.

My psychology colleagues were unhappy that I was offering free services at a time when we were all struggling to legitimise our profession. In the second year, however, the music department created for me an official part-time position as researcher and therapist. Then, to my happy surprise, Leon Schidlowski, my former composition teacher, was hired onto the faculty of music as a professor of composition. I was thrilled that he was finally recognised in Chile and that I would be able to see more of him. Once, while walking me home after a concert, he confessed that he felt guilty from having steered me away from a musical career. Although he offered to teach me composition for free again, the circumstances in my life did not allow me to accept his offer—a decision that I shall always regret. Eventually, Leon and his family immigrated to Israel, and in 2015 he was awarded the Chilean National Prize for Music, even though he had been living in Israel for some years. I called him in Tel Aviv to congratulate him and he let me know that lately he had been painting more than composing!

After my work with the music faculty at the University of Chile, I became fascinated with psychological research on creativity, and with a Fulbright Travel Fellowship I went to study at the University of California at Berkeley. My interest was in the work carried out at IPAR (Institute of Personality Assessment and Research), an organisation on campus dedicated to innovative studies on creativity, particularly the research by Frank Barron and Donald McKinnon.

Despite that painful year of being separated from my family, and especially from my two children, I managed to earn a master's degree with a dissertation entitled "The personality correlates of musical taste". For my thesis I used data I had previously prepared in Chile—sixty excerpts of classical and popular music, for which I carefully selected unrecognisable passages rather than the well-known main themes. The subjects responded to these excerpts with "like", "dislike" or "uncertain" responses, and then described themselves with a checklist of adjectives. I was very lucky that professor Jack Block, an exceptional researcher and music lover in the psychology department, supervised my work.

In the middle of my thesis work, I somehow lost the source list of the sixty musical excerpts. This was not a major problem, because I could recognise the music, all except for one, which no one in UC Berkeley's music department could figure out either! I then took the recording to a nearby record shop and played it for the Moroccan salesman with whom I had often enjoyed talking with about music. He listened, and to my amazement, he immediately brought out an LP of Beethoven's *Archduke* Piano Trio, and placed the arm of the turntable on the exact spot of the excerpt! What a moment that was! So taken with his knowledge, I asked him to recommend a list of forty essential recordings of contemporary classical music with which I was not yet familiar. With the money I painfully saved from my assistant teaching position, I was able to bring this unknown treasure of LPs back to Chile, a treasure I eventually lost later during my divorce. But, life went on, and something quite magical happened years later during a family reunion in Chile in 2012. After my first husband passed away, his second wife prepared a festive lunch celebrating her husband's life. At the end of the meal, one of their sons, who was finishing architecture training, sat next to me to tell me that thanks to my recordings (he knew they had been mine), he had gotten an amazing musical education. I was quite moved to know that this young person had discovered my long-lost treasured LPs and, in turn, he had been initiated into music's magic.

My involvement with music continued after I was remarried. My husband, Harold Gerard, was a professor of social psychology at the University of California Los Angeles (UCLA). We met at an Inter-American Congress of Psychology in Montevideo, Uruguay, where we both presented papers. Eventually, my children and I ended up in Los Angeles, where I continued my psychology studies at UCLA and received my Ph.D. in clinical psychology a few years later. I was very fortunate that my husband loved music and art as much as I did. He was a well-known professor and researcher in social psychology, but after listening to tapes of my psychoanalytic training, he decided to start psychoanalytic training at age fifty nine! Thus, we were able to share our passion for art, music, *and* psychoanalysis! After he died in 2003, it was art, music, and my work with patients that helped sustain me after my loss.

Art emerges again

Painting became my primary creative focus from the time I began to paint in 1971 to overcome the stress of the clinical psychology training at UCLA. But my paintings had not yet become integrated with music until I painted *Le marteau sans maître*. It consisted of nine paintings inspired by the nine movements that Pierre Boulez composed, based on poems by surrealist poet René Char.

In 2012, in conjunction with the opening of an exhibition at Corinne Bonnet's Galerie Dufay/Bonnet in Paris, I performed with the model Maria Clark to the music of Boulez's *Notations*. Unfortunately, Boulez was in Chicago and was unable to attend my Paris performance. Since then, I have had several performances to the music of Shostakovich, Boulez, and Los Angeles composers William Kraft and Jane Brockman.

The Los Angeles Psychological Association sponsored my Los Angeles performance art debut in 2013, but amusingly imposed the requirement that my "nude" model wear a flesh-toned bodysuit. Despite the restriction, they funded a new aspect to enhance my performance: the addition of a real-time image of my hands projected onto a large screen serving as the backdrop for the stage while I painted. The audience was able to experience the creative process coming from the music, the model, my working hands and the resulting paintings themselves.

Music to painting: encounters with Pierre Boulez

When I first met Pierre Boulez I was only nineteen years old, singing in the University of Chile choir. As a fledging conductor, he was the music director of the famous theatrical company of Jean-Louis Barrault and Madeleine Renaud. (Barrault played the role as mime years later in the French classic film, *Les enfants du paradis*.) During his time in Chile, Boulez needed a small choir to sing the music of Darius Milhaud for Claudel's play, *Cristobal Colon*, acted out by Barrault and Renaud. I was selected as one of the sixteen musicians from our university choir to perform with Boulez during the play at the Teatro Municipal de Santiago. Many years later, after I had settled in Los Angeles, I met Boulez again and told him that I had sung for him in Chile. He replied that the time he spent there was the happiest in his life.

Sometime in 1984, Boulez was in Los Angeles and I attended a lecture he gave on creativity. I had found the lecture so compelling and inspiring that I later wrote him a detailed letter with my thoughts about it (see Appendix A). At the event, I asked him permission to "paint" his nine movements of *Le marteau sans maître*. With his *logique francaise*, he responded that because René Char had given him permission to write music to his collection of poems, and to even use the titles for his composition, he was now delighted to grant me a similar permission—to translate his music into art.

Le marteau sans maître (The hammer without a master) was published in 1954 and premiered the year after. Scored for alto voice, flute, viola, guitar, vibraphone, and percussion, it is comprised of nine movements based on a collection of three poems with the same title by surrealist poet René Char. The poems appear in four of the movements for voice and instrumentalists; the remaining five are instrumental commentaries on the poems without text. *Le marteau* became one of Boulez's early "trademark" pieces that further distinguished him as a composer of modernist and serial music.

My attempt to do a visual translation of Boulez's musical ideas had to do with my wish to deeply comprehend this musical masterpiece. I was fascinated with *Le marteau*'s complexity and beauty. I would take long walks at Palisades Park in Santa Monica, listening to it many times. Then back at my studio, I would listen to it again, striving to understand each of its movements thoroughly, as if I wanted to somehow get into Boulez's mind and relive his creative process with him.

This particular intimacy with Boulez's mind called for small format work, so I used paper measuring eighteen by fourteen inches with watercolour, micro pens and coloured pencils as media. I drew what I heard. The overall colours were the result of my subjective experience of each movement. For example, in three of the paintings I used a golden yellow for the background, in four I used a soft green for the background, and in the last two I used a soft magenta. The colours were applied unevenly, leaving enough visual elements to encourage me to play and invent new shapes. These areas without colour or small areas of different and subtle pastel colours were meant to represent the irregularities of the sound events. Using a deeper shade of the same colour, I created a subtle frame so that events could extend outward and beyond as if "breaking outside the box"—a feature of Boulez's music that I had wanted to portray for some time. This was to be the most important visual feature (see Figures 9.1 and 9.2). In addition, and perhaps more importantly, these paintings represented my wish to forget my own subjectivity in order to pursue a more objective depiction of Boulez's sounds. My desire to connect with Boulez's creative mind called for a smaller and more personal format than the large canvases I was working with at the time.

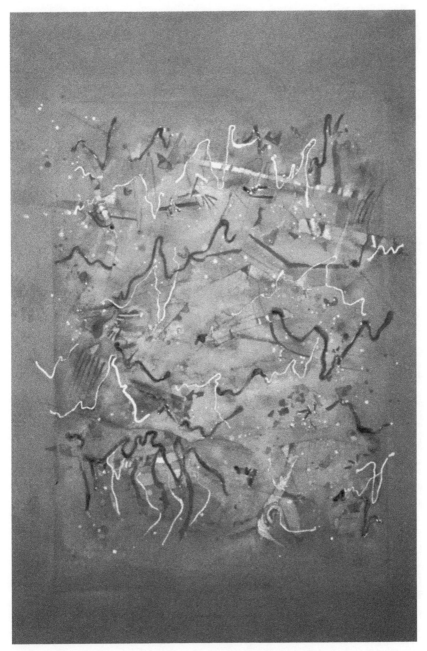

Figure 9.1. I Avant L'Artisanat Furieux, 1989, watercolour on paper, 18″ × 14″.

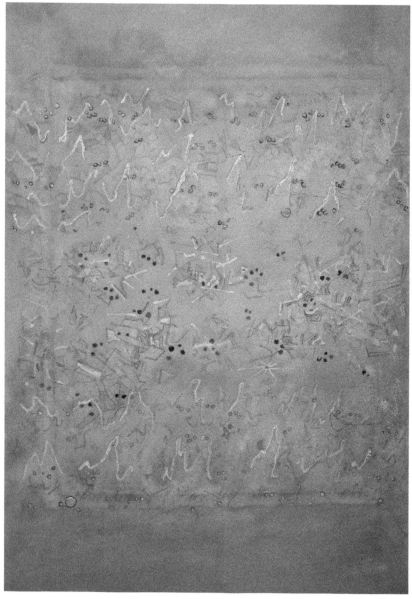

Figure 9.2. Il Commentaire I de Bourreaux de Solitude, 1989, watercolour on paper, 18″ × 14″.

Within the framed areas I searched for a visual equivalent of each sound. It became clear to me that a thin silver line, moving irregularly up and down with the music, would represent the flute. A thick burgundy-coloured line that moved rather slowly would represent the bassoon, and a thicker gold line would represent the viola and cello. An even thicker burgundy line would represent the alto voice featured in the final two movements.

As in much of Boulez's music, Le marteau calls for many percussion instruments. I attempted to represent the reverberation of these instruments with concentric circles drawn from a point at the centre. Different lines crossing and coming together in various areas depict the complexity of their polyphony. I allowed the accidental happenings on the paper to help me guide the intersecting lines. In spite of my desire to be loyal to Boulez, I felt tremendous freedom to invent visual elements as needed (see Figures 9.3 and 9.4).

Several years later, Pierre Boulez, now a world-renowned conductor and composer, returned to Los Angeles to conduct Bruckner's Ninth Symphony. My husband and I visited him after a rehearsal, hoping to entice him to visit my studio to see my finished Le marteau. Due to his tight schedule, he requested that we bring them back stage after an upcoming rehearsal. So we did. In two large suitcases, my husband and I lugged those nine paintings and lined them up against the wall of his dressing room. To our surprise and delight, he pointed to one of them matter-of-factly saying, "That's my number four," and to another, "That's my number six," and so on until he identified each of my paintings with the corresponding movement of his music. I was blown over that he could respond so accurately to my paintings, as I must have managed to capture the structure and the affect within each movement. I was elated that my attempts to translate his music had been worthwhile and rewarded with Boulez's acceptance and validation (see Figures 9.5 and 9.6)!

My collaboration with Boulez and painting Le marteau represents a major shift and breakthrough in my relationship to music, painting, and even my psychoanalytic work (see Figures 9.7, 9.8, and 9.9). Listening and responding to the many nuances found in musical expression have expanded my capacity to respond to a wider range of human emotions as expressed by my patients. It is uncertain whether an analyst's sensitivity to patients stems from an intense involvement with music, but in my experience I wouldn't doubt that music has played a big part.

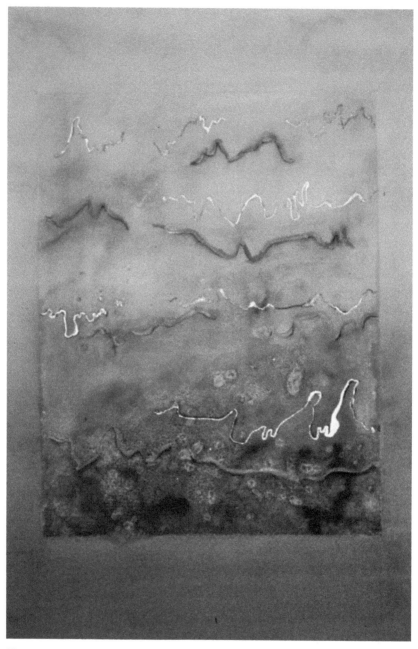

Figure 9.3. III L'Artisanat Furieux, 1989, watercolour on paper, 18″ × 14″.

Figure 9.4. IV Commentaire II de Bourreaux de Solitude, 1989, water-colour on paper, 18″ × 14″.

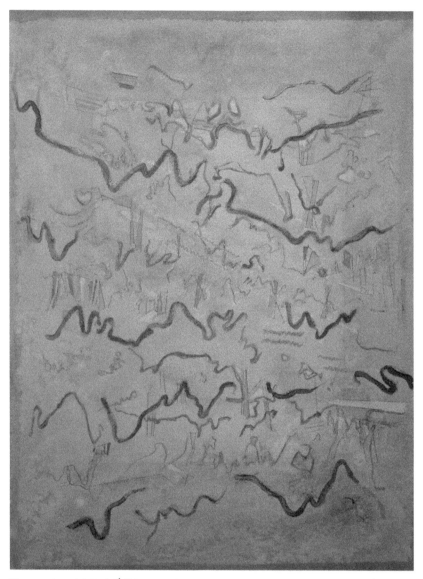

Figure 9.5. V Bel Édifice et les pressentiments, 1989, watercolour on paper, 18″ × 14″.

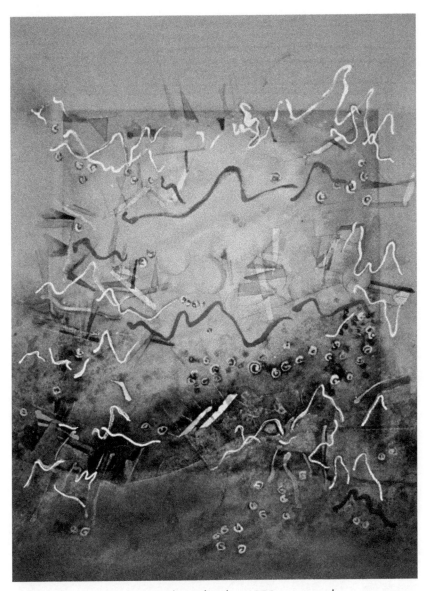

Figure 9.6. VI Bourreaux de Solitude, 1989, watercolour on paper, 18″ × 14″.

Figure 9.7. VII Après l'artisanat furieux, 1989, watercolour on paper, 18″ × 14″.

Figure 9.8. VIII Commentaire III de Burreaux de Solitude, 1989, water-colour on paper, 18″ × 14″.

Figure 9.9. IX Bel édifice et les pressentiments, 1989, watercolour on paper, 18″ × 14″.

Music has offered my painting a method to renew itself. Quite aware of the ubiquitous projecting that goes on in the viewer and the listener, I think that what appeals to me in the music that inspired my paintings is something that I have always sought in my other paintings, the right combination of discipline and freedom, structure and chance, the Apollonian and the Dionysian. In Chapter One I describe this particular interplay. This is, of course, a notion shared by many artists and musicians. Boulez took it to a new level when he asserted that we have to take the interior essence of a work as our only guide. Likewise, Keith Finch, who was my beloved art teacher, talked about the need to follow the discipline required by the work itself. However, in these paintings based on music I need to do more than follow the music's internal logic. I need to place myself as an intermediary between the discipline of the music and the discipline of the related canvas in front of me. This requires a hard-to-come-by flexibility: to follow the musical events in themselves while accommodating the chance events on the canvas.

In contrast with the Romantic notion of the necessity of a plunge into oneself, there emerges a new concept of beauty outside the subjective, a forgetting of our moods, our passions, ourselves. I believe that in my translation of Boulez's *Le marteau sans maître*, I was trying to free myself from my own subjectivity and from the inevitable repetitions born out of my own intuition. Boulez was once asked if, in his creative process, he follows his own intuition. He replied, "Oh no! If I did, I would be repeating myself. In fact, I would do the opposite from what my intuition tells me. This would open new possibilities."

Appendix A: letter to Pierre Boulez, June 1984

What follows is my letter to Boulez with comments in response to his 1984 lecture in Los Angeles on creativity. It contains my developing views on the subject.

Dear Pierre,
I want to share with you some of my reactions to your lecture on creativity here in Los Angeles, which was so very rich in ideas. You were putting to rest in a compelling way some ongoing myths about the creative process and warning us of the perils of thinking that we know something about it. You were so right when you said from the start that we can be "right on" or "way off" in trying to analyze it and/or explain it. A while back, I wrote a paper on the evolution of a painting, trying to understand the motive

behind all of the choices, and I am still not sure if I was right on or way off! My interpretations were greatly limited by my theoretical orientation and my own motivated blindness, but one has to start somewhere ... and I wouldn't care to try to do it better.

You suggest that the value of analyzing other composers is to find oneself in the work. One cannot help but project oneself into aspects of the work that may not have been critical for the composer, like the case you described of your analyzing Debussy's intervals, which were important to you, but may not have mattered to him. Some of my research years ago seems to validate this notion. Studying the relationship between musical taste and personality I found that, by and large, people like what is similar to them or what reflects them. Musical analysis may also provide an opportunity for a composer to find himself. You suggest that amplifying and deepening the understanding of a part of the work allows for an understanding of the mechanism of invention. In the same way, I would add, this mechanism of invention may belong to the one doing the analysis rather than to the composer—another way of finding oneself in discovering what one can do with one's mind and tools.

The three steps the composer goes through—not knowing, knowing, and not knowing again when the work is finished—are very suggestive to me. The composer ends up not knowing because he cannot explain the irrational aspect of his solutions. "He would be in despair if he knew" you added mischievously. This despair, I gather, would have to do with the recognition that the finished work represented all that one did. You would like to feel that a part of you that you don't know very well has contributed its hand. This may provide the mystery you alluded to. When you claim not to like the obvious, you were confirming this view, weren't you? And now I am discovering something about myself in trying to understand and analyze what you said!

You talked about being suspicious of your "instinctive" solutions. Part of my interest in doing paintings to your music is that I want to stretch the limits of mine by finding what happens to my painting as a result of trying to follow solutions that are, in a way, alien and unknown to me and, in another way, so very compatible. You have done and keep doing your stretching, and it would be a great change for me to allow someone else as a mentor of sorts, for my own. In my work with creative people, both individually and in groups, I am the agent for their stretching. So far, none has performed that function for me in the art world with the exception of my first and only art teacher and his function was somewhat different. He was there for me as a resource, as a background object saying "Yes, go ahead, make a fool of yourself ... get in trouble," and I was lucky indeed.

I find myself completely agreeing with your idea of the double mirror of imagination and technique because for me, they have always gone hand in hand. My teacher allowed me to find my own path while he helped me with technique as I needed it. This is not the case at all in most art schools. As you probably know, they seem to stress discipline in order to eventually free the imagination. By the time the students have developed the techniques, their imagination has dried up. American composer Mel Powel, who was teaching at CAL ARTS when I taught there, had a similar experience with composition—he had a few very difficult years trying to find his own freedom after he became a craftsman. To become an autodidact after learning the tools and studying the past, as you suggest, becomes quite difficult for those who, while studying the great, demand such greatness from themselves. To become an autodidact means that one has to know what one knows and at the same time acknowledge that in terms of oneself one knows nothing. That is the only place to start learning by oneself—becoming very hungry again. My work with artists who cannot find such freedom to learn revolves around their reluctance to become aware of these needs, this hunger. It shows up in particular in their relationship to me, their analyst, but the work is surely the counterpart. Acknowledging their need of me allows them to also need something from and for the work.

It was nice to hear you say, "A good composer is a thief." This year I wrote a statement about stealing from others and from myself for an exhibition of some painting collages. As you say, many creators expect complete originality from themselves not allowing themselves to feed from someone else. This is also related to an unwillingness to need. Program notes on the First Symphony by a New York composer, John Corigliano, stated with no apologies who he had taken from beginning to end throughout the piece, and ended up with a most original piece. You took from Klee's lectures, and I will be taking from you, and so it goes. However, there are different ways of stealing something. Superficial, magical appropriation won't produce anything of value, since the artist won't have found any personal truth in what he's feeding from. You had to understand the structure of Mallarmé's poems to be able to do what you did with them. You stated that the sources of inspiration could be many, "from a model to a sunrise," and that all sources, cultural or not, are valid. Each composer, each artist, has his own process, and the first inspiration may come in a different way for the same composer. This is such an important point, since so many have tried and keep trying to generalize about the conditions of inspiration or the sources. Your description of how you started playing with the notion of resonance of the different instruments and the things you could create with that, ending up with the conception of time, is especially pertinent. It underscores the idea that one never knows where one is going when one starts, which may be a surprise for those who are impressed by the lucidity of your compositions and believe you distill everything down from an overall conception perfectly worked out ahead of time.

You also talked about how much freedom one starts with. Constraints seem to have a paradoxical effect on freedom. As you mentioned, Donatoni seems to have loved them (two oboes, great)! The less choices the more stretching, I suppose. When it comes to my own work I tend to agree as I often start a painting with an accident that gives me a "no choice" starting point: I've got to make that work! Pretty soon your music will be my restraint, my no-choice position. And your lecture today is my constraint now, which keeps me up late, but this is freedom—to allow myself to just respond to you.

Your wish for the work to be unfinished and your notion of the spiral form is a wish I share for my painting, is very appealing to me. Room to continue, space to go on, freedom to expand even more. The unconscious fantasy, I suppose, is that you cannot destroy the work no matter what you do to it. As with many artists, I play with construction and reconstruction, chaos and control. There has to be great relief to confirm that despite all our aggression, the work will continue to be alive and, in our case, ready to be continued. As you say, "darkness to start and will end in darkness." In the middle is where the exploration is taking place. We go through the labyrinth and we know we are lost. Yet, we remain in it, in spite of the hunger for a solution, for knowledge, and in spite of the pain. But the labyrinth affords us a myriad of mini steps that can be exciting and can offset all the pain, all the waiting.

Finally, someone raised the issue of time in music and painting and you talked about how the background of Klee's painting conveyed to you the notion of time, because it seems random and accidental, as opposed to the figures he adds later on. This was unclear to me, especially since I, and other artists, work on figure/ground at the same time. Also unclear because it is an issue I have been struggling with for some time, and will have to struggle with again when I follow your music. A slide show of paintings in evolution and what happens to paintings over time has been an attempt to disclose what went into it and when. You hinted about being aware of the figure/ground relationships between different instruments and how you will be using this awareness. How is this related to time? Would love to hear some day what you discover with that.

Thank you again for your ideas, for your music, for your conducting, and for being such a wonderful trigger for me. Will let you know of my developments with my stealing from you: what I stole, what I'm learning from it, when I will have it ... or it has had me.

Warmest regards,

Desy

Appendix B: music to the eye

"Music to the Eye" was an exhibition and presentation that took place during the opening of my exhibition of the same name at LA Artcore at Union Center for the Arts in December of 2003. The show featured paintings inspired by and based on musical compositions. Underneath each of the paintings hanging in the gallery was a recorded excerpt of the corresponding composition so that viewers could listen to the music that gave rise to the visual interpretation. For the presentation, the Los Angeles Chapter of the American Composers Forum sponsored a panel discussion with special guests: Getty curator/musicologist Nancy Perloff, composer William Kraft, and percussionist/composer David Johnson, who also performed during the event.

What follows are descriptions of my work shown at the "Music to the Eye" exhibition. The title of each painting is comprised of the composer's name and the title of the original composition from which I derived my artistic rendition.

Boulez's *Le marteau sans maître*, 1989
Set of 9. Watercolour and mixed media on paper, 18" x 14"
(See the section above entitled "Music to painting: Encounters with Pierre Boulez" for an account of the nine paintings of this work.)

Shostakovich's *String Quartet No. 15*, 2002
Set of 6. Acrylic on raw canvas, 48" x 48"
For some years I wanted to depict the barren and lonely quality of Shostakovich's quartets. I didn't expect that I would be

doing them through the movements of Sara, my first model in Los Angeles. Trying to depict Sara's slow movements without the use of music and having the quartet number fifteen softly playing, she asked me one day if I would want her to move to it. This started a new body of work with watercolour where I used a different colour pencil in each hand, my deft hand and my clumsy hand, providing the right combination of smooth and jagged lines. With Shostakovich sounding in the studio, and Sara gracefully moving to his music, I found myself experiencing the juxtaposition of life and tragedy, the shadow without which there can be no light.

Several sessions later, I decided to move this work on to large canvases (see Figure 9.10). There were six in all, representing each of the movements of Shostakovich's longest quartet. They all had to be prepared with washes ahead of time before I could begin my session with Sara. The paradoxical result is that the barren, lonely quality of the quartet ends up in lively canvases where red predominates, a colour I had not particularly used before (see Figures 9.11, 9.12, and 9.13). Perhaps a true immersion in the despairing quality of the quartet allowed the emergence of the opposite quality on the canvases.

Figure 9.10. Floor painting with Sara moving.

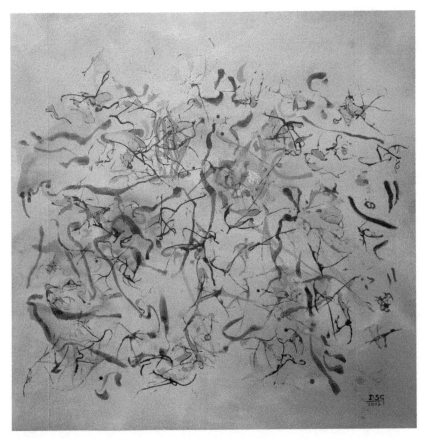

Figure 9.11. On Wings and Wheels, 2002, acrylic on raw canvas, 48″ × 48″.

Appendix C: Kraft and Piazzolla

William Kraft's *Vintage Renaissance*, 2003
Watercolour on paper, 16″ x 12″
When I heard Vintage Renaissance, I immediately realised that the Renaissance theme was merely Kraft's excuse to engage in the elaborate developments that fanned out of that era. I was struck by the crisp, measured quality of the theme as opposed to the grand gestures emerging from it. It seemed to me that the music was about the interplay of construction and deconstruction or, in other words, libido and aggression. Throughout the piece the Renaissance theme keeps emerging with the piccolo in bits and pieces here and there

Figure 9.12. The Terrors Flew Around, 2002, acrylic on raw canvas, 48" × 48".

as the chaotic and orchestral sounds give way to it with dissonant sonorities of modern times. It would seem that, in this interplay, there is a gradual integration of libido and aggression, not unlike what I found to be the case in Piazzolla's tangos. Kraft's piece reminded me of a similar construction/deconstruction in Charles Ives's *Three Places in New England*, and I have found this interplay in other music such as a melody that would take off in a different key. It was as if the first line would be leading into an infinite, disembodied space and the second line was providing a ground or platform on which things could now stand firm again. In Sur, these two lines are carried out by the bandoneon and the cello, which at times alternate. How to represent visually this musical shift was

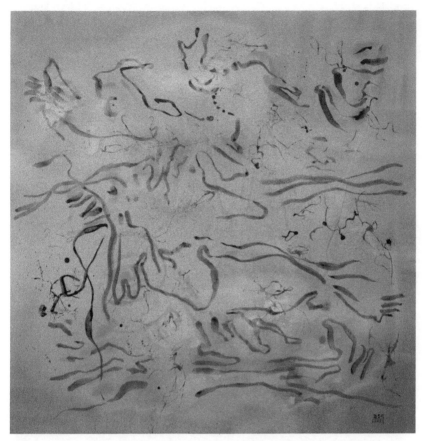

Figure 9.13. Bliss is Ripe, 2002, acrylic on raw canvas, 48″ × 48″.

my challenge. I finally ended up with two lighter areas framed by circular lines encompassing these shifts (see Figure 9.14).

Piazzolla's *Sur regreso al amor*, 2003
Acrylic on canvas, 48″ x 36″.
"What is this?!" was my first reaction to listening to Piazzolla during a flight years ago. This depiction of a tango is not only extremely romantic and over the top, but also invokes the darker side of one's emotional life—aggression in all its forms. This mixture of libido and longing on one hand with aggression and destruction on the other hand seemed to encompass a full spectrum of our passions. Particularly striking was the way a line of feeling and thought was suddenly abandoned in mid-air, giving way to its re-enactment in another key (see Figure 9.15).

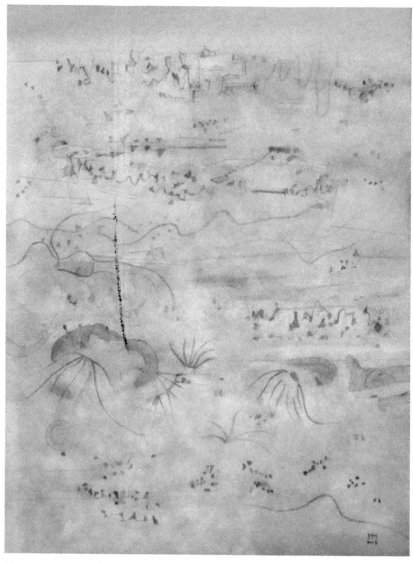

Figure 9.14. Kraft—Vintage Renaissance, 2003, watercolour on paper, 16″ × 12″.

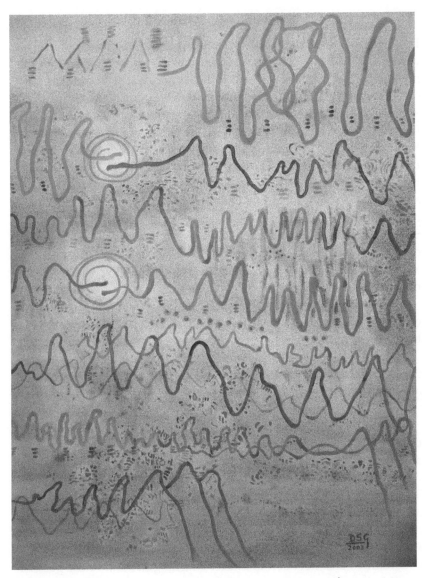

Figure 9.15. Piazzolla—Sur—regreso al amor, 2003, acrylic on canvas, 48″ × 36″.

Latest and future involvements

Having gone through various accounts of my relationship to music I would like to end this chapter with what is happening now in this involvement. It has been a treat to listen and watch live stream concerts from the Berlin Philharmonic with Sir Simon Rattle conducting and also listening to interviews with the various conductors and performers involved. To my delight, they had a film in their archives about Rumanian conductor Sergiu Celibidache and his triumphant return to the Berlin Philharmonic. He had been my favourite conductor and I had not seen him in years. He was now an older man who had to sit on a high chair to conduct but he had the same passion I remember from his conducting in Chile. The film shows him rehearsing Bruckner's Seventh. Just watching the careful and insisting translation of his vision of the beginning of this symphony to the musicians is an inspiration to any conductor or performer. That Seventh's beginning has been running in my head for weeks!

Most recently I have discovered on YouTube a whole array of videos of Sergiu Celibidache's rehearsals with different orchestras. What a treat! Engrossed in these videos I thoroughly enjoy his commentary during the rehearsals, which gives the listener access as to how he conceives every work. These videos remind me of the thrill I experienced as a teenager each time I was allowed to watch, from the pit, his rehearsals with the Filarmónica de Chile in Santiago.

One particular night concert from the Berlin Philharmonic consisted of Kurt Weil's songs with Canadian soprano Barbara Hannigan, who is an outstanding performer of contemporary music. She has been a great discovery for me as a singer and a conductor and her musicianship is just superb. Her renditions of Weil's "Youkali" and "Je ne t'aime pas" accompanied at the piano by Sir Simon Rattle are particularly arresting. She details in a video what it took for her to prepare for the role of Lulu in Alban Berg's opera. Her account shows her enviable complete commitment and devotion to music. Watching her and Rattle perform together I come to feel once again that there is Nothing like Music! She recently obtained an honorary doctorate at Mount Allison University in Canada during the 100th Anniversary of their first bachelor degree in music. At the end of a most inspiring speech addressing the students she said, "I wish you all many unexpected mistakes, that you always have a million questions; that you find and feed your passion with the discipline to support it. And that every once in a while, when you least expect it, you might just fly."

Bela Bartok's four quartets, rarely offered, were marvellously played by the Calder quartet at the Ojai Music Festival of Contemporary Music in California four years ago. I made a vow then to translate them into paintings and it will be one of my projects when I finish this book.

The moment when a composer shifts keys to go into some disembodied place constitutes one of the ultimate pleasures for the listener. Prokofiev and Shostakovich engage in these unexpected shifts, which I so value. At a recent seminar on Prokofiev and Shostakovich here in Los Angeles, gifted composer/conductor Russell Steinberg illustrated at the piano one such moment from Shostakovich's Fifth Symphony, pondering out loud towards the audience, "Where is he going here! To some unknown Universe?" The utmost pleasure of such a shift in the music is hard to describe and I wonder whether a lucid death could feel like that. There would be nothing to fear in such a blissful passing. Other than the Bartok quartets, my future challenge will be to translate such passages into paintings.

It is strangely satisfying that, whereas my memory for dreams has almost disappeared—and I used to remember up to five distinct dreams every night—and my memory for names is also failing, my memory for music has remained intact. Remembering the next movement in a chamber or a symphonic piece playing on the radio, I delight in the fact that I not only remember the melody coming up, but even the key of that melody. More than pride about this, I feel a welcomed reassurance that I still have room for music and its treasures in my aging mind.

CHAPTER TEN

How painting became a passion

A dumpy, middle-aged woman lumbered into Keith Finch's studio carrying two large shopping bags filled with clothes, shoes, and feathers. Pearl would go change in the bathroom and emerge transformed: a push-up brassier forcing out extra flesh, dark stockings with garters, excruciatingly high heels, and a huge feathered hat. She would lie down on a low wooden table in the middle of the studio. When Keith switched the floodlight on her, she was suddenly transformed into a beauty. It was like a miracle! That was the first time I dealt with realism, and in the process, I came to love this Pearl! I later learned that she was a beloved model by artists all over Los Angeles.

In 1971, I discovered Di Chirico's print, *The Soothsayer's Recompense* (1913), a metaphysical work conveying absolute desolation. I suddenly felt a pang of pain and thought, "What am I doing with my life?" My creative impulses demanded an escape from the daily grind of studying for a doctorate in clinical psychology at the University of California Los Angeles (UCLA). Years later, psychoanalytic training introduced me to the marvel of exploring inner life. Similarly painting reveals the magic of the artist's inner life to herself and the viewer.

The first time I went to visit Keith's class, I followed him around as he gave feedback with no academic jargon to the artists working there.

Amazed, I felt as if he had the words to express what I was thinking. The artists seemed to admit to not knowing what they were doing, and this was refreshing compared with the seriousness and pretentiousness of some of my fellow students. Not knowing turned out to be at the root of all creative work and, together with destructiveness, another pivotal theme of this book.

Attending Keith's Tuesday afternoon class became a MUST. For the second class I brought watercolour papers, paints, and pencils. He suggested I use a pencil and follow my line. This time there was no model so I was puzzled as to what he meant. He said, "Just put the pencil on the paper and let your hand guide the movements of the line. Let your line explore the space on the page as if you were taking a stroll on it. You can also go over the line if you want." For me, this was a delicious doodling exercise, the perfect way to stop thinking … and I was so tired of thinking! Keith came around once more suggesting that I put colour in the spaces created by the line. Later, he suggested that I could begin to draw on top of what I had done, exploring the space once more with the pencil. I was in a trance experiencing delight at the crossing of boundaries, going over pristine coloured space and discovering new shapes. Keith again suggested that I could now put more paint in the new spaces created. "Don't be afraid of painting over what you have done," he said. A tapestry was forming on the paper where I was finding many recognisable objects and people, some quite bizarre.

At the end of this first class he said, "Now you have to do 200, 300 of these. We have to find out what your line is like because you ARE your line!" Incidentally, the artist Paul Klee has been quoted as saying that "a line is a dot that went for a walk". Keith would later laugh and say that he didn't mean the 200 literally, for I couldn't stop what had been started. Even during my internship at Children's Hospital Los Angeles a year later I managed to draw and follow my line while sitting in boring staff meetings discussing insurance forms. I was thrilled to find out that the experience I had years earlier during my studies of musical composition was being replicated while drawing.

I also remember my early fascination with the shapes formed by the receding ocean when, as a teenager, I would spend hours observing the shapes left by algae at the water's edge on the beaches of Papudo or Algarrobo in Chile during the summer. My friends would be pointing to the beauty of the sunset, but I would prefer to watch these fascinating and ongoing creations on the sand.

Observing the artists' powerful transference reactions to our art teacher, I was quite intrigued. One of them would turn to me and ask, "Why is he so angry with me today?" when Keith didn't appear angry at all. I also became quite intrigued witnessing the obstacles to creativity at work and I believe much of my ideas about creative blocks stem from my initial observations at Keith's studio. Some of the artists expressed disgust towards their work in progress when an accidental happening took place on it and they would rush to cover it up or erase it. I found myself suggesting to them to wait and see how they could capitalise on these accidents. They were also amazed that I could disagree and argue with Keith, the great master! He would say, for example, that I should stop, that my painting was finished and I would insist that I wanted to continue because it was not yet where it could be. Invariably he would later come around to admit that I was right and that was my most welcomed validation. For most of the time we could see eye-to-eye on what the painting needed.

The feeling came to me after these sessions with Keith that I could do anything—painting, sculpture, composing, and writing—only if I created the space to engage in them. As I wrote earlier, Tuesday afternoons became a "sacred time". I didn't take any seminar or class at UCLA that would conflict with that special afternoon and, when challenged, I told family and friends that my sanity depended on it.

Even when, after a few years, I stopped going to Keith's classes and I worked on my own, my teacher's opinion of what I was doing or planning to do was very important to me. I went back to taking his class in his studio each time I was left without a studio, since in those days I was only subletting studio space from other artists. Going to Keith's class was my way to ensure that I would continue to paint in spite of my other commitments, professional and personal. He died over twenty years ago and I made a vow to myself to never, never see patients on Tuesday afternoons! And I have kept that vow. It has been a way to honour him by making room for the continuity of my work. I have been so fortunate to have had such a gifted and beloved teacher! This book represents the final outgrowth of what I initially learned from Keith on those Tuesday afternoons.

I also want to honour psychoanalyst/artist Marion Milner, because, as I hope you will see, Finch and Milner were kindred spirits and I am lucky to have had both of them in my life. I hold clearly in my memory the magical conversations Marion and I had over the years. It was her book, *On Not Being Able to Paint* (1950), that enticed me to write to her in 1981, which led to my visiting her in London almost every other year. She was more interested in showing me her recent collages and sculptures than discussing her ideas about art and psychoanalysis. Marion had an irreverent and refreshing sense of humour about the controversies in psychoanalysis. Feeling something in "one's bones" and being "behind one's eyes" are metaphors Milner used in her quest for awareness as opposed to living only in one's conscious mind. She writes about the "answering activity", referring to the dialogue with her unconscious mind that results from her opening herself to it, "like suddenly remembering to open a kind of little trap-door inside and finding a great expansion of spirit" (p. 52). A thread in her writings was her ongoing, relentless attempt to keep that communication open (Milner, 1987). These were ideas I had toyed with, especially with regard to the inspiration phase of a creative project and the beginning phase of an analysis.

Milner was clearly trying to broaden Kleinian concepts to make room for a feeling that goes beyond confidence or wellbeing. She wrote about praying for an answer from her unconscious, a praying that would free her from egocentric preoccupations. With her interest in states of fusion, un-differentiation and soft boundaries between self and others, Milner finds her place with Winnicott, Balint and others in the object relations Middle School of psychoanalysis, also referred to as Independents. A still life she gave me when we exchanged paintings has been hanging in my office since 1988 (Figure 10.1). It is a painting that I treasure and it will always be a reminder of our friendship. Upon hearing of her passing, I made a collage painting of her incorporating the portrait used in her obituary (Figure 10.2). Emma Letley has reproduced this painting in her marvellous biography *Marion Milner: The Life* (2014).

Around that time I experienced painting with four Chinese artists during a retreat at the Wuyi Mountains, near Nanking during 1985. I had found out that a Chinese Tai Chi instructor in Los Angeles was taking a group of his students to a cultural retreat during his first visit to China. I decided to join because I had often heard people say that my paintings revealed an Oriental sensibility. I was also enticed to go when I was told that some Chinese artists would be attending the retreat and painting there as well. Perhaps I would be able to find out if we shared a similar sensibility! Once at the retreat I had the unique experience of painting together with four artists on the same piece of rice paper placed

Figure 10.1. Still Life by Marion Milner, mixed media on paper, 8" × 10 3/4".

on a large table. We each did our work. The artists, who talked a lot as they painted, seemingly ignoring me, created mostly small figurative motifs, while I was doing some abstract inventions. At one moment, all of us went with our brushes to the same right hand corner and that unusual concordance felt like such a unique meeting of the minds that it suddenly became a celebration. The artists were crying and hugging me and I burst into tears responding to theirs.

In 2000, I used the Chinese rice paper I had brought with me from China and did some paintings on them. Through a Japanese artist friend, I contacted a master framer near Tokyo, who mounted them on scrolls. Of course they were a follow up of my Chinese experience. However, I entitled these scrolls *Tenganan Series* out of my visiting this amazing old village near Ubud in Bali a few years later.

So what is painting for me after all these years? In *Music and Imagination* (1952) Aaron Copland seems to say it better than I can:

> The reason for the compulsion to renewed creativity, it seems to me, is that each added work brings with it an element of self-discovery.

Figure 10.2. Marion Milner, mixed media collage, 15 1/4″ × 10 1/4″.

> I must create in order to know myself and since self-knowledge is
> a never-ending search, each new work is only a part-answer to the
> question, "Who am I?" and brings with it the need to go on to other
> and different part-answers (p. 41).

The artist also experiences his creation as happening to him beyond his control.

Like Copland, Stravinsky, and many artists, I feel like a vehicle for the expression of something that is quite beyond my control. Paul Klee believed that the artist is a channel and does nothing other than gather and pass on what comes to him from the depths (1924). In a similar vein and about the *Rite of Spring (Le Sacre du Printemps)*, Stravinsky wrote in his later years, "I am the vessel through which le *Sacre* passed" (Copland, 1952, p. 58). For me, the process is nothing short of miraculous. I never know where it will end up. This process can't be rushed. It must grow by itself and be given the space for it to happen, a space that is more and more precious and has to be protected from life's other intrusions. Sometimes I leave the work for a time while doing something else, but I am always aware that the process is continuing somewhere in my unconscious. When I approach the painting again I will have found new solutions for its dilemmas. This is not unlike what happens to me with the work on a psychoanalytic paper or on this book for that matter. One starts work on it, a few ideas develop, and the process has begun. It is something that goes on quite independently of one's will. It is at these times that my dual commitment to art and psychoanalysis is reaffirmed—my life will forever be split between these beloved paths!

CHAPTER ELEVEN

Creativity: from the painting studio to the consulting room

People often ask me if my psychoanalytic life and my work with patients affect my work as a painter. I tell them it is rather the other way around—that is, my painting helps me in my work with patients. This is what I am mostly aware of, but in all fairness, I believe the self-knowledge acquired through my personal analysis and the work with patients must have an effect on my work as a painter as well. There seems to be a dialectic relationship between the work of an artist and the psychological vigilance required in working with unconscious and projective processes during an analysis.

From the very beginning (over thirty years ago) I mainly painted abstraction, even though there was a period when I ventured to work figuratively in watercolours using a live model. In my work with abstraction, I typically start by creating an accidental happening on the paper or the canvas and then follow the dictates of that accident. It is here where the work with a painting resembles the work with a patient in that I need to follow the patient like I follow the accident on the canvas. In both cases I have to be able to tolerate a state of not knowing that can be quite unpleasant for most people. When learning to paint in my teacher Keith Finch's studio, fellow students at different levels of competence would often say, with a mixture of irritation and acceptance, they didn't know what they were doing. The English Romantic poet Keats called this not knowing "negative capability", the capacity to stay in contact with the work without reaching for a resolution. In the work with patients, this translates into a tolerance of this *not knowing* state without reaching for theory or for other material in the patient that could explain what is going on in the present. In other words, this negative capability results in an ability to abstain from trying to reach conclusions that lead to an interpretation, along with a special kind of patience to wait for clarification from the material emerging in the session.

Another poet whose poetry and writings can be related to psychoanalytic work is Rainer Maria Rilke. When reading *The Letters of Rainer Maria Rilke: 1892–1910* one sees that they are a chronicle of his thoughts and emotions, an autobiography of sorts, while also revealing his desire for friendship and his need to participate in emotional exchanges with his friends and family (Rilke, 1969). His letters were also his means of easing the pressures of life. They became his handicraft, the tool that could keep him at work in constant preparation for the creative moment:

> An intention to write never turns into a letter. A letter must happen to one like a surprise, and one may not know where in the day there was room for it to come into being … For the many experiences and impressions are still heaped up in me in such disorder and chaos that I do not want to touch them. (1969, p. 31)

Rilke's approach to letter writing and his avoidance of acknowledging his thoughts can be compared to a patient who is troubled by the emergence of disturbing associations or the artist who is confronting some unwanted aspect of himself in the work. Additionally, his way of waiting for the words to happen can also be related to the patient's waiting for an association or the analyst's waiting for an appropriate interpretation. In the same way, waiting for the next step of a painting in progress has helped me to wait for the right time before formulating an interpretation.

As Rilke's letters and poems expressed so much of what was going on in his mind, it is important to look at how Melanie Klein's notions can be applied. His poems succeed in showing the fluctuations from

Ps (paranoid-schizoid) to D (depressive), concepts that Klein (1946) created to account for changes that take place in early development. The paranoid-schizoid refers to the attacks and fear of attacks by the other person, while the depressive refers to the sadness and regret about having attacked the beloved other. The goal of an analysis is a move from the paranoid-schizoid to a depressive position, which indicates an affective maturity where love is in the ascendance in the patient's life. In a letter to his ex-lover, Lou Andreas-Salomé, Rilke writes "in one of my poems that is successful, there is much more reality than in any relationship or affection that I feel; where I create, I am true, and I would like to find the strength to base my life entirely on this truth, on this infinite simplicity and joy that is sometimes given to me ..." He then complains to her about his shortcomings, a common complaint among creative people: "I still lack the discipline, the being able to work, and the being compelled to work, for which I have longed for years ..." (1969, pp. 121–122). Later in the letter he continues to criticise himself: "I am similarly clumsy about events that come and go, without the gift of selection, without the calmness for reception ... that is why it is so frightfully necessary to find the tool of my art, the hammer, my hammer so that it may become master and may grow above all noises" (1969, p. 124). This is an idea also voiced by surrealist poet René Char, who wrote a series of nine poems entitled *Le marteau sans maître* (1934) (The hammer without a master), that compelled composer Pierre Boulez to base music on them (more about this in Chapter Nine). Artists have this need to not only create, but to find their own "tool" with which to do the creating. Like most artists, Rilke was quite demanding and critical of himself and learned the value of "always working" from the sculptor Auguste Rodin.

Rilke's admiration for other artists is expressed in a letter about Rodin to his sculptor wife, Clara Westhoff, who had studied with him. He writes:

> ... You see, Rodin has lived nothing that is not in his work. Thus it grew around him. Thus he did not lose himself ... because what he experienced did not remain a plan because in the evenings he immediately made real what he had wanted during the day. Thus everything always became real. That is the principal thing—not to remain with the dream, the intention, with the being-in-the-mood, but always forcibly to convert it all into things. (1969, p. 59)

Or into *words* in Rilke's case. In one of his letters to Lou Andreas Salome he continues to write about his admiration of Rodin:

> Oh what a lonely person is this aged man who, sunk in himself, stands full of sap like an old tree in autumn! He has become deep; he has dug a deep place for his heart, and its beat comes from afar off as from the center of a mountain ... He has become blunt and hard toward the unimportant ... But to what is important he throws himself open ... For him, what he gazes at and surrounds with gazing is always the only thing, the world in which everything happens. (1969, p. 118)

In a later letter Rilke writes, "... it is becoming apparent to me that I must follow him ... not in a sculptural reshaping of my creative work, but in the inner disposition of the creative process ... I must learn to work, to work, Lou, I am so lacking in that!" (1969, p. 123). And still in another letter he continues, "... I want so ardently and so impatiently to find work, the workday, because life, if only it has first become work, can become art" (1969, p. 126).

Converting experiences into work can lead to a total immersion, which can result in confusion with the work. These states of confusion with the work can be followed by a certain detachment from it, where the artist does the necessary editing or corrections. The states of fusion and confusion with the work alternate with a separation from it that leads to a certain objectivity to do to it what is required. This also corresponds to Melanie Klein's paranoid-schizoid and depressive positions. I write about my own experience in my paper "The evolution of a painting" (1981) (see Chapter Twelve, where I attempt to document the work on a large painting on canvas by taking photographs of its progress, recording my conscious thoughts after each "session" with it, and writing about my dreams during that time. I only put these elements together when the painting was finished and concluded, in amazement, that the combined effort with this one painting represented a few years of analysis. In the same way, poets such as Rilke offer us their poems and their commentary, far more transparent than my work in the painting studio and its effect on my analytic work.

The poetry of Wordsworth, Rilke, Blake, Milton and others is examined from a psychoanalytic perspective by psychoanalyst Ronald Britton in *Belief and Imagination: Explorations in Psychoanalysis* (1998). He argues that Wordsworth illustrates some aspects of Klein's depressive position and mourning, whereas Rilke's poems illustrate Klein's paranoid-schizoid position or Herbert Rosenfeld's clinical descriptions of psychotic states of mind (Rosenfeld, 1965). This verse from Wordsworth's "Ode: Intimations of Immortality", a well-known poem completed in 1804, illustrates the depressive position:

> Though nothing can bring back the hour
> Of splendour in the grass, of glory in the flower;
> We will grieve not, rather find
> Strength in what remains behind;
>
> (Wordsworth, 1995, pp. 70–71)

As compared with Wordsworth, a poet of the depressive position, Rilke's writings exemplify the paranoid-schizoid position. Britton is not describing Rilke as in the mode of the paranoid-schizoid position, since, in order to be able to write as Rilke did, he had to be functioning in the mode of the depressive position. He goes further to suggest that, for Rilke, the act of writing was the means of moving himself from the paranoid-schizoid to the depressive position. In another letter to Lou Andreas Salomé, Rilke accused himself of destructiveness, for which in the past he had always blamed others, and he made it clear that he could no longer entertain a sense of persecution. Here he is clearly moving towards the depressive position with less projection of his own aggression, and thus less persecution. Hanna Segal has suggested that, "for the artist, the work of art *is* his most complete and satisfactory way of allaying the guilt and despair arising out of the depressive position and of restoring his destroyed objects" (1952, p. 198). She also writes that, "in a great work of art the degree of the denial of the death instinct is less than in any other human activity" (1952, p. 204).

I have chosen to extensively quote from Rilke's letters because he describes so well the difficulties involved in carrying out a life engaged in creative work. His letters convey the travels from the paranoid-schizoid position and the confusion with the object to the depressive position where there is true separation from it. Rilke's writing demonstrates this shift from confusion to clarity. It is certainly the same as it happens with painting, only that in a painting it is more difficult to follow its evolution. One has to wonder if for the artist the use of words makes self-analysis more accessible than working on a painting. Rilke writes to

Lou Andreas Salomé on 24 January 1912: "I know now that analysis would have sense for me only if I were really serious about not writing anymore" (Rilke, 1969, p. 45). His statement raises the question of whether analysis inhibits or encourages creativity, and whether creativity is in itself therapeutic. While it is true that Rilke did not undergo a proper analysis, his letters to Lou show that he engaged her as an analyst, disclosing his ongoing conflicts to her, and responding well to her letters in return. And she was clearly operating as an analyst, having been one of Freud's disciples. Another example of Rilke's reliance on Salomé as an analyst comes in an earlier letter where he writes:

> For I am dissatisfied with myself, because I am without daily work, tired, although not sick, but in anxiety. When, Lou, when will this miserable life begin to be effective, when will it grow out over inability, inertia, and opacity to the simple, reverent joyousness for which it longs? Is it growing at all? I scarcely dare ask about my advancing steps, because I am afraid (like that man in Tolstoy) to find that their tracks run in a circle, keep coming back to that notorious disconsolate spot from which I have already so often started out. (1969, p. 133)

I believe that if the analyst is aware that changes from fusion and separation will happen of their own accord and with their own rhythm, he or she will be able to wait for these changes and will not get discouraged when things seem to revert back to a more hostile and unreceptive place. The notion of waiting reminds us of Rilke's waiting for a moment of clarity that leads to the drive to share both his conflict and resolution in a letter. I have learned about these unpredictable fluctuations from my work in my studio, where a painting seems to go towards success or failure outside of my control.

Another element comes to the surface at this time, a certain ruthlessness facing the work where the artist engages in actions that put the work in jeopardy. From time to time I find myself destroying the existing work, which has become stale or contrived, to make room for something different and new. This is sometimes frightening, as I may have spent a lot of time developing the work up to this point. But the ruthless action seems absolutely necessary to move the work to a different level. This ruthlessness shows the artist's capacity to face death insofar as the work is always in danger of being destroyed. In the work with a patient, this ruthlessness may manifest in interrupting the patient's discourse at the risk of appearing rude; dropping a line of inquiry to make room for something new the patient is bringing up; or in responding to the patient's non-verbal communication. I believe that I can exercise this freedom because of the freedom with which I can destroy a painting in progress. Patience at times and ruthlessness at other times are capacities that come to my analytic work directly from my work as a painter. The difficulty with becoming ruthless is ultimately a fear of death. In the consulting room this is reflected in the analyst's capacity to tolerate long periods of silence in the patient, of nothing going on, and the fear that analysis is being nullified.

Another aspect where the work as a painter has helped me in my work with patients is the capacity to use mistakes and not discard them or correct them prematurely. This translates in the analyst's capacity to use what appears irrelevant and out of sync with what the patient is saying. Ever since Winnicott (1971) wrote about the use of the object, there has been an interest in the fate of an interpretation. Does the patient take it, does he seem indifferent to it, or does he reject it? How much of the analyst's work is used by the patient? The possibility of creativity during a session arises when both therapist and patient can use what is available to them without too much editing in the listening. And, as I have said earlier, this can be coupled by the courage to disturb things; by the analyst interrupting the patient with a different idea or the patient interrupting the analyst with a new association that contradicts the analyst's interpretation. This ruthlessness runs counter to empathy, a sine qua non of analytic work, but is a necessary ingredient of my work with a patient that originates directly from the ruthlessness with which I engage my artwork.

CHAPTER TWELVE

The evolution of a painting

I would like to offer an inside view of the creative process through an examination of my work on a single painting from beginning to end. I performed an experiment with a painting by taking photographs as the work progressed over a four-month period, by keeping notes on my ongoing reactions to the painting before and after each session with it, and by keeping a journal of my dreams during the process. Since my work is abstract, I had no idea if there would be any dreams clearly related to the work on the painting rather than to other circumstances in my life. I knew that in the past there were such dreams, but I was not sure how often I had had them.

It was not easy to change from immersion in the painting to writing about it, and trying to remember what I had gone through. I did not want to analyse what I was seeing in the painting, since I felt this would interfere with the work itself. So, I recorded my reactions as candidly as I could and only occasionally looked back to see what I had written earlier. This "reporting" slowed things down and I resented it at times. However, it was quite enjoyable to make some new discovery or to find out what I thought about the painting in this unselfconscious way. I did not make any effort to analyse my dreams, afraid again of the effect this would have on the work. Only when the painting was finished did I do that and I began to put the pieces of the puzzle together: the slides, the ongoing report, and the dreams—now analysed and dated.

I also began to wonder if I was willing to communicate what I was finding out about myself—after all, this effort was purported to be an exploration of the creative process and psychodynamics, not of my own psychopathology. By now, I have enough distance and am willing to talk about both. My experience with life had been transformed in the painting and was no longer my experience. In the same way, my own conscious reactions and dreams also transformed as I wrote about them. As Susanne Langer said: "Even the personality called 'I' in an autobiography must be a creature of the story and not the model itself" (1953, p. 254). So here is the story of what happened to my painting—my own story is now what happens in this chapter.

This is the fifth of a series of large paintings measuring sixty by forty-two inches. I have used acrylic paint on raw canvas, which allows for very little control over the paint, but can give the quality of watercolour that I like. I let the work evolve by putting paint on the wet canvas, painting and doodling on it while dry, pouring more paint, and doing this in many layers to the finished state. I had a work by Chilean artist Roberto Sebastian Matta (1911–2002) in mind when I began this painting. This is probably why I began to stain it with green paint (Figure 12.1). Soon after, I seem to have forgotten Matta, because I started adding some orange and warm tones to it. I wanted to depart from my earlier paintings that were predominantly green and blue. The doodles in the upper centre bothered me: they seemed too structured, packed, and messy, yet they had some of the raw canvas showing through, which I liked (Figure 12.2).

The mess probably represents an unwanted aspect of myself and that may explain my aversion to it (Ehrenzweig, 1967; Safán-Gerard, 1982). I spent some time getting it under control or trying to obliterate it all together. I wanted to pour paint over the troubled areas in the middle in an attempt to get rid of them. I found some leftover paint in a jar, a soft orange I had used in another painting, and poured it over the upper centre, moving the paint down with a squeegee. I did the same in an area below, where it worked well.

When I came back to the painting after a break, I realised that the orange had spread badly (Figure 12.3). As I was trying to fix this by adding water and trying to erase the edge left by the spread of the orange, I remembered a dream I had a few days earlier.

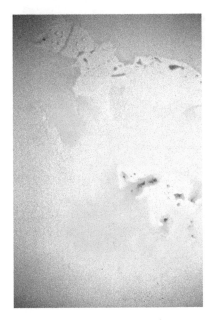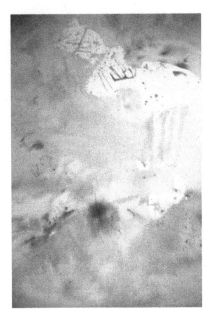

Figure 12.1. Matta in mind.

Figure 12.2. Departure from previous work.

A circle like a balloon in a translucent white had three or four soft tubes or connections coming off of one end. On the right side there was an organic-looking protuberance (like a tear) with some gold-yellow intense colour on the end of it. It was translucent and mysterious and I had awakened with a good feeling, wanting to retain the image. In remembering it now and drawing it in my notebook, I thought, "This is the image of creation itself". It is interesting that this came to mind as I was trying to erase an edge, a boundary that I had not intended. Edges and outlines tend to keep things separate and in their place. For Marion Milner, the outline represents the world of fact, of separate solid objects (Milner, 1950). Clinging to it is a way of protecting ourselves from the world of imagination, which stirs up the fear of going mad. I have noticed that I tend to use more lines and drawing when I need a certain hold on things and myself, and that they become less necessary when I'm feeling in harmony with myself. This time I did not want the separation, I wanted the mating, the transition of the two colours equivalent to birth itself. In this case, the unintended outline suggested more than a separation, a rupture. Bloodstains leave an edge like that.

Figure 12.3. Creation itself.

Figure 12.4. Swastika figure.

By this time, I liked the top and the bottom of the canvas, but not the middle section. I thought a deep green over the entire middle area would unify the painting, but it would darken it and I liked the softness of the background and wanted to keep it. Then, I thought light lavender would be better, since this would not darken the whole thing and would get rid of the middle area as well. After working for a couple of hours, I realised that the soft purple in the middle had taken the strength away from the painting and made the green areas at the top left and lower right feel isolated. This was distressing to me. It was as though I myself had become disconnected. Besides, there was this small figure in the upper left that reappeared after the soft purple was in. It looked like a swastika, which troubled me (Figure 12.4).

A couple of days later I began to cover two areas that showed the raw canvas. I hesitated. "I am losing the light, but they *have* to go under. Otherwise, it would be an array of interesting areas, but not a whole painting". I soon realised that my destroying these raw, valued areas for the sake of the painting was not only helping the painting, it was creating a new mystery in it. I was delighted. I wondered now if I should do the same with the canvas in the lower right and to the left, but I was not sure if this other area was going to survive so nicely.

By this time, the painting had nine distinct areas. I made a diagram in my notebook and numbered them to be able to refer to them later. It was clear that there was too much fragmentation and that these areas had to be pulled together somehow, but that would saturate the space and I wanted to retain some of the open areas I had at the beginning.

I began to put wet green paint on top of the soft purple. The turquoise green was too intense anyway to go over it alone. The superimposition of soft purple and green began to feel very exciting (Figure 12.5). I wrote in my notes: "This is what I'm here for. This is what feels pleasurable and where the surprise is for me". What I had been doing so far was "like adding ingredients to a stew with my mind only half in it". The painting was beginning to have a life of its own and I was discovering an *other* in it. It was at this point that I got something from it, something that felt like nourishment.

A couple of weeks later I had a vivid dream. There was something in a burgundy colour that meant anger, war, or death. Someone was saying that turquoise green was the only way to counteract its effects. When

Figure 12.5. A life of its own.

I woke up, I remembered the dinner of the previous evening where someone I knew wore a wine-coloured dress and that the night before, someone else did also. These are two very accomplished, but self-centred and aggressive women. I wondered whether the wine colour stood for the more aggressive, narcissistic part of me that needed to be balanced or mitigated by some other qualities represented by the turquoise green. At the time of the dream, the painting was predominantly green and I wondered if this neutralisation by the colour had actually happened inside me, or was I using the canvas to cover up unacceptable feelings.

Turquoise green is for me the epitome of life, nature at its best, the mixture of green foliage and the ocean. It seems to also stand for the young, uncertain, and not-knowing part of me. The burgundy is the wine that one takes to get rid of the pain of being young, producing a state of certainty, and filling the space. When I am burgundy, I know everything and don't need anyone. Whereas, when I'm green, I am alive and can grow, but envy those who have certainty and knowledge. My conflict is then between this young part of me that suffers envy and the omniscient, smug part of me that says: "I can do it myself." Burgundy is the cure for the pain of envy, but is destructive of the child part of me and the chance to grow. My excitement at the superimposition of colours may have been a response to the encounter between these two parts of me and the sense of acceptance or integration of them inside me.

Two days later I had the following dream: I'm sitting behind Otto Kernberg and there is the notion that he is also Einstein. He's lecturing from his seat in an auditorium and I am able to see his notes. Then he turns the page and there is a drawing in the upper left hand corner, an abstract design done with charcoal representing a person. He calls it "the sculpture" and is using it instead of concepts or words. Somebody challenges him from the audience asking, "Why a sculpture?" and he replies "Why not a sculpture?" and people laugh. Then I have a plastic bag on my lap. It looks like it doesn't have anything in it and my neighbour to my right gives me some lettuce to feed it and we both laugh. The sculpture that Kernberg/Einstein is talking about and what is in the plastic bag represent the same thing. In the next scene, I'm telling this dream to an analyst friend of mine, who is also a painter. He comments that my dream could not be more omnipotent: I only need to sit behind Kernberg and I become him. We both laugh. Then I have to go to the bathroom. I hear a man outside who's breathing deeply and he looks at me through the keyhole. I try to cover the keyhole, but to no avail.

The sculpture in the dream stands for the section in the upper left of my painting, the area I liked that turned out right from the very beginning with no effort. I take possession of what Kernberg/Einstein has—handwriting and ideas, but the sculpture (the drawing on his page) is from my painting. Otto Kernberg was my analyst years ago in Chile and Einstein may stand for my mentor, whose names is Albert, too. It appears that in fantasy I have taken possession of what he has, but this creates a problem. While it makes me think that I am acquiring a lot, I never feel quite safe with it: someone is already looking at me and watching me for my productions or my shortcomings. Most importantly, taking possession of his ideas leads me to confusion about my own creativity. Whose sculpture/painting is it? Is it Kernberg's or is it mine? I see it in his notes and it is also in my painting and in my plastic bag. I don't know any more if it is truly mine or if I took it from him. An early tendency to take in too much, too quickly, to get away from the pain or terror of my hunger and feeling of inadequacy continues. The plastic bag has a sculpture and nothing at the same time. This reminded me of my young sister, who opened a cheese empanada and (not seeing the cheese that had stuck to the inside of the dough) remarked, "It seems it is made of nothing." The plastic bag in the dream may stand for this seemingly empty empanada, the Chilean younger part of me. Of course, there is also a sexual symbolism here in the plastic bag needing to be filled. Do I need a sculpture from them or do I make my own by painting? My solution came a couple of weeks later. I saw my son in a dream, very young, playing with his penis. It had a strange shape with something like flowered pistols at the end, very beautiful. My son, as an extension of myself, didn't need a sculpture from somebody else.

When I resumed work on the painting, I realised that leaving all these areas in would have felt like crowding the open space I needed. I felt claustrophobic and wanted the painting to breathe and to be free. I wanted nothing locked in by lines, but things should exist in a state of transformation and becoming. Therefore, some areas would have to go, but which ones? I was taking a picture of the painting at that stage and thought that if I were to show slides for a presentation, the audience would be seeing things in them. This is not something I do when I paint or even when I sit to evaluate my work. This time (and for the sake of this experiment) I was going to take the trouble.

In my notes I wrote that I was bothered by what looked like a bird's eye and also by something like a nipple next to it (Figure 12.4). I had already covered what had been the breast, and the eye seemed to be looking now towards the nipple. Soon, the latter became the right arm of an amoeba-like figure with three stick legs (Figure 12.5). So here I was, being watched by an eye, already persecuted for my attack on the breast. That the nipple, the desired object, becomes transformed into a right arm suggests a manic reversal: the baby part of me can now reach out and get things by herself. Not only do I have an arm, but three legs in which to move around or I might even have two legs and a penis: "I'm all set!" But, this manoeuvring to get away from needing was not to last. For then I wrote, "Now I see the former eye as one of the breasts of a larger female figure with a very large head, like the ones in cave paintings. The breasts are not as large as they ought to be for that size head". Who was to say how they ought to be? No doubt I wanted them and I wanted them big.

In the lower left hand corner I saw something like a medieval figure dressed in a big cape with a weapon rising from his head or his left side (Figure 12.5). It reminded me of those mythical figures from Australian cave paintings that have a phallic pole/hat going from the head forward. He also had some blue weapons on his right side, like a sword hanging to the left corner, and seemed to be sliding on skis or skating. I had clearly gotten away from my vulnerable place. I was a warrior and in control. In the lower right hand corner, I saw a figure like an astronaut with one eye in the centre (Figure 12.5). He seemed to be travelling in space in his own capsule. He also had some strange weapons in his right hand. I liked him. He surely didn't need anyone, had travelled far, and was surrounded by his own shell. As for autonomy and control, this was better than the warrior, and certainly much better than the amoebic figure with three legs.

The painting looked washed-out and I didn't like it at all. I began to wonder if I should add some scribbles to give it some of the structure it seemed to be lacking or if I should just pour paint over it. The problem with this latter option is that I liked the background and didn't want to lose it. I painted out the messy spot in the centre with the more intense green to obliterate it. I eliminated the connection between part of the body and breast of the large-headed figure, which left the head alone. This separating of head and body may be once again my way of dissociating from my own dependency: I destroy the object of my need by breaking it up into unrecognisable parts. The mystery of the upper right area had now become isolated and I liked it, except that the bottom of the figure seemed too contrived, tense, and entangled (Figure 12.6).

Figure 12.6. Large-headed figure.

I kept wetting the painting, blending the purple and green, changing my mind, and then going green over purple in certain parts or vice versa in other parts. The lower left corner was practically untouched while I managed to get rid of the middle area. I left the studio that day knowing that there was much to do to have it all come together. It takes courage to be able to withstand looking at a painting that is not what one wants it to be. It is like being in the gap between subject and object, where the awareness of our needing the object is inescapable. This is very different from the situation of being in the transitional space between self and object. In this latter case, one is in the middle, but still connected to both, and it feels wonderful. The painting was there, but it was wrong and it was failing me. In my case, it was up to me to make it right and I had to wait for the next "session" with it, another gap to endure.

For Bion, there has to be a gap between subject and object for thinking or creativity to develop (Bion, 1962). The pain of experiencing this gap is not tolerated for too long and one needs to retreat to states of fusion to regain strength. Alternating between fusion and separation may be necessary, not only for the development of the creative process, but for the development and growth of the self (Rose, 1980).

A couple of weeks before, I had a dream in which I had had to wait. It was unclear what it was I was waiting for, but simultaneous with the idea of waiting, there was the image of a half circle, which may represent the breast. That I have to wait for the painting to nourish me again after that exciting moment of discovery seems to confirm the idea that, in a way, the painting becomes the breast we have created and that it has the potential for feeding us. We give life to the object and "the created object is experienced as life-giving" (Jaques, 1970, p. 60).

As we can see, there were some other changes and the painting felt more balanced now (Figure 12.7). The astronaut had turned into a flying Santa Claus. I not only seemed to fly away from the troubles of earth and reality, but I had also turned myself into the helper and giver. In the upper right, I now saw a face, a young being, a dear little monster. I wrote in my notes: "It has a questioning look as if asking: What am I supposed to do here, Desy? Why do you put me here without a body, just an arm-ladder to my right?" It seems that, after the destruction of all the sources and turning myself into creator or Santa Claus, the needy, infantile part of me had returned. You may remember the amoebic figure with one arm and three legs. I was back

Figure 12.7. Monsters.

in the scene, clearly more helpless and this time asking someone for something.

A dream I had at the time seemed to add to this picture. There were two lions, one young and the other old. The old one was jealous and was attacking the young one and I wanted to protect it. I wanted to put him up on a branch of a tree and asked my mentor to tell me which was the best way to hold him and he suggested from the seat. I put the young lion, in the tree, by wrapping his wooden leg (that was made up of several sticks strung together) around one of the branches to help him stay there. The young lion, like the young being in the painting, was clearly the infantile part of me that was finally getting attention and being protected.

By now, the painting needed more structure and I did this by moving a string dipped in black paint around the canvas. I wanted to retain the feeling that *nature* was creating it, not me. The face I had seen before had now turned into a turtle, a benign figure flying over Santa Claus. I wrote: "The flying is suspicious now. Where is it going? What is it escaping? Did it also decide to fly away from need? The turtle seems to want to fly away from the painting. Santa Claus seemed to now fly in". *In* may stand for the belly of the painting and, in that sense, Santa Claus is closer to accepting needing something, whereas the turtle is the part of me that is still fighting the recognition of vulnerability. My ambivalence is well portrayed by these figures moving in opposite directions: one towards the source; one away from it. All of a sudden, the turtle looked like Popeye. On its way out, the turtle seemed to make a last display of phony strength. I felt a special warmth towards this poor turtle that extended towards the painting in general.

When I came back to work on it, I wrote:

> It's so structured now, it makes me sick! The only thing I have achieved so far seems to be the connecting of the different parts, but connecting for what?! I haven't the slightest idea how to pull it out from where it is. Should I go with a white wash and pull it together that way? Should I insist on the turquoise green? Should I bring in the burgundy I dreamt about? It's time to pour paint, not time to fuss over it.

In several areas of the painting there were movements like swirls that also looked like foetuses.

I have always liked swirls. Swirls, foetuses, life. There was a movement from left to right and back again. The whole painting was becoming a self-contained swirl, too comfortable, too static, no need there, but no life either. I wanted it to flow out of itself rather than to curl upon itself. I wanted it to grow. Later on, as I took a photograph of it while it was still wet, I realised that the painting now had the wine and the green colours I had seen in a dream where I was mixing coloured powders. In an earlier dream, there was the warning about the meaning of burgundy. I had a sense that the painting was becoming what it had to be (Figures 12.7 and 12.8).

The astronaut in the lower right corner now seemed like a mythical bird carrying a child upward. I wish I were the child and could trust the bird. The bird has one eye and is looking towards the warrior. Earlier, there had been an eye looking to the left. That one was against me, this one was for me. The warrior now looks like a female dancer in movement with ruffled clothes. Then, it turns into a woman on a horse facing left and moving out of the painting. I had the feeling that the bird was watching and waiting for her to leave and only then would he carry the child upward with him. The dancer seemed to represent the omnipotent, smug part of me that creates a lot of movement and

Figure 12.8. Bird and child.

noise in order to get away from the child part of me that wants to be helped. The bird cannot help me while this restless lady and horse are still drawing attention to their vigorous presence. Besides, the lady on the horse part of me is already finished with the painting and can now leave the scene.

I had a problem to solve: the painting needed to be rooted. The blue came down straight from the luminescent area over the bird's head, so I decided to extend it to the right corner and below the child (Figure 12.8). I also wanted to give more weight to the lower left corner, under the lady on the horse, but decided later that it had to remain lightweight.

The last time I worked on the canvas I toned down the intensity of the cobalt blue with a purple wash (Figure 12.9). In my impatience, I stood the painting up in order to take the final picture and the purple paint ran over the bird and child, who then looked imprisoned behind bars. For a moment I thought all the struggle had been for nothing.

Quickly, I put the canvas down and blotted out the streaks of colour, freeing the bird and child. The next day, I went to my studio to see it finished (Figure 12.10). It had lost some of the mystical quality it had

Figure 12.9. Freeing the bird and child.

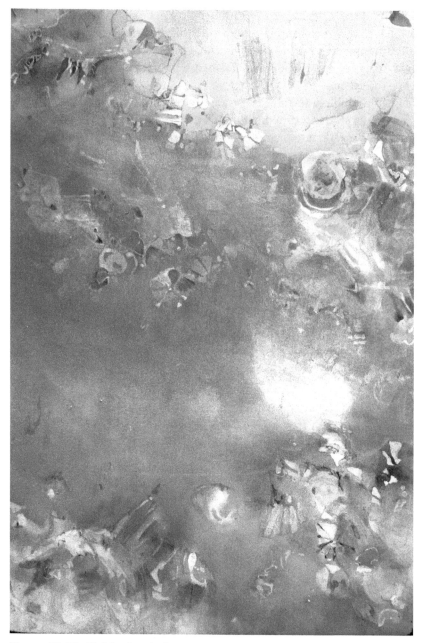

Figure 12.10. Finished painting.

when wet and I was trying to resign myself to this disappointing result. Still, I felt some warmth and contentment. It was not what I wanted, but it was alright. While looking at the slides a couple of months later, a friend pointed out that there was an interplay between the old swastika up above and one just like it in the lower right corner in the child's body. I was startled, since I had not noticed it. Is it possible that I had placed my destructive impulses where they belonged, but didn't want to know? I knew of my unconscious attacks on the source by the evidence appearing in dreams, like the one about the destruction of the contents of my office. Now I had a symbol of this aspect of myself and wore it directly on myself, like a stamp. I would have to accept that as undeniable truth.

Conclusion

The relationship between the conscious dilemmas, the decisions, and the dream material that seemed to relate to it opens many old questions and some new ones. To pose a few: Is creativity the inevitable outcome of a relatively healthy personality or is it a way of dealing with internal conflicts? Does creative work always promote growth and integration or only when the unconscious conflicts have become conscious during or after the work? Given that a capacity for symbol formation indicates this growth, where do the ones in the painting, or the ones in the dreams, stand in a concrete-abstract dimension? Is the symbolism of the elements of the painting more accessible to consciousness than those of the dream? Does it matter?

As I was finishing this chapter, I was struck that the turtle/Popeye and the lady on the horse images ended up on their way out of the canvas. As those images stand for the defensively omnipotent part of myself, I would like to think that (as a result of my deep involvement with the painting) this aspect of my personality has become less salient and that I have come to accept the infantile, not knowing and needy part of me represented by the little monster. However, these images are still on the canvas as well as the colours and what they stood for, even though they went through a series of transformations (Figure 12.11). At any rate (at least for now), I have been humbled by this experience and even more so after writing about it. Would this have happened if I had painted without the notes, the dreams and the work of putting it all together?

Figure 12.11. Desy working on painting in Venice studio.

I go through many different feelings while I work and I know that much is going on within me. Is it possible to reach new levels of integration without having to transform these feelings into thoughts or everyday language? Perhaps so, at least insofar as creative work keeps the door to one's unconscious open and that the chance of rigidifying defences is lessened. I have been struck by the mobility and successive alternation of images and colours that suggested power and destruction, those that suggested helplessness, and by those that indicated the masculine and feminine sides of my nature. For a while, as I wrote about it, I thought the painting merely served as a screen to argue for and against these images.

Opposite elements or forces seem now to stand side by side on the canvas. This may account for the unsettled, unresolved feeling one has after a painting is finished. There is the sense of having stirred something up, coupled with a sense of hope. It may be that other thought processes, such as induction and logic, carry out actual reconciliation of these opposites. Not that I recommend that artists do this. I could not wait to finish this chapter so I could paint, just paint.

CHAPTER THIRTEEN

Love and hate in the creative process

In a letter dated 24 July, 1953, the great American writer Norman Mailer complains to fellow writer William Styron about his anxieties with his creative process.

> I'm at a funny place with my book. I gave up the draft I was pushing in third person, deciding finally that while objectively it might be a better book, I just didn't have the enthusiasm to write it. And so now I'm back to my first draft which is in a curious shape. I've finally been able to see it, and I think all of it which is minor (minor characters, minor themes, etc) is the best I've done, but the heart of the book, which I've finally boiled down to a key sixty pages is bad, slovenly, and what have you. So if I can write sixty new pages which are right, I've got a book. It's maddening because if I can find what to do, I've got a novel in sixty days or so, and if I can't, I suppose I can fritter away another year or more. It's the old business of not knowing just what I want to say— there are so many half-formed things I feel about love and sex and the boundaries and demarcations of them, and other themes too, all very worth-while, but I don't know where to grasp them, and I've got to make up a brand new sixty pages or eighty or whatever they'll turn out to be.

So as we always are before work, I am scared stiff, especially since I
can't put it off any longer—all the reasons for not working are now
gone ... I've always found it terribly hard to write something better
in a second draft than in a first. One's book is alive in the first draft
as it never is again, and to be sloppy with it then is to pollute the
whole book. (Mailer, 1953, p. 140)

Creative work is as demanding of creative people working in all
fields as analysis is of psychoanalysts. A painful process or struggle of
thinking about, evaluating or considering each new thing must take
place in order for the right or best new thing to be recognised—that new
intervention that allows the work itself to grow and mature. When this
new solution has been found, the analyst and the artist (or musician,
programmer or business negotiator) may notice that something quite
magical has just transpired. It is for these moments that we choose to
endure the ordeal.

Similar difficulties are experienced by creators in many fields; even
in fields outside the scope of the arts—those not readily associated with
creativity but require creative thinking nonetheless. For example, the
process of labour negotiations requires negative capability and creative
thinking. Many of the points made here can be applied to those fields as
well. From my own experience as a painter and as an aspiring composer
earlier in life, I have been able to see first-hand how analysts have much
more in common with the creative and performing arts than one might
generally realise. There are no formulas, neither for artistic creation nor
for psychoanalytic work. Every solution is unique.

Wilfred Bion has pointed out how both types of work require one to
enter into the "not knowing" state—that courageous openness, which
invites the unknown and spawns the exploration of various connections in the search for possible solutions. Even with "negative capability", Keats' term for the capacity to tolerate and remain in the "not
knowing" state despite the inherent feelings of anxiety and discomfort,
one is faced with making choices. One must draw from one's intuition,
sensibility, best judgement, training, and experience.

In the introduction to a volume of art critic Adrian Stokes' writings,
noted art scholar Richard Wollheim eloquently describes the beginnings of a painting with accidental markings. He states, "... the notion
finds acceptance that art is a form of externalization, of making concrete

the inner world, and the evolution of Stokes' criticism can largely be accounted for by the increasingly richer view that is taken of the inner world and of how and by what means it works its way out" (Stokes, 1972, p. 11). Influenced by his analysis with Melanie Klein, Stokes writes, "I believe that in the creation of art there exists a preliminary element of acting out of aggression, an acting out that then accompanies reparative transformation, by which inequalities, tension and distortion, for instance, are integrated, and made to 'work'" (1972, p. 110).

His ideas are similar to those of Hanna Segal for whom "there can be no art without aggression" (1991, p. 92). For Stokes, an artist should be able to carry out defacement in order to add, transfer, create, or restore. He claims that if the attack is reduced below a certain minimum, creativity ceases. A good artist has to reckon with the conflicting emotions that underlie his aggression, power, and control, as well as a concurrent belief in his own goodness. Stokes believes this is more clearly shown in music than in other arts (1972, pp. 110–111).

Along with the pleasure of reading Stokes, I again became aware of my own process and my own destructiveness. I had kept a detailed journal of my work in a yellow notebook during the 1980s. I believe I did this to better understand how ideas came to me, as a way to respond to people asking me often how I developed these paintings; also as a way of disabusing them of the notion that creating the paintings was easy. What will follow turns out to be a conflictual, feisty kind of self-analysis while working on some abstract paintings. These notes are equivalent to psychoanalytic sessions, where I am both patient and analyst. Having recently rediscovered what I thought was lost (unfortunately the photographs are still lost), I was amazed to reread my notes, reliving the painful dilemmas experienced in creating those paintings.

As with most of my work, the abstract paintings I will be talking about today were born out of some accidental markings that I imposed onto the blank canvases. What followed was an intimate, challenging, and rewarding relationship and discourse with each work. The thoughts recorded bring to mind Bion's "not knowing" state as well as Keats' "negative capability". Noticeable are my on-going struggles to work things out as well as the frustrations and disappointments of faulty solutions. As it turned out, writing about the ups and downs while painting didn't make things any easier in the studio. It rather highlighted the conflict alternating between assertion and doubt, confidence and despair, love and hate, as I added or destroyed elements in the work.

Notes from the yellow notebook

I would work on three or four canvases at a time each referred to by number and measuring 48 × 72 inches. By doing this, I respected the timing of the painting and the fact that I had no control over when it would be finished.

DAY 1, Tuesday 17 June, 1986
I have been working for a while on three paintings after photographing them. The rust colour I started a while ago took a good turn on Saturday. (Notice that I am not taking credit for this good turn). Applying gold and red paint seemed to put it together finally. It is almost done now, except for some discordant cool purples and light green. Will have to let it go for a while.

Painting #2—I poured some blue across to bring some unity, but it seems I can't get rid of details! There are some interesting things on the left corner. Actually the left side below, that I cannot part with yet. Some of the goodness of the figure on the right side got lost, especially that it is now enclosed from down below. I can see I have a lot of work to do ahead on this one.

Painting #3—I'm trying to ground this one also. I have to get rid, or subdue completely, the figure on the left, otherwise everything seems to float up. I would have liked to keep the pink feeling soft, the pink-purple I put on the left lower side. It changes the mood and I don't like it as much now. This one will have to be washed with white-pink and I ran out of the white! Frustrating day.

DAY 2 (Two days later)
Started by taking photos of all three, outdoors. A nuisance!

Painting #2—It's getting rich and there are some exciting spots such as yellow on lower right with sparks under it. The lower centre is very unformed and black. The dark blue I poured last time is too thin and seems to cut the painting in half (upper and lower). Is this a tendency of mine? Will continue to add—don't think the time has come yet to eliminate anything.

I was waiting for the painting to let me know what it wanted.

Painting #3—Did it or didn't it get more grounded? It doesn't seem it did! Maybe this is not possible with this one. The shapes on the top half are interesting but too disjointed. No sense of skeleton or structure to hold it. I like the grey colour in the centre, but it is divisive. Left on top is all muddy and dirty, but not when you see it from afar. Don't know what to do with this one—I suppose I can only work on the parts and wait.

Again I was waiting for the painting itself to guide me.

At 5 PM and exhausted!

Did some detail work on it especially in the lower middle with red-pink. It is too rich now and something will have to go! Either raw canvas in the middle, which I like, or area on the right, which I also like. I didn't mean to emphasise this but can't get rid of it! I want to keep the yellow on top as is. It definitely needs editing!

Painting #3—Did something completely drastic here. Turned it upside down, dropped intense yellow on open area on left side and let it run upward in streaks. Looks wild! Changed colour on left bottom to unify. Now there may be a problem with the nice pink. Does it go with it? The pink seems so light on the right side, light and transparent, whereas the green-blue on the left side is more solid. It has changed considerably but there is something so familiar on the left lower corner!

DAY 3 (Two days later at 11:00 AM)
Just took them out to photograph …

Painting #1—The light comet-like shape in the centre bothers me. Would have to connect it to light area on left-hand side with the halo going across to feel OK. The centre halo, as it now stands, seems to divide or pivot all painting on top in a balancing act. It reminds me of the penises in the Belmer book I was looking at earlier. Is it why I want to deny their importance?

Painting #2—I am still stuck with this one. Unable to let go of the goodies. Maybe when I start mixing paints I'll get the courage.

Painting #1—The opaque green on the bottom is too dark, too opaque and too green. Will have to cover it with a light blue, as I intended earlier. It is such a relief to get away from the world of words! Was reading Susan Deri's book on symbolism yesterday, also Pontillis, André Green and others on aesthetics. Words, words, words! Would rather get something done!!!!

DAY 4 (The next day)

Painting # 4—Came in before lunch to photograph #4 after the work I did last night. I don't like at all what happened after last night. I created more elements and confusion. I will have to work with that now. There are too many interesting things, but it got too busy and complicated. I am not sure I like that shade of yellow in the yellows. Is that what creates the problem? The pearlescent light purple is too discordant. I like very much the subtlety of the changes in the dark area. There are so many ways to go to reduce its complexity—they all imply LOSS and I have to be in the mood for that.

DAY 5 (Two days later)

Painting #4—Don't like it at all! I think the mustard yellow is what gives it this ominous feeling. The dark grey is dull and lifeless. Some of the gold in the upper right seems pasted in, especially the one attempting to link toward the centre. Will have to start by changing the mustard yellow. There are problems with the shapes too! Nothing seems to work today!

DAY 6 (Three days later)

Painting #4—This is definitely wrong! I can't stand it now!!! Will have to do some drastic killing of some areas. It is just too full of details! The blue-green spot where I covered the gold portion is wrong!!!

Painting #5—Even though it needs a lot of work, it doesn't feel as hopeless as #4. It is open, rich with possibilities. I intend to allow this one to breathe!

Up to this point, the paintings and I are in good condition. We both seem to be surviving the ongoing conflicts that come up during the creative process. However, my own destructiveness and self-doubts became apparent to me when I reread my notes from the yellow notebook. For Stokes, the artist, writer, composer, or dancer is often afraid that his difficulties creating will reveal some basic and hopeless shortcomings in one psychological make-up. Norman Mailer reveals this fear in a subsequent letter to Styron from 24 April, 1953, without any idea that he was soon to become one of America's most celebrated literary idols:

> At the moment what's killing me in my work is that dilemma of point of view. I find that when I write in third person I'm so bound, so constipated, that I can't seem to enter people's heads—I write as if the damn thing were a play, scene, dialog, entrance, exit, and of course it's very wasteful. It takes forever to get to the point that way. First person is even worse. The moment I have a character in first person, I tighten up, my narrator becomes a stiff, haughty, cold young man whose relation to myself I've never been able to discover.
>
> In a way I think I understand why. To write well in the third person, to be omniscient, one has to have a life-view, and if one is a serious writer, it has to be a life-view of some depth and some capacity for embracing entities, contradictory people, etc. etc. The thing which is so bad about the average third person novel is that the matter, the interpretation, is absolutely without life-view, it's written the way everyone else sees it, and that irritating maddening business of pop, pop, pop, in and out of the minds we go, comes because there's no mind directing it. I think that's why writers like Maugham as they shrivel turn so naturally to the first person narrator—it's the perfect substitute for a life-view. One's form is given by the sole perceiver, although unhappily it's the exact opposite of the expansive life-view of the major novelist. And it's so binding as well. Anyway, these days, trying by an act of will (which I don't disapprove of entirely) de me mêler dans le monde [to be out in the world], I find that I actually sweat from the fear of getting loose in such a book and revealing my fundamental poverty of imagination, and so for this first month, I've been rushing virtually on alternate days from third person to first person and back again, disgusted in first person by the artificial barriers I set up on a book which shouldn't have them. Do you ever suffer from this kind of thing? (Mailer, 1953, p. 138)

Yes, Norman. We all suffer from this kind of thing.

Endnote

I am including here composer Lucky Choi's unexpected and creative transformation of what took place during these ten sessions with three paintings in my studio, as described in this chapter. It has been a privilege to receive from such a dear and gifted friend these unusual and insightful graphs about my work (Figure 13.1).

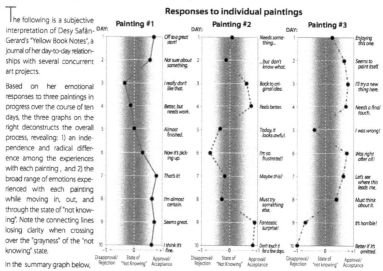

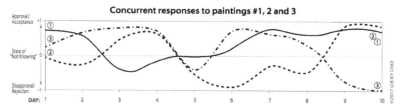

Figure 13.1. Composer Lucky Choi's graph of my responses to my working on these paintings.

CHAPTER FOURTEEN

Destructiveness and reparation: a retrospective

This chapter is primarily a presentation of some notions about the creative process using myself as the subject of inquiry. The ideas presented are expounded by describing the development of my own paintings, which I made over a span of nearly thirty years.

The main idea here is that destructiveness in its various forms is an intrinsic part of the creative process. In 1912, Sabina Spielrein advanced this thought in her seminal contribution, "Destruction as the cause of coming into being". Her publication anticipated Freud's conception of the death instinct by eight years and Freud in fact acknowledged Spielrein's contribution in his 1920 paper entitled *Beyond the Pleasure Principle*. Spielrein's paper, with many examples from both biology and mythology, placed destructiveness not only at the centre of psychopathology, but also at the centre of personality development. Her destructiveness is not fuelled by hatred of the good object and the wish to attack and destroy it, as described later on by Melanie Klein, but by the desire to destroy something that is not satisfying in order to give birth to something that is (Kerr, 1993). Spielrein's destructiveness is akin to the ruthlessness Winnicott described as the necessary destructiveness in order to allow the emergence of something new (1971). I believe both kinds of destructiveness are reflected in my work: destructiveness in the accidents with which I start some of my work and the ruthlessness in the execution of that work. Moreover, one could say that the ruthlessness Spielrein referred to is motivated by love for the love object, so that it may have a better life, a true life, and an independent life. Thus, even though this chapter focuses on destructiveness, we have to keep in mind the love underlying it, as it is the love that translates into what we call beauty.

An initial review of my paintings for this analysis made me realise that major themes kept coming back at different times. So, I have sacrificed strict chronology by reorganising the images around themes. As a preview I can already tell you that the themes in the earlier work are accidents and repairing them, the mother–baby pair, the inside of the mother's body, the father, and a pictorial comment on relationships. These themes reappear in later works: my blue period (why not?), the exuberant work, my *Boulez series*, and the *Totem series* (collage on paper, large canvases, and monoprints).

Before telling you about how I have interpreted this work, I want to emphasise that the psychodynamic formulations were nowhere in my mind while I was painting. In addition, I no longer have access to the associations or fantasies that accompanied them. In fact, I ended my first attempt at understanding and interpreting the evolution of a single painting with the realisation that my analysis was interfering with the work (Safán-Gerard, 1983) (see Chapter Twelve). It is only in retrospect that I can now look at my early paintings the way one would look at a child's drawings. Klein's "Narrative of a child analysis" (1961) has been very present in my mind. I have become both the Richard who did those paintings and the Melanie Klein who interpreted them. She was in a better position than I am, however, because she was interpreting Richard's paintings in the context of the events of the session and the child's associations. I can only do it in relation to the larger events of my life. One piece of biography that can account for some of my destructiveness (at least to some degree) is having been the oldest of four sisters and having been asked many times to look after them. These sisters, born one after the other in rapid succession, led to a special curiosity about my mother's body as well as to an early turning away from my mother to my father as a replacement.

I began to paint during my graduate training in clinical psychology at the University of California Los Angeles (UCLA) by attending an unstructured class with Keith Finch, a gifted teacher who allowed me to develop at my own pace and in my own way (see Chapter Ten). His class was on Tuesday afternoons and I protected that time from any intrusion. Now, years after Keith's death, I have made a vow to keep Tuesday afternoons free of patients to pursue my painting. My training was not formal and I never took anatomy drawing lessons with a model. I started directly with abstraction.

Accidents and repairs

One of the ways I got started with a new work was by creating an accident on paper or on canvas (the uglier the better!) and by using paints at random while working flat on a table, initially only with watercolours. Once I had an accident on the paper, I had a problem to solve: how to make it work. This involved a close scrutiny of the accident and trial and error in pursuing the work.

In addition to the initial accident, there were unwanted accidents that took place at various times throughout the work. These accidents are the pictorial equivalent of a slip of the tongue, revealing unconscious impulses. Artists have to contain their first inclination to eliminate them by distancing from them for a while. I, for example, tend to work on other areas of the painting or by putting the whole painting aside for a later time when I am more ready to work on it. In both cases, I seem to be lowering my anxiety enough to be able to look at the accident again and confront my projections in it. In his *Reminiscences*, Kandinsky states that, for him, accidents allow a puzzling play of forces that he experienced as alien to himself. As he put it, "I owe much to these accidents: they have taught me more than any teacher or master" (1913, p. 34). I believe that "working on a painting offers the opportunity to bring back into the self what has been projected into it" (see Chapter Twelve).

It appears that the accident with which I start new work carries my aggression and, as Adrian Stokes discusses in *The Invitation in Art* (1965), the first step in starting artistic work contains aggression and explains the painter's or the writer's anxiety facing the virgin canvas or page. In searching internally for material to put on the canvas or the page, the painter and the writer may come in contact with destroyed or damaged internal objects or with impulses to destroy the object, which give rise to anxiety. Stokes argues that, "A painter, then, to be so, must be capable of perpetrating defacement; though it be defacement in order to add, create, transform, restore, the attack is defacement none the less" (1965, p. 23).

Along similar lines, both Ella Sharpe (1930) and John Rickman (1940) relate the "ugly" to the fragmented and destroyed object, while they relate the "beautiful" to the experience of the whole object and its goodness. However, what is aesthetic is not only what is beautiful. For Segal, the "aesthetic experience is ... a particular combination of what has been called 'ugly' and what could be called 'beautiful'" (1991, p. 90). In working through the accident and repairing it, one adds beauty to what is ugly, reparation to what was damaged or destroyed, but the traces of the destructiveness are still embedded in the work. To quote Segal once again, "True reparation, in contrast to manic reparation, must include an acknowledgment of aggression and its effect. And there can be no art without aggression" (1991, p. 92). By this, she means that the aggression may have been carried out in phantasy prior to creating: "One may need to create because one has destroyed" (Segal, 1998). Thus, traces of the destroyed object must be part of the painting and coexist with its reparation.

One can then begin to understand the motivation fuelling these accidents and what the page or the canvas represents. For Kandinsky the "pure canvas ... is as *beautiful* as a painting", yet he remarks, "Each work originates just as does the cosmos—through catastrophes" (1913, p. 35). Perhaps implied in Kandinsky's statement is a phantasy-level recognition of the canvas as the primary object. The pristine canvas, insofar as it is the colour of milk and acts as a container of our communications, may stand for the primary object, the mother. The spilling of paint on the pure canvas could be seen as representing incontinence and an attack on or even the destruction of the mother with urine and faeces. This is not unlike the phantasies of young children during play, as revealed in child analysis. The attempt to make something of the accident is clearly related to restitution and repair of the damage. So when I paint, I seem to be recreating cycles of destruction and reparation, going from a state of unintegration of love and hate where hate leads to phantasised attacks on the object, to the painful integration of ambivalent feelings when one repairs the damage, even though, according to Segal, "the artist's reparative work is never completed" (1991, p. 94).

Another way in which this cycle is expressed is in my abstract landscapes, where it became a challenge to extract light out of the darkness, something quite difficult to do with watercolours (Figure 14.1).

I believe the challenge was again related to repair, since darkness is often associated with dark passions and destructiveness. Artist and art historian Roland Reiss, when writing about my work, pointed out that I am first and foremost a luminist. He concludes, "In actual fact, her

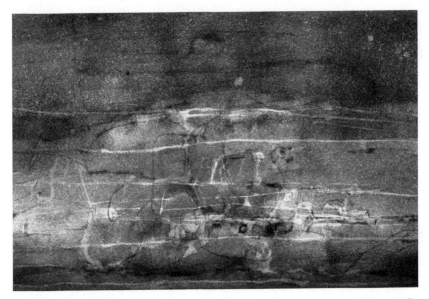

Figure 14.1. Abstract landscape, 1972, watercolour on paper, 11″ × 15.″

paintings appear to emanate an internal light which suffuses pictorial space and imagery" (Reiss, 1998, p. 2). He was certainly pointing to the reparative aspect of my work and to attempts to turn chaos into something integrated. The accident may then represent the manic destructive attack, leading to guilt and reparation. In her seminal paper "Infantile anxiety situations reflected in a work of art and in the creative impulse", Melanie Klein (1929) concludes that, just as painter Ruth Kjar's compelling urge to paint was based on the desire to make reparation, other paintings of hers were more directly an expression of a primary, sadistic desire to destroy. Similarly, as you will notice later on, some of my paintings represent the wish to repair, while others more directly give expression to my destructiveness.

Mother–baby

I realise that many of my earliest watercolours contain a large figure on the left and a small figure on the right (Figures 14.2, 14.3, 14.4, and 14.5). Even in my later attempts at realism this seems to hold true, as is the case with the barn with a big window and a little window (Figure 14.6) or the big courtyard and the small courtyard on the right (Figure 14.7). This one represents an attempt to put together different photographs

Figure 14.2. (a): Untitled, 1972, watercolour on paper, 9″ × 12″.

Figure 14.3. (b): The Pet, 1972, watercolour on paper, 9″ × 12″.

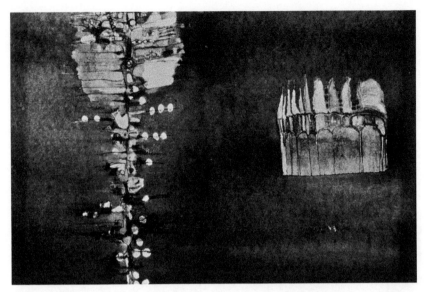

Figure 14.4. (c): Ice, 1972, watercolour on paper, 11″ × 15″.

Figure 14.5. (d): Untitled, 1972, watercolour on paper, 11″ × 15″.

Figure 14.6. Barn, watercolour on paper, 11″ × 15″.

Figure 14.7. Courtyard, watercolour on paper, 11″ × 15″.

of a trip to Brittany, creating something new out of disparate scenes: a broken up mother and the attempt to bring the parts together suggests reparation.

Destructiveness

In the abstract landscapes that follow, I believe what is being depicted is the inside of the mother's body. As Roland Reiss observed, "The idea of landscape which underlays many of [Desy's] compositions, is quickly transposed into the idea of internal landscape as well" (1998, p. 3). Some of these paintings seem to show a harmonious inside, while others have ominous undertones of disaster (Figure 14.8).

The disaster follows the sadistic attacks on the harmony. While reviewing these images for this chapter, I discovered that there was what could be thought of as a birth canal between the happenings at the bottom and the space above (inside and outside) (Figures 14.9 and 14.10). In fact, I was surprised to discover that the last painting of this series seems to have a sketch of a baby in the aperture (Figure 14.11). I do not remember having intended that.

Figure 14.8. Abstract landscape—disaster: Untitled, watercolour on paper, 11" × 15".

Figure 14.9. Abstract landscape—birth canal (a): Under the Boat, 1978, watercolour on paper, 11″ × 15″.

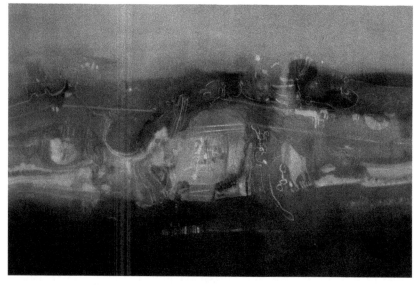

Figure 14.10. Abstract landscape—birth canal (b): Untitled, watercolour on paper, 15″ × 20″.

Figure 14.11. Abstract landscape—baby: Untitled, watercolour on paper, 15″ × 20″.

In the following images one can also see how the attack on the mother or on the parental couple results in mutants or bizarre objects (Figure 14.12). This is envy at work at all levels: the mother's body, the father's penis, and the baby inside the mother. Even in the loving feelings there is damage because of the devouring quality of this love and the wish to possess. The following painting is perhaps the most primitive (Figure 14.13). My son had started a drawing that intrigued me and I finished it. The big fish has eaten the little fish. One can see how the attack on the mother's body leads to a powerful attacking mother-fish that can swallow up the little me. One could say that the painting represents the outcome of projective identification in which the attack by the little fish caused the big mother-fish to eat the baby fish. Either in love or in hate, the relationship to the mother is devouring. Therefore, the mother object is now felt to possess the child's projected mouth. Klein's ten-year-old patient Richard's drawings in "Narrative of a child analysis" came to mind while reviewing my drawing. Richard drew his fish in the fifteenth session. In the analysis of this drawing, the fat fish on top stands for mommy. Klein believed, "The starfish also stood for the greedy and frustrated baby—himself—injuring and eating Mummy's inside when he wanted her and she did not come" (1961, p. 79).

Figure 14.12. Destruction: Untitled, watercolour on paper, 11" × 15".

Figure 14.13. Mauricio's unfinished painting: Untitled, watercolour on paper, 11" × 15".

She implies here that her patient's attacks were partly due to the frustration of an unresponsive mother. I have noted earlier that I was the oldest of four sisters and I can well imagine that, like Richard's mother, my mother was frustrating to me, busy as she was with my younger siblings. This may account in part for the evidence of unmitigated destructiveness in my early paintings.

The next watercolour has an amazing story. During my graduate work at UCLA I had an internship at Children's Hospital. I worked for a while in the dialysis unit, having the children and their mothers communicate with each other through drawings. I used to bring my own materials and once, by mistake, I took a watercolour pad with a painting I had just been working on (Figure 14.14).

The little patient I showed it to said, "There is a baby here calling Mommy!" The hair on the back of my neck stood up because I had just had a miscarriage. That the young patient could respond to the baby I had lost, and that the baby was felt to be in distress calling for me, was utterly amazing. In retrospect, we could say that the painting depicts my attack on my mother's body that has a counterpart in the attack on my own creativity. Because of my attack, I now had a vindictive

Figure 14.14. Mommy! 1973, watercolour and pencil on paper, 16" × 20".

internal mother who attacked my baby. These are persecutory (the vin-dictive internal mother) and depressive (the destroyed internal mother) versions of the outcome. The depressive solution, namely the identifica-tion with a damaged mother, leads to unconscious guilt, which makes me suffer the damage I feel I have produced.

Is there some way to support these interpretations? In the absence of associations or the context of a session, I turn now to a dream I had at the beginning of my second analysis some years ago that seems to illustrate a similar dynamic and offers some validation for the interpre-tations of the paintings. In the dream I am looking for an apartment for my son Mauricio. I enter through a courtyard into a sophisticated place, not elegant, but full of books. "How would they rent this to Mauricio?" I thought. My husband and I explore the place. There is a huge grand piano with rich brown colour in the living room. I move an ashtray on it and, to my amazement, there is a hole that reveals water underneath it. The inside is lit up and there are little bugs, like ants, swarming in there. I quickly cover the hole. I subsequently find something inside my mouth, something grainy, and I try to spit it out but can't. I go into the bathroom and look in the mirror. I try to get it out of my mouth with a towel when I realise that what I have in my mouth is what is inside the piano. The bugs are breeding inside me and I am horrified. In terror, I call for help and wake up.

As you can see, this dream illustrates how the attacks on the mother have an effect on my own creativity. I identify with a damaged mother—bugs instead of babies in her body—by having the bugs inside my mouth. If we look closely at the elements of the dream, we find that looking for a place for my son may stand for a search for a place for the me who would not benefit from the sophisticated elegance of the place, especially from the books and learning from them; the me who, out of envy, is unable to feed properly. The boy part of me is envious of the mother and the babies the father puts inside her. This me won't take things in my mouth in a good way, but what I do take in will be filled with envy and greed. The large piano may stand for my mother's body, the ashtray covering her vagina. I fill the lit space with these ants and bugs breeding there instead of live babies, an attack on my mother's generativity. I cover the space again with the ashtray to deny what I have done and to either say to myself, "I didn't do it" or "It's full of shit anyway." Then I find that the same bugs and ants are in my own mouth, part of my own body, which reveals that I was in fact the perpetrator of the crime. By projective identification I end up experiencing and identifying with the attack directed at my mother.

Since this was an early dream in the analysis, we can speculate that the new situation with this new mommy/analyst is stimulating phantasies of the earliest attacks on my mother and they are being relived in the transference. I had recurrent primitive dreams about trying to get hairs and gunk out of my mouth unsuccessfully, but up to this point it had never been clear to me that what I created inside the piano was the antecedent (the cause) of these recurrent dreams. In other words, I always felt that these awful things I had in my mouth were replicating my mother's attacks on me that I was trying to get rid of. Now I could see the role I had played. The analysis of this dream shows how attacking my mother's creativity may interfere with my own creativity. This consequence has also revealed itself in my not pursuing opportunities to exhibit my paintings because of "lack of time". My attacks on my mother's babies results in miscarrying my own babies. One is tempted to ask whether this dynamic has affected my work as a painter. Were my attacks on the primary object affecting the paintings themselves?

I believe that evidence of the attacks appears both in the content of these paintings and in the neglect of the work itself.

A second dream around the same time depicts in more detail the insidious attacks on the mother's body and its consequences. It shows that, in killing my mother's babies, I kill the fruits of my parents' relationship, which means that I have also attacked that relationship and my father as well. The result will be an internal couple that can't create new babies.

But not all is destructiveness. A recent dream shows how love is, at times, in the ascendance. I am in a place like New Zealand, debating whether I should swim or not. The water looks fantastic. Some people in our group are snorkelling near the rocks. I wonder whether they have wetsuits to bear the cold water. I am aware that there is a rich life underneath, as rich as in the Great Barrier Reef in Australia. It reminds me of years ago in Hawaii going into a trance snorkelling in Hanauma Bay. After that vacation all of my paintings would turn blue, regardless of the colour in which I started working. The beautiful ocean must stand for the inside of my mother's body, the rich life inside it.

One of the startling things about this retrospective is that just bringing those early paintings to mind stirred up the early destructive phantasies that must have instigated the paintings in the first place. Recently, when I was examining the earliest images, I had a dream that seems to again portray the conflict between the destructive forces and the loving, reparative ones. This is probably what fuelled the early paintings, a wish to represent this conflict and have the loving me win in the end, a conflict that may be ongoing in all my paintings. The different stages I have gone through in my work may end up representing many variations on the same theme of destruction and reparation.

Reparation

The next painting shows how the bizarre objects of earlier paintings begin to get organised around a mandala type shape (Figure 14.15). According to Jung, mandalas represent attempts at reconciling opposites and achieving personality integration (Wilhelm & Jung, 1931).

Perhaps, out of guilt, these mandalas are my attempt to put together the hate and the love for my objects. As you will see, some sixteen years later I would be doing totems that seem to fulfil the same quest for integration. The next painting appears to represent the clearest attempt at reparation (Figure 14.16). It is an abstract depiction of surgeons at

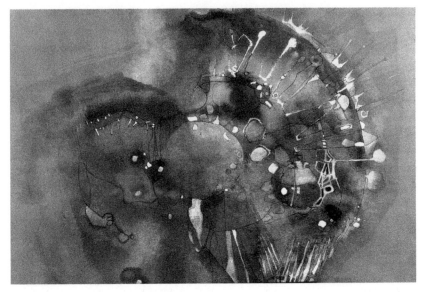

Figure 14.15. Mandala, 1973, watercolour on paper, 16″ × 20″.

Figure 14.16. Reparation, 1973, watercolour on paper, 16″ × 20″.

work. One day, ready to resume work on this watercolour, I noticed a beautiful epiphyllum bloom in the garden, took it to my studio, and suddenly decided to paint it in the place where the patient's flesh could be seen. The second epiphyllum to the left was a response to the requirement of balance in the painting. At the time, I felt that at this juncture the painting had acquired a life of its own—the surgeons at work that had fascinated me had given way to a separate painting that was telling me what it needed. I now can see that the second epiphyllum may stand for the daddy. Mommy was restored—a flower instead of her sick body and daddy was with her. The parents were now together, he on the left, she on the right, just like the mommy and baby of earlier paintings. A happy ending!

Mother as a whole object

In some sessions in Keith's studio we had two-minute poses of a live model. We were supposed to use the model's body as a stimulus to superimpose drawing upon drawing in order to create a design (Figure 14.17).

Figure 14.17. First model: Bringing in the Light, 1973, pencil and watercolour on paper, 18″ × 22″.

The pleasure in carrying out these paintings may have to do with Winnicott's (1971) view of the use of the object. In this case, the mother is shaped and manipulated at will in order to create a total structure that may, in turn, represent the "good enough" mother. Then there are versions of the mother that seem to provide evidence that the attacks on the mother's body have given way to an appreciation of her beauty. The first is an attempt at the Three Graces, the mother from various angles (Figure 14.18). In some of these nudes the drawing predominates, while others are done with a minimum of drawing, where the goal is to create volume with different shades of sepia. Another attempt is to paint the woman with one's touch, rather than by seeing her.

The pleasure here is having a body emerge on the paper as a result of the minimal use of paint and to recognise one's capacity to create it without what I have come to see as the envious attacks of earlier paintings (Figure 14.19).

Figure 14.18. Three Graces, 1979, watercolour on paper, 20" × 14".

Figure 14.19. Minimal figure: Pregnancy, 1978, watercolour on paper, 20" × 14".

But, just as things would seem to get better in relation to my destructiveness and as I seemed to be allowing the mother a life of her own, we encounter this painting, which appears to represent absolute possession and control over the mother (Figure 14.20). The work seems to have been an afterthought. I remember I didn't like the rendering of the reclining woman and, rather than discarding it, I began to play with lines going into and out of her body.

Control appears as a manic defence against a recognition of the mother as a separate object, a mother with a life of her own. However, the control mitigates the destructive feelings towards this mother. There is no guilt as yet over the control and no reparation. So, just as I seem to allow the mother a life of her own, I revert back to controlling her. This back and forth movement brings to mind Bion's (1963) correction of the Ps→D equation to a Ps←→D, from a state of unmitigated love and hate (Ps) to the integration of ambivalence (D) and back again in a constant to and fro. In his contribution to the book *Belief and Imagination* (1998), Ronald Britton studied the movement from D to Ps as it applies to the generation of new knowledge. For Britton, a return from D to Ps does not simply imply a regression to an earlier organisation. Each time there is a return to Ps, there is the possibility of new

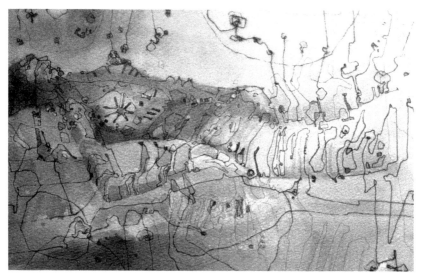

Figure 14.20. Control over the mother: Untitled, 1978, watercolour and pencil on paper, 22" × 30".

knowledge and an increase in the capacity to search for it. One can conclude that these shifts from D to Ps and back to D are essential to enrich
and further one's creative work.

Double paintings

The two figures in the early watercolours later gave way to what I have
come to call the "double paintings". Seven years into painting I hired
my own model and always managed to put two poses on each sheet of
paper (Figures 14.21 and 14.22). This is no longer a mother and baby, but
it may rather indicate a manic defence against depression and mourning,
the result of my destructiveness. I may lose one, but I still have another.
This idea of the double has extended to a tendency to paint in pairs with
perhaps the same motive (Figure 14.23).

Migraines

As an afterthought, I have decided to add to this account the fact that
I have suffered severe migraines all my life since childhood. Perhaps

Figure 14.21. Double (a): Lying Women, 1979, watercolour on paper,
14" × 20".

Figure 14.22. Double (b): Sitting Women II, 1979, watercolour on paper, 14″ × 20″.

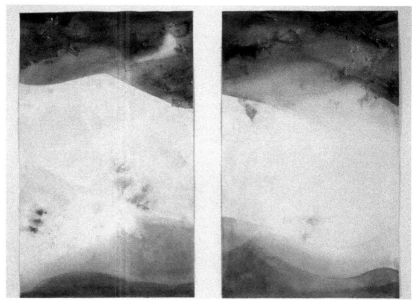

Figure 14.23. Pair: Untitled, 1986, watercolour on paper, 39″ × 25″.

they are due to a fall I had at age eight, the result of my game of slid-ing down the side of the long set of stairs where we lived. I must have tripped and tumbled down onto the concrete pavement below, hitting my head, and breaking my nose. I lost consciousness and came to when my bloody face was being washed at a lavatory. Headaches, which were quite severe at times, began shortly after that fall.

My mother took me to various specialists and I tried different medi-cations prescribed by them, but nothing seemed to work. I remember taking a bus to school at age thirteen or fourteen with tears running down my face, as the bus's vibrations exacerbated my pain. I continued trying various specialists and treatments throughout adolescence into adulthood. Some of them were orthodox, while others experimental, and until very recently I experienced no relief.

My mother told a specialist in allergies (one of the various doctors I visited as a teenager) that she thought my migraines were the result of my hours of listening to so many dissonant sounds, like those in Stravinsky's music. "The music my daughter listens to," she told him while showing him one of her arms, "makes the hairs on my arms stand up!" As you can imagine, I didn't like these visits. Complaining again about my listening to so much music, she told another doctor that now I even wanted to study the flute! This doctor asked me which was my favourite piece of music that featured a flute soloist and I told him that it was Bach's Second Suite. He seemed to be familiar with it because he smiled in recognition and this delighted me. Of course my mother never took me back to THAT doctor!

I have to thank the migraines, however, because at college age they brought me into my first analysis and sparked my interest in psycho-analysts. Years later, already studying for my doctoral degree in clinical psychology at UCLA, I attended a workshop with Stanislav Groff at the Esalen Institute in Big Sur, California. The interesting description of the programme intrigued me, as it seemed quite revolutionary. Stan had participants pair up, with one person lying on his/her back, and engaged them in heavy breathing in response to loud and powerful music. The other participant sat next to the one undergoing the experi-ence, functioning as a mindful caretaker. Straining as this experience was, it was the only treatment that, at the time, relieved my migraines for a while. When I returned from that experience with Dr Groff I did the following painting. It depicts a fantasy that my head had opened, allowing a baby trapped in my brain to become freed up. It is surprising

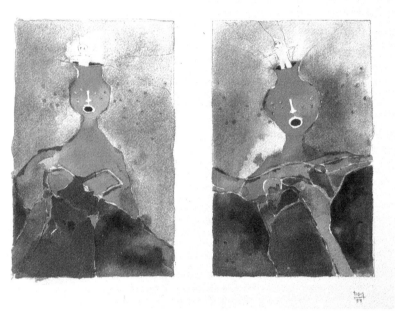

Figure 14.23a. Migraines: Relieved, 1983, watercolour on paper, 11″ × 16″.

to me how many people have loved this painting! My youngest grand-daughter, Hannah, asked me a few days ago if I could make a copy of it for her, and she referred to it as "the painting of the volcano woman" (Figure 14.23a).

I still suffer from these severe migraines. Because they have been so central in my life, I believe that this retrospective chapter would not be accurate and honest if I were to fail to mention them. As of late, they seem to obey a certain rhythm: two days on, one day clear. Today is my day on, but here I am, still working. I have often felt that finishing this book will be a miracle of sorts because of it being created IN SPITE of these migraines!

Father

As I was reviewing the photos of my paintings, I kept finding this vertical format landscape that stood out and didn't seem to fit with any of the themes I had so far developed (Figure 14.24). There were several other pieces for which I found the right place, but this one was an irritation. I thought of deleting it from this chapter, but I also knew it was one of the good watercolours and I had been quite thrilled with it when I painted it. I finally realised, "this strong tree keeps sticking out! But of course it sticks out. It's the penis!"

Then I found these other two paintings with objects that seemed quite different from the tree, but in the same position on the paper: a collage painting (Figure 14.25), and a small watercolour (Figure 14.26). The irritation at the images probably mirrors the earliest irritation at an awareness of the father and of his relationship to the mother. A later turning towards the father may have been the result of the frustrations with the mother, especially due to weaning and toilet training, but also in relation to the new babies, who were demanding her attention. My father's presence as a whole object may have helped facilitate the problems of mourning in relation to my mother. As Segal notes, "It is an important aspect of the depressive position that the recognition of mother as a separate person includes the recognition of father as her partner, rather than as a part-object seen as her possession or as an object confused with

Figure 14.24. Vertical (father): Driving back from Palo Alto, 1979, watercolour on paper, 24″ × 18″.

Figure 14.25. Vertical collage: Untitled, c.1978, watercolour and collage on paper, 24″ × 18″.

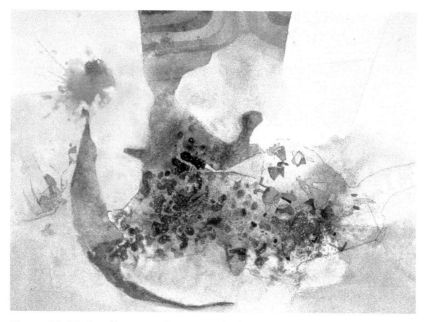

Figure 14.26. Small watercolour: Untitled, c.1978, watercolour on paper, 18" × 24".

her, as in the phantasy of the combined parents" (Segal, 1991, p. 46); for example, the paintings with a penis inside the mother's body is seen in the painting entitled *The Kiss* (Figure 14.29).

As I write this, it is puzzling to me that in comparison with all the paintings about the mother and mother's body there is a paucity of examples of my relationship with my father. This is particularly strange because of the strong oedipal ties I had with my father as I was growing up. As a young girl I became the "little wife", who shared music with him in a way that my mother never did. His love of life and music was inspiring not only to me, but also to most of my young friends who wanted a daddy/husband like mine. An old friend called me from Chile when my father died and told me that he had been the model of what she wanted in her own husband. His importance in my life is revealed in my later paintings, which are examined in more detail in the Totems section later on. Starting with the collage paintings, the *Totem series* is (in a way) a monument to my father after his death as Meltzer suggested to me when he visited my studio (1998). The importance of the internal father for the women writers that Susan

Kavaler-Adler (1993) studied may also be the case for women artists in general.

Relationships

The following watercolour (Figure 14.27) depicts an abstraction of a painting class with Keith, my teacher, dozing off on the left while three students paint from the model. He used to sit like that during our classes, a bit out of it, but ready to help if we needed him. He probably represented what Grotstein (1981) has called the "background object of primary identification", while we were the siblings venturing into the outside world. The next painting, ostensibly a further abstraction of the class, is already an envious attack on the father and his studio (Figure 14.28).

He had what the children needed, what I needed to continue to develop as an artist. As Segal noted, "Once a higher mode of mental functioning has been achieved, it is of course not achieved once and for all. There is always the potential for regression" (Segal, 1991, p. 48).

I now believe that the next painting depicts the primal scene (Figure 14.29). It is a bizarre depiction of a kiss with the couple entangled in such a way that you don't know whose mouth or whose body it is. I believe this is the infantile version of the parent's intercourse, tinged with aggression and sadism, for we don't know if they are kissing or devouring each other. With its oral component, the parental couple is clearly depicting my own aggression and sadism towards them.

This attack on the parental couple is followed by a painting I entitled *The Fight* (Figure 14.30). This was supposed to be a demonic machine held by a witch-like creature, who was keeping my husband and me turning around and around in an interminable fight. Conveniently, my husband was losing—he looked apoplectic—and I have a mischievous smile revealing my triumph as I am winning. I vividly remember when I did this painting that everything turned out this way quite accidentally and to my amazement. The child's envy and jealousy leads to a triumphant attack on the couple and particularly on the father. One could say that, by projective identification, this attack on the parental couple in *The Kiss* leads to an identification with a couple that devour each other in *The Fight*. My husband and I are the victims of this attack now turned towards ourselves in the form of a demonic machine that will make sure that we cannot get along.

Figure 14.27. The painting class, 1974, watercolour on paper, 14″ × 20″.

Figure 14.28. Abstracted class, 1974, watercolour on paper, 14″ × 20″.

Figure 14.29. The Kiss, 1973, watercolour on paper, 16″ × 20″.

Figure 14.30. The Fight, 1973, mixed media on paper, 16″ × 20″.

Blue canvases

At a certain point my watercolours got larger and larger, making framing them a problem of weight and cost. I began to explore the possibility of working on canvases with acrylic paint, doing it in such a way as to capture the fresh and improvisational quality of watercolours. Emulating Helen Frankenthaler, the New York based artist who developed the staining technique, I began to use acrylic on raw canvas by staining rather than actually painting on the surface with brushes. I diluted the medium, poured it on the canvas, and manipulated the paint to create stains. Most of the time I worked on layer upon layer of diluted paint, as I had done with the watercolours. The staining gave me very little control of accidents, just like the watercolours. Once again, the accidents may represent incontinence and the infantile phantasy of damaging the object with urine and faeces. I seldom used brushes, preferring squeegees to move the paint around. It was a period of expansion and more freedom. I worked on the floor, often on two or more paintings at a time so if one needed to dry I could move to the other (Figure 14.31). I worked mostly in a vertical format and many of these paintings ended up turning blue, even though I often started them in other colours. As I said earlier, snorkelling in Hawaii had a powerful effect on my paintings and their colour. These paintings may represent the inside of the mother's body without the earlier attacks on it; I was simply peering into the mother's body and recognising the rich life inside it (Figures 14.32 and 14.33). Fifteen years ago, I used one of these paintings to study the creative process by photographing it at various points in its development and by keeping a journal of dreams (see Chapter Twelve) (Safán-Gerard, 1983).

Exuberant series

Then something strange happened. I emerged from my blue period with the use of exuberant colour on canvas done with the same staining technique, but this time by using more concentrated paint instead of the diluted washes of the blue paintings. I also worked on the floor, pouring paint and leaving the accidents intact rather than working them over with layers of paint. This change may have been caused both by external artistic influences and by internal dynamics. At the time, I was sharing a studio with a very imaginative Swedish artist, who created banners and unusual flags in very bright colours. I also remember a two-person

Figure 14.31. Blue painting, Untitled, 1983, acrylic on raw canvas, 60″ × 42″.

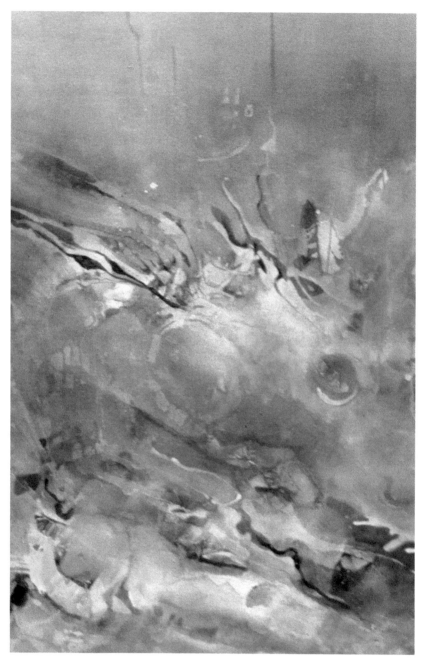

Figure 14.32. Blue painting (a): Untitled, 1983, acrylic on raw canvas, 60″ × 42″.

Figure 14.33. Blue painting (b): Untitled, 1983, acrylic on raw canvas, 60″ × 42″.

Figure 14.34. Large diptych: Anticipating Bali, 1986, 48″ × 108″.

show I had some years earlier with Keith, my art teacher, and how I thought that my subtle palette felt weak compared with his stronger paintings. However, a couple of years later, perhaps the most important determinant was that I had temporarily separated from my husband around that time. The intensity of the colour might be related to the manic sense of freedom I was experiencing.

Towards the end of this series, I again began to work in pairs that would be hung together to form large diptychs (Figure 14.34). It was a challenge to create two objects that, like the collage works and paintings before, had their own integrity, yet could be put together to give integrity to the whole. This pairing, however, is different from the pairs of models or the pairs of paintings in the past (the doubles). This time the emphasis was on creating two separate paintings, each of which could be one. It makes me think of two separate individuals coming together and creating a couple. And yet, you can separate them and each has its own life. In retrospect, this work was perhaps related to a new-found harmony in my pairing with my husband.

The Boulez series

What follows is a series of paintings based on music, the *Boulez series*. I tried to paint the nine movements of his *Le marteau sans maître*, wwhich were, in turn, based on poems by surrealist poet René Char (see Chapter Nine, Figures 9.1–9.9). I believe this mixed media work on paper represents my way of getting inside the composer's mind and doing pictorially what he did musically. After all, as Walter Pater (1893) said, "All art constantly aspires towards the condition of music". Music was my first art and will forever be linked to the memory of my father (see Chapter Nine). During my youth, music was my means of artistic expression and creativity. Later, this included music composition, which I had to interrupt when my teacher left the country. The *Boulez series* seems to represent my return to music and my wish to bring it back into my life.

In these small paintings I went back to working on paper using mixed media, watercolour, and acrylic. I prepared a "frame" within the edges of the paper and had the musical events, as I translated them into pictorial form, noted within this frame. However, I took pleasure in breaking the frame here and there as much as I enjoyed staying within it. The frame seemed to control what it contained: if it was too rigid, it annihilated, and if it was too loose, it failed to contain. Something destructive was at work, blowing apart the creative coupling between painting and music. However, there was playfulness more than destructiveness in my attempts to loosen up the frame—like a toddler who wants to get away from mother, but needs to keep her in sight. I was trying to find the right amount of loosening up to create a sense of freedom without chaos. The reassurance lies in the fact that, even though there were transgressions of the frame, the events were kept within it, for the most part. In addition, it is worth remembering my struggle creating this work. I set out to follow the music as faithfully as I could by listening to it many times and by following the printed score. But, oftentimes I felt trapped by that resolve and wanted the painting to take off on its own. Throughout the process I felt that I was struggling with the wish to follow Boulez on the one hand, and the wish to forget Boulez and serve the painting on the other. Was this the result of my claustrophobic anxieties of feeling trapped inside the object? After all, as I said, I wanted to get inside of Boulez's mind and I must have done so in fantasy. The pleasure in doing this work was connected, at least in my conscious mind, with a sense of a true collaboration with Boulez. I was thrilled to find out I had done his music justice: when Boulez saw my paintings in person, he immediately recognised which one corresponded to each of the nine movements (see Chapter Nine).

Totems/Monochromatic collages

The next set of paintings represents a drastic departure from my former work. I had lost the lease on my studio, so I decided to go back to Keith's to make use of his studio on Tuesday afternoons, taking advantage of his unstructured class. I was thinking of paintings I could easily take with me back and forth and came upon the idea of using collage on paper, so I began combing magazines and newspapers for interesting images. I would do this while watching TV at home so the work was done "on the side" without much thinking. The first time I went to Keith's studio with these clippings, I suddenly drew a vertical line on a sheet of vertical paper along with some horizontal lines to guide my pasting over the vertical axis. Then I began to paste along the vertical line and to cut out shapes from the clippings that could be placed on each side. I was discovering symmetry (Figures 14.35, 14.36, 14.37, and 14.38)! I still remember the excitement of this discovery. It felt so different to anything I had done before. No sooner was I done with the first one, I did a second one and a third one, and so on.

Figure 14.35. Totem (a), 1994, mixed media collage on paper, 20″ × 16″.

Figure 14.36. Totem (b), 1994, mixed media collage on paper, 20″ × 16″.

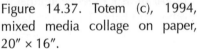
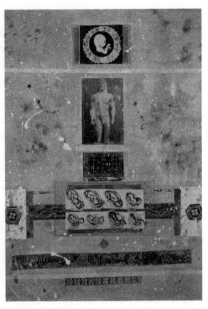

Figure 14.37. Totem (c), 1994, mixed media collage on paper, 20″ × 16″.

Figure 14.38. Totem (d), 1994, mixed media collage on paper, 20″ × 16″.

Something amazing happened when, in a daring act that felt potentially destructive of the work, I began to paint with grey washes over the whole thing. These washes were unifying and integrating the space. The darkness of the figures had to be replicated by darkness in the surrounding areas, which I created by splattering dark paint here and there. As they dried, I began to paste over them. I was doing the familiar layering (like my other paintings), building up the surfaces, and making sure that the whole thing would work together. I never thought of the meaning of the images I had selected, since I chose them for their shape and value, not because of their content, although unconsciously this must have been critical. I would later be quite surprised by the readings people made about these paintings. What I was after was the total feeling.

I so enjoyed the monochromatic nature of this work that I thought I would never again go back to working with colour. I ended up doing twenty-eight of these 20 × 16 inch images over the course of a year and a half. On one occasion, I had a series of them lying on the floor of my new studio space to make corrections on the lightness/darkness dimension, so that the whole group would work together when my son Mauricio came to see them. He said, "These don't look like paper. They look like stones, like tombstones." Startling to me, this was the first time I linked this work to the death of my father two years before I started this new series. I thought that surely the absence of colour had to do with mourning him. That they looked like stones made me think of the Jewish tradition of leaving a stone at a graveside as a sign of remembering the dead person. Perhaps in these paintings I was visiting his grave.

The symmetry may be another version of the earlier mandalas in which the attempt at integration was evident. What was I bringing together here? Was it the mother's body after daddy's death? Was it the parental couple? I believe that the penis is clearly represented in the totem in the centre, while the rest represents the beauty and symmetry of my mother's face and body. Perhaps the pleasure associated with this work had to do with allowing my parents to be together. An alternative way of looking at symmetry was in the earlier mother–baby paintings. In this case, the symmetry could be thought of as a defence against a recognition of the disparity between mother and baby. This interpretation points to a defensive use of symmetry rather than another attempt at integration. An additional piece of information may shed light on my use of symmetry: my repeated trips to Bali and my exposure to the symmetry of the Balinese temples. On one of these trips with my husband, my teacher Keith came along, and when he saw for the first time one of the numerous temples he exclaimed, "There are your paintings, Desy!"

It is interesting to note that my use of symmetry seems to also go along with contemporary painting and a return to the sense that symmetry is more basic than composition. In an interview by Bruce Glaser in ARTnews, artist Frank Stella claims that, "In the new American painting we strive to get things in the middle and symmetrical, getting rid of composition effects which carry with them all structures, values, feelings of the whole European tradition" (1966). This seems to be the case in cultural development. Primitive sculpture makes use of a strict frontal symmetry, which also persists in Egyptian and early Greek styles (Sobel, 1982). There is something especially appealing to me in Greek Cycladic sculpture (circa 2600–2500 B.C.) and the Dokathismata type (circa 2400 B.C.). The simplicity of the frontal view says to me, "This is it. Here I am, take it or leave it". As Ronald Fairbairn remarked, "It is hard to imagine an any more convincing attempt to establish the integrity of the object than that represented by the symmetry of Greek architecture and by the perception of form and purity of line, which are such obvious features of Greek sculpture" (Fairbairn, 1938, p. 297).

An outgrowth of this work some years later led to playing with symmetry and asymmetry with colour on vertical canvases, where events were again organized around a vertical line at the centre. I experienced the same pleasure I had experienced with the monochromatic paintings when tracing the vertical that would keep everything in place (Figures 14.39, 14.40, 14.41, and 14.42). Paintings from this series were exhibited in Stuttgart, Germany, in 2009, by curator Walter Bischoff (who had visited my studio in Los Angeles) and by Gustavo Bocaz in Montreuil, Paris. One work was selected for the permanent collection at the Museum Villa Haiss in Harmersbach, Germany.

Continuing the series, I kept copying reduced images I particularly liked and recycled them in other paintings. On one of these trips to make copies, I looked at one of the images and saw a very large canvas with colour and texture in it! I told Keith of this discovery and he concurred with me, adding, "Yes, but scale is important. They have to be very large." By this time, my husband and I were building a house in Venice, CA, where I would finally have my own studio with enough space to work on large paintings.

Totems/Large canvases

It took a while to work out the surfaces of these seven by five foot canvases, as there are no prescribed ways to do this. I wanted the surface to be like the mossy walls of the Balinese temples that so fascinated me. I also wanted to show the viewer the history of the painting by revealing the layers of paint that went into it. I did this by creating a frame, but unlike the Boulez paintings, it would be a one-inch linear dent on the canvas that would show the successive layers and act as a grid over which the image would be placed. I wanted the central totemic image to be totally immersed in the background, where figure and background would reverberate and shift easily. The ones I'm featuring here are close to this ideal (Figures 14.43 and 14.44).

Following my assessment of the monochromatic collage/paintings, this attempt to bring closer the figure-ground nature of the work is still the reparation of the parental couple and a more intense wish to get them together in harmony, something that had not been apparent

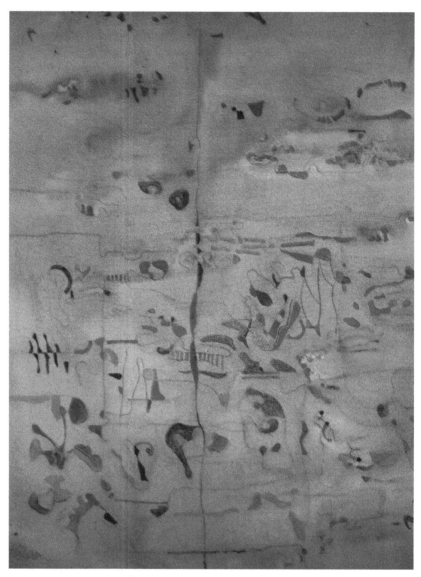

Figure 14.39. A Method to Its Virtue, 2006, acrylic on raw canvas, 36″ × 24″.

Figure 14.40. Awash in Promises, 2006, acrylic on raw canvas, 36″ × 24″.

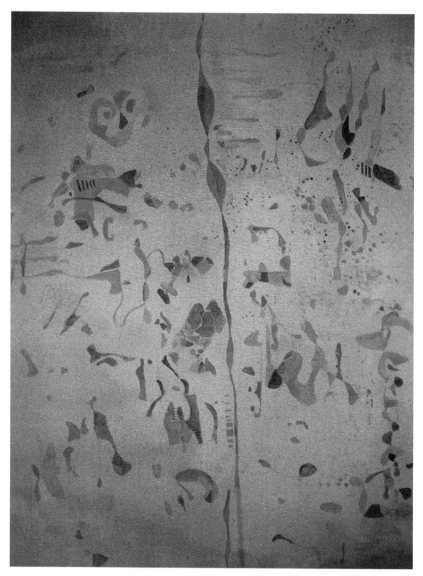

Figure 14.41. The Wrong Side of the Sky, 2006, acrylic on raw canvas, 36″ × 24″.

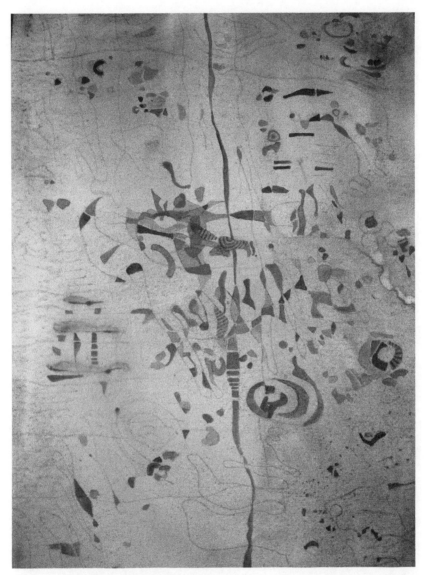

Figure 14.42. Against All Odds, 2006, acrylic on raw canvas, 36″ × 24″.

Figure 14.43. Large totem (a): Pichilemu, 1998, mixed media on canvas, 84" × 60".

Figure 14.44. Large totem (b): Concepción, 1999, mixed media on canvas, 84" × 60".

Figure 14.45. Texture (a): Green, 2002, acrylic and kitty litter on canvas, 20″ × 16″.

in my parents' marriage. This perception must have fuelled my wish to separate them in the monochromatic series.

Texture itself became the object of my next work. I discovered the technique accidentally by telling a friend that I was after something like semolina that could be placed in a thin layer over a work on paper, glued to the canvas, and then removed here and there to barely reveal small areas of the painting underneath. I had seen an exhibit of work like this by a French painter that was very exciting to me. A friend suggested scoopable kitty litter. I mixed it with water and gel medium and applied it with some difficulty to a small canvas as a test.

Two weeks later, it had totally dried creating the most interesting crevasses and shapes, like a dried-up lake or riverbed. I bought myself a big box of kitty litter and I began work on a series of imageless paintings in which texture was the object (Figures 14.45 and 14.46). I realised I was close to my idea of the accident of earlier work. In this case, I had

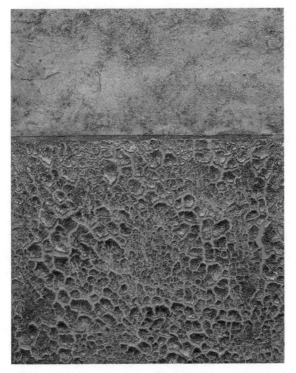

Figure 14.46. Texture (b): Red, 2002, acrylic and
kitty litter on canvas, 20″ × 16″.

to deal with this accident of nature by allowing time, temperature and
the process to take place without my intervention; then to make do with
the accident, just as I did in earlier work.

Totems/Monoprints

I came upon the idea of bringing the totem work into a different medium,
monoprints, with the help of a fellow artist, Renata Zerner. The first
time working in her studio I took some of my unframed collages in an
attempt to translate these images into this new medium. I painted on
a Plexiglas plate, selecting the pigments from sticky and unpredictable
gobs of oil paint that Renata had set out for me. I picked the colours
randomly. In this way, I figured, I would be exploring unknown territory rather than repeating myself by choosing colours I was attracted
to. I had to stick a palette knife into the paint and spread it thinly over

a piece of paper to realise what colour it really was, which was always very different than the gob of paint it came from. So in a way, I felt as if I was painting in the dark, not having any idea of how the monoprint would turn out.

To make things even more difficult, I wanted to slightly break the images and get away from what looked like a solid totem (a figure against an uninteresting background). I sprinkled alcohol over the whole thing, along with a bit of turpentine. You could see the paint on the plate reacting to these substances. What this would do to the monoprint was an absolute mystery. After pressing, there was a completely strange painting that seemed to have no relationship whatsoever with what I had been doing. For one thing, the image was reversed, the right was on the left and the left was now on the right. Then, the colour was too strong and bizarre. Renata suggested that we use a second sheet of paper on top of the same plate for a ghost copy. She set the pressure to be stronger than the first time. After we ran the press, we finally had something closer to what I had in mind, quite miraculously so in fact. Then we made a third image with the same plate, applying still more pressure to the press. This time, what emerged was very delicate and beautiful, a wispy reminder of the second one. These three (and sometimes four) versions of the same image needed to be corrected. This could be done by using pastel sticks: releasing the powder in them by scratching them against a piece of cardboard and applying the powder very lightly over the needed areas with a tissue or cotton tip. I also used colour pencils to emphasise areas or to change the colour of other areas. This work required a critical eye and focused sensitivity. The changes were ever so subtle, but very significant. Artists sometimes do the first copy on newspaper to dispose of it because the colour tends to be too strong. I wanted to do them on regular paper to challenge myself to make something out of these "difficult" versions and I did. So what you see here are strong and subtle versions of the same image (Figures 14.47 and 14.48).

I realise in hindsight that by working on these monoprints I was enlisting Renata with her gobs of unknown paint and the printing press to create the accidents for me. Other than my initial laying of the paints on the plate, I retained the task of working it out and repairing the accidents, a very satisfying task. At the end of a successful print we would spontaneously hug. I had never painted in collaboration, but this went beyond collaboration—Renata was playing the destructive me, while

Figure 14.47. Monoprint, 1997, monoprint
on paper, 30" × 20".

I was repairing the damage. She was also the "good mother", paying
close attention to what I was doing and ready to give me a hand when
I got in trouble.

In working over the third version of an image, I began to play with
the idea of breaking the symmetry by deviations from it. This seems
to be a repeat of my experience with the *Totem* canvases and their grid
and the *Boulez series* when I was breaking the frame. There was a new
interplay between the underlying fixed structure and the freedom of the
new shapes emerging in opposition and away from the symmetry. I felt
quite mischievous doing this and anticipated that this would be my
new direction. However, upon seeing this monoprint, an artist friend
said: "That's a mother with her children," which brings to mind Hanna
Segal's remark referring to the depressive position, "... one cannot
restore a mother without restoring the whole family she is related to"
(Segal, 1991, p. 100).

Figure 14.48. Monoprint "Ghost", 1997, monoprint on paper, 30" × 20".

Conclusions

I have taken advantage of my dual role of subject and analyst in trying to understand the creative process. To counterbalance the limitations of such an approach, I have access to the best biographical source: myself. I have somewhat limited myself to descriptive elements in my paintings, which could visually relate to known objects. Naturally, a whole body of interpretation may deal with the non-representational pictorial elements such as form and colour, which cannot be recognised as objects, but have an importance of their own derived from the earlier connection with objects. The overall approach throughout my work reflects the duality of chaos and control. As you might have noticed, most of my paintings are made up of a vague, undefined, fluid background against controlled and direct elements made out of lines, brushstrokes, and interwoven with deliberate areas devoid of colour. The latter, without necessarily representing identifiable objects, seem to reflect the need to control the object. My breaking the frame, as I have done in the *Boulez series* and in the large *Totem series*, may indicate the need to defy such control from the object. This interplay of forms is surely a precipitate of an older content. My fear of being controlled has to do with my own control of the object and the workings of projective identification that make me feel controlled by it.

An important question raised in Chapter Twelve, "The evolution of a painting", was whether it was possible through artistic activity to reach new levels of integration of the personality without having to transform the feelings awakened by the work into thoughts or everyday language. I was then struck by the mobility and successive alternation of images and colours that suggest power and destruction and those that suggest helplessness. I thought that the painting served as a screen to argue for and against these competing sets of images. Opposite forces ended up standing side by side on the canvas being studied. My conclusion was that "actual reconciliation of these opposites is carried out by other thought processes such as induction and logic" (Safán-Gerard, 1983, p. 17). In other words, creating doesn't in and of itself produce integration, but merely reflects whatever conflicts exist with as much splitting, projection, denial and idealisation as is present in the artist's life at the time. The perspective of time has allowed me to change this view, as I have come to believe that opposites standing side by side constitute a form of integration. Staying with the work also leads to integration even though, as artist Francois Gilot has said, "works of art are traces of an artist's quest" (1997, p. 125). I hope that both the quest and my own development as an artist have become apparent in this chapter. I seem to have moved from the expression of unmitigated attacks on the mother and the mother's body of the earliest paintings to an appreciation of the mother's beauty, her relation to the father, and to siblings in the later work. In one way or another, all these latter motifs seem to appear as we get closer to my current work. The importance of the father has become more and more apparent in my latest paintings along with the importance of the parental couple that are allowed to have a life of their own, just like the paintings. But was this change in my work the result of painting alone? Or was it the result of my two analyses? I believe that these questions can be answered by recognising that to face the truth about one's psychic life involves depressive pain and the willingness to endure it. How this shows up in the work is out of the artist's conscious mind. As Oremland puts it, "art provides the meta-autobiography of the artist's subjective life of which the artist is only dimly aware or completely unaware ..." (1997, p. xvi). If the artist undergoes an analysis, however, the art is affected in unknown ways, but conceivably will also reflect the patient's development. One could safely argue that both art and analysis support each other in promoting psychic development.

The efforts at integrating good and bad and love and hate in the later paintings give the impression of growth and development insofar as they represent the movement from the paranoid schizoid to the depressive position (Segal, 1991). But, during the progress of any given painting there is a fluctuation between these positions. In closely studying the evolution of several early paintings, I have recognised four to five cycles of destruction and reparation in every painting examined (Safán-Gerard, 1983). Meltzer corroborates this observation when he states, "... if we say that the artist performs acts of reparation through his creativity we must recognize that in the creative process itself, phases of attack and phases of reparation exist in some sort of rhythmical relationship" (Meltzer & Williams, 1988, p. 209). According to him, there comes a point when mature artists achieve a sense of stabilisation in their relationships to their own primal good objects in their inner world, which leads to feelings of concern for "all the mother's babies". At this time the impulse to exhibit works of art functions as "a sermon to siblings", a sermon that is not only intended to show what has been accomplished by this brother but is also intended to project into the siblings both the restored object as well as to project those capacities for the bearing of depressive pains which have been achieved by the artist in his own development" (1998, p. 219).

As I said at the beginning, destructiveness and reparation is the running thread in all of these paintings. In her book, *On Not Being Able to Paint*, Marion Milner (1950) analyses the all too common restrictions by which the creativity of the average adult is held in check. In her experiments with free drawings, she tried to paint as the hand liked it, without much conscious control, and discovered the aggression hidden in her inhibitions "... my mind was trying to tell about the angry attacking impulses that are an essential part of oneself, but the existence of which I had persistently tried to deny" (Milner, 1950, p. 41). When, for example, she allowed her hand to do as it pleased, a supposedly peaceful scene turned, to her surprise, into a raging fire. One is reminded once again of Sabina Spielrein's seminal paper "Destructiveness as the cause of coming into being" (1912), where, paradoxically, she saw destructiveness as an intrinsic part of all creation. At this point, it is important to keep in mind the difference between the destructiveness in which the aim is to spoil and annihilate from the destructiveness that aims to create a new life. There is also the destructiveness of the object that fails to be ideal. This third kind is related to the artist's narcissism in that he or she cannot accept the limits of idealisation for any given painting.

The first kind of destructiveness, more related to envious attacks, finds its way into the content of my own paintings, which has been especially illustrated by the abstract landscapes depicting the inside of the mother's body (where destruction and reparation become apparent). As for the second kind, perhaps the term "ruthlessness" best expresses what Spielrein meant by destructiveness. This ruthlessness takes place in the creative process itself where destruction is carried out in the service of development. An example is the grey wash over the surface of the monochromatic totems. This is the destructiveness Spielrein is talking about. She mentions the fact that many lower creatures (e.g., the mayfly) forfeit their lives in favour of new life. In her own life, Spielrein's letters to Jung and Freud demonstrate a unique effort in the history of psychoanalysis of someone using intellectual incisiveness to forge a synthesis, trying to help Freud and Jung to overcome their mutual destructiveness in order to bring their ideas together (Carotenuto, 1980). The letters can also be seen as motivated by her reparative urge to bring about the reconciliation of the parental couple. In going through them, one finds several instances of the sermons to siblings Meltzer writes about in that Spielrein tries to project into them her own restored objects and her capacity to bear depressive pain, like an artist with his or her work. As for the third kind of destructiveness, the destruction of a painting that fails to achieve perfection, I can only say that there are many instances where I have had to painfully resign myself that a newly finished painting didn't quite "make it" and fight my impulse to destroy it.

The artist not only finds his or her way back to reality, but, in a way, he or she never leaves reality (Segal, 1991). However, with the exception of the artist that circumvents truth through a compulsion to idealise the work, the artist primarily seeks psychic truth (getting in touch as deeply and truthfully to the contents of his or her mind), which is therapeutic (Chasseguet-Smirgel, 1985). The finished work has to be able to reveal this psychic truth, meaning that, in showing the work, the artist leads the viewer into and out of the world of suffering. In order to carry out the work, he or she needs to allow that suffering. To quote John Rickman from his paper "On the nature of ugliness and the creative impulse", "... unless the artist can reach down to the experience of deep anxiety and find the way out, his work will not give us a deeper understanding of ourselves or a fuller enjoyment of life ... [the work of art] is a living proof that the artist himself has stayed the course of havoc and has himself made life come out of dust and confusion" (1940, p. 310). What is true for the artist is also true for the viewer. As Meltzer points out, "... the viewing of art is an expression particularly linked to this component of the breast situation, that is, the feeling of looking and listening to the events going on inside the mother, of seeing either the intactness of her inner world, or conversely, of seeing the destruction that has been wrought there. It means an experience of allowing, in the first case, the introjecting of this goodness and intactness and, in the second case, exposing oneself to having destruction projected into one" (1988, p. 216). His conclusion is that "... the experience of viewing art can be extremely taxing and extremely hazardous ..." (p. 218) and I am most appreciative of any reader taking a chance with me.

CHAPTER FIFTEEN

From mistake to mistake: the creative process in four large paintings

When I began to use the camera to register stages of work in progress, I had no idea that Henri Matisse (1869–1954) had engaged in the systematic practice of photographing his paintings. He hired a photographer to document his work on *The Dance*, the famous mural Alfred Barnes had commissioned for his suburban Philadelphia residence, in the early 1930s, but had had his works photographed in the early 1900s as well. Matisse liked the surprising effect of the resulting photos and even framed some to exhibit alongside his paintings to formalise his methodology. He came to believe that a photograph revealed the true nature of a painting or a significant stage in its development. He attributed such importance to the photographs of the stages of a painting that he seemed to begin to paint for the camera, using the photographs as motivation for the next phase of the work. The photographs were his ideal way to preserve "versions of an image that would otherwise be lost". In a 1944 interview with Leon Degand Matisse stated: "'I work from feeling. I have my conception in my head, and I want to realize it. I can, very often, reconceive it. But I know where I want it to end up. The photos taken in the course of the execution of the work permit me to know if the last conception conforms more to what I am after than the preceding ones, whether I have advanced or regressed'" (Aagesen & Rabinow, 2012, p. 10).

Matisse shared his photographs of the various stages of his paintings with friends and collectors. In fact, his *Large Reclining Nude* (also known as *Pink Nude*) was sold to American collector Etta Cone in 1935, who was enthralled by the photographs that Matisse had sent to her (Figure 15).

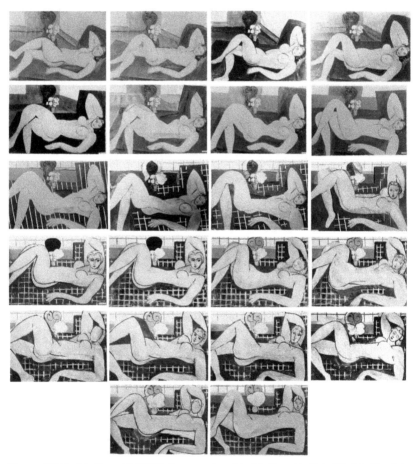

Figure 15.0. Matisse © 2017 Succession H. Matisse/Artists Rights Society (ARS), New York. Photographs of *Large Reclining Nude* by Henri Matisse in process, states 1–22, May 3–October 30, 1935. Dr Claribel and Etta Cone Papers, Archives and Manuscripts Collections, The Baltimore Museum of Art. CP30.6.1-22.

This series of twenty-two photographs of the successive stages of this painting are a captivating review of Matisse's process. The painting is now in the Baltimore Museum of Art along with the rest of the Cone family collection. Matisse was criticised for using his photographs as a means of promoting his work. However, I think sharing his creative process with others was not Matisse's "marketing strategy", as his detractors proclaimed. It was rather a reflection of his intense wish to share his discoveries and musings about his creative work, an instance of "sermons to siblings" (Meltzer, 1988), evidence of his generosity with other artists.

In 1945, Matisse explained that his photographs helped him determine whether he had advanced or regressed with respect to an imagined goal. With a similar purpose, I have used photos of my works-in-progress. Sometimes a photo is also my way of holding on to a version that would be lost during the painting's development. One of my paintings from 2010, *Doorway to Becoming*, (Figures 15.1 and 15.2), may be seen as two separate paintings, but, in fact, they are two versions of the same painting, one at an early stage, which I took and saved as a way to hold on to it. I wasn't sure that my continuing to work on this painting would result in an improvement. I had also developed an attachment to the earlier version.

Accidents and mistakes play a critical role in one's development as a painter. Over thirty years ago I presented a paper entitled "The role of the accident in the creative act" (1982) (see Chapter Three) and some fifteen years later I began to photograph my paintings in progress (see Chapter Twelve). Like Matisse, I thought that by examining them with my camera hours later, the images would give me some insight into what to do next, and what might need to be changed. The camera gave me a new perspective that seemed to reveal the unconscious nature of the work.

This chapter was born out of two desires: to share what I have learned from examining paintings in progress, and to debunk the negative connotations attached to mistakes, both in art and in psychoanalysis. The most important fact that I have come to understand with these photos is that a mistake stands for an unwanted aspect of oneself. Sometimes I am tempted, for truth's sake, to let it remain there as a self-confrontation, but it creates a restlessness within me until I get back to working on that painting again. Eventually I follow the impulse to rework the emerged content so it becomes integrated into the rest of the piece, suspecting that a similar experience exists for writers, composers, and analysts at work. A correction of this nature is different from the compulsive need

Figure 15.1. Doorway to Becoming I.

to get rid of what is perceived as an error. Instead, it assimilates the error and the resulting sense of relief comes from the recognition that something important has developed, and that a new truth has been unveiled. This is, in turn, followed by the larger pleasure of seeing that the work as a whole is beginning to make sense.

Since artwork doesn't unfold predictably, artists constantly face unsatisfactory developments in their work, which can lead to a sense

Figure 15.2. Doorway to Becoming II.

of inadequacy when approaching a project. As artist Agnes Martin wrote, "To feel confident and successful is not natural to the artist. To feel insufficient, to experience disappointment and defeat in waiting for inspiration is the natural state of mind of an artist" (1992, p. 32). Yet, insufficiency can itself be a source of inspiration. For artist Francis Bacon, accidents were an essential part of his art making. When being interviewed by David Sylvester around 1975, Bacon said: "I think that accident, which I would call luck, is one of the most important and fertile aspects of it, because, if anything works for me, I feel it is nothing I have made myself, but something which chance has been able to give me ... I never know how much it is pure chance and how much it is manipulation of it" (Sylvester, 1975, p. 52). Like Bacon and others, artists rely on accidents to move a painting forward. Bacon put it succinctly when he said, "If anything ever does work in my case, it works from the moment when consciously I don't know what I am doing" (Sylvester, 1975, pp. 53–54).

An earlier paper of mine, "Chaos and control in the creative process" (1982) (see Chapter One), deals with aspects of this progression of creating accidents and following them. As suggested in that chapter, excessive control over the medium will lead to a tight structure that will become lifeless. The artist will have to destroy this structure and generate a new chaos in order to start afresh and find renewed value in what he or she is doing. This tension between chaos and control is characteristic of most creative work and it is beautifully apparent in Beethoven's musical sketches (see Chapter One).

What now follows is an examination of four of my large paintings in progress: *Homage to Ferrari, Euclid to Lunch, Uncompromised Subtleties*, and *Red Revenge*. By describing my own mental process, I confirm Matisse's approach and Bacon's beliefs in showing how mistakes can be useful, as they displace control from conscious to unconscious levels of mind. Like most artists, I feel a need to expand my point of departure and welcome the independent life of the medium. The shapes that result seem to grow and interact before my eyes. A frustrating mistake can lead to a welcomed spur and to more flexible planning, more inspiring work, and unexpected new beginnings.

"Homage to Leon Ferrari"

Starting on a new painting seems to require random action by applying paint here and there indiscriminately and I did so while remembering Leon Ferrari's work. Beginning to fill the canvas with new shapes, I began by placing one on top (Figure 15.3). Remembering Ferrari's lines, I took oil sticks and began to develop my own lines (Figure 15.4). It felt good to run down the painting with the lines and extend them to cover the canvas (Figure 15.5). Turning the canvas upside down I began to enter lines into the existing shapes (Figure 15.6). When I turned

Figure 15.3. Beginning of Homage to Leon Ferrari.

Figure 15.4. Ferrari in progress (a).

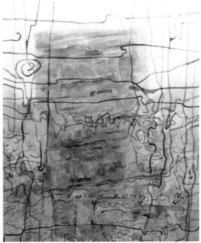

Figure 15.5. Ferrari in progress (b).

Figure 15.6. Ferrari in progress (c).

the canvas back, I incorporated some small black areas (Figure 15.7). Progress seemed apparent with no mistakes yet! Changing the colour of the black shapes, I added zigzags on top on both sides. So far, the feeling was that I just needed to continue to develop the canvas (Figure 15.8).

Adding a number of black lines, they seemed to take over and asphyxiate the painting in the centre. This was the first major mistake and I was feeling uneasy about this new turn (Figure 15.9). An immediate sense of regret of having lost the previous version was followed by opening up the space with lime green shapes here and there, interrupting the lines. Filling the canvas with them, I covered the shapes with soft green washes, beginning to feel better about these lines and the new development, realising that it would not have happened without the mistake. However, even though some new soft shapes emerged, the mistake was still present (Figure 15.10).

Seeking a drastic solution, I created a white square over a black shape and continued to open up various places on the canvas. The red shape next to the black seemed to float there, which was another mistake (Figure 15.11). So I changed the red shape to black and brought back the lines inside the white square, developing a new appreciation for them. The shapes were becoming more integrated. I began to use white and let it run over the black. However, the white seemed unrelated to the rest and constituted another mistake. A solution had become a mistake!

Figure 15.7. Ferrari in progress (d).   Figure 15.8. Ferrari in progress (e).

Figure 15.9. Ferrari in progress (f).

Figure 15.10. Ferrari in progress (g).

Figure 15.11. Ferrari in progress (h).

Figure 15.12. Myself with Homage to Leon Ferrari in progress.

In order to bring balance to the painting, I developed another white shape on the right side of the work (Figure 15.12). Holding it in the image, I washed the top with white and lime green, softening other areas with wash as well. These final steps brought the painting to completion. The great relief was the feeling that the major mistake had not only been corrected, but had guided me into a more satisfying solution (Figure 15.13).

"Euclid to Lunch"

This painting was started the way *Homage to Ferrari* had started, wanting to play with the oil sticks again and let the red run down the canvas by creating a dark column on the left, continuing to develop the upper portion of the canvas (Figure 15.14). In my deep involvement

Figure 15.13. Homage to Leon Ferrari, 2009, oil on canvas, 72" x 60".

with this painting I failed to document its early development during two four-hour sessions with it, so illustrations for this particular work are limited.

Continuing to create the shapes on top, I used oil sticks on the bottom from right to left (Figure 15.15). Playing with geometric shapes in the lower half was the outcome of a conversation with a New York gallery owner who specialised in work from Latin American artists. She told

Figure 15.14. Beginning of Euclid to Lunch.

Figure 15.15. Euclid in progress (a).

me that my work was beautiful and strong, but that their collectors bought only geometric abstraction. My impulse was to give geometry to those collectors—"I'll show them!"—and further developed the lower half. Filling the shapes with soft green and adding small shapes on the top led me to not liking this one bit! The green shapes were a mistake with the red outlines throwing them off, as they had become too solid (Figure 15.16).

Filling up the geometric shapes with various colours felt like it solved the problem of the previous mistake (Figure 15.17). A drastic deletion of all the lines behind the geometric shapes was achieved by covering them with white. A big mistake! "Where did the painting go?" I asked myself (Figure 15.18).

The phantom shapes left underneath the white needed to be covered with soft green. Doing the same over the upper half was also necessary (Figure 15.19). Strengthening the green all over made me happier, because it integrated top and bottom (Figure 15.20).

By brightening and strengthening the green I felt I had recovered from the mistake, amazed at how far I had departed from the beginning stages of this work. Once again, the mistake is what led me to this final outcome (Figure 15.21). I became grateful to the curator of that New York gallery for her comment regarding her collectors, since that

Figure 15.16. Euclid in progress (b).

Figure 15.17. Euclid in progress (c).

Figure 15.18. Euclid in progress (d).

Figure 15.19. Euclid in progress (e).

Figure 15.20. Euclid in progress (f).

Figure 15.21. Euclid to Lunch, 2010, oil on canvas 72″ × 60″.

is what instigated this work. Of course, it was disappointing that there was no response to the photo of the finished painting I sent to her.

"Uncompromised Subtleties"

To start this painting I first drew lines inspired by Willem de Kooning and Cy Twombly using charcoal sticks (Figure 15.22). Filling up areas using green as an underpaint I continued to fill the shapes using blue, brown, and black (Figures 15.23 and 15.24). Oil sticks to go in and out of the shapes felt like play, as there was something naughty about crossing and disrupting them (Figure 15.25). Softening the areas with white, I immediately recognised a familiar mistake—just too much white! It washed out the interesting shapes that I had just created (Figure 15.26). I started correcting the washed out forms by adding dark colours again (Figure 15.27), but it still felt far from finished. My mentor at the time suggested creating luminosity by adding white and green shapes (Figure 15.28). The luminosity worked out, but I considered the green areas a mistake and I deleted them. He then suggested adding a red shape as an element of surprise. I didn't agree with him but I was willing to give it a try (Figure 15.29). Unhappy about the red, I changed its shape thinking it might alter my judgement, but for me it was still a mistake. Playing with the shape again I added an orange element on top. That was also a mistake (Figure 15.30).

So I got rid of the red and replaced it with green. I needed to redevelop the area where the red existed, and managed to finish the painting (Figure 15.31) feeling quite happy with the result. At the time, I felt this painting was the best of my large paintings thus far, but that feeling has since changed. By now I have over sixteen works measuring 72 × 60 inches, all with mistakes, ultimately resolved. My predilections over this body of work seem to change over time.

Figure 15.22. Beginning of Uncompromised Subtleties.

Figure 15.23. Uncompromised Subtleties in progress (a).

Figure 15.24. Uncompromised Subtleties in progress (b).

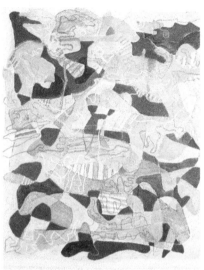

Figure 15.25. Uncompromised Subtleties in progress (c).

Figure 15.26. Uncompromised Subtleties in progress (d).

Figure 15.27. Uncompromised Subtleties in progress (e).

Figure 15.28. Uncompromised Subtleties in progress (f).

Figure 15.29. Uncompromised Subtleties in progress red shape (a).

Figure 15.30. Uncompromised Subtleties red shape (b).

Figure 15.31. Uncompromised Subtleties, 2010, oil on canvas, 72" × 60".

"Red Revenge"

Again inspired by de Kooning and Twombly, I began to draw with charcoal sticks (Figure 15.32). When red and crimson shapes appeared, I knew the red from *Uncompromised Subtleties* had come back to haunt me (Figure 15.33). Being so against that red spot in my previous painting seemed to have led to revenge, where this colour seemed to invade the new canvas. Then I added pink, orange and crimson to build the

 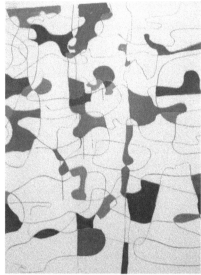

Figure 15.32. Beginning of Red Revenge.

Figure 15.33. Red Revenge in progress (a).

surface, a rather mindless doing (Figure 15.34). Adding purple and more of the orange I developed a bit more of the red. Continuing to add orange and strengthening the lines (Figure 15.35), I painted a grey wash over the top, which was the first big mistake (Figure 15.36). It made me feel regretful and mad at myself for having allowed it.

However, I continued the destruction by covering the right hand side with white and a darker wash on top (Figure 15.37). This constituted another mistake, because the painting lost the nice original structure and became muddy. However, some luminosity appeared through the muddy areas and this made me happy. Drawing in and out of the shapes with a white oil stick I tried to recover some structure. Still worried about the muddy grey, I incorporated a red circle where the red spot had been in *Red Revenge*, as a "souvenir" from it. The purple, red and orange were also brought back from under the grey (Figure 15.38).

What has happened with this painting is not unlike what has happened with other paintings, where I make the mistake of drastically washing over it, risking total destruction. As you see in *Red Revenge*, this typically leads to reparation, where a much richer solution is obtained than would be the case if no mistakes were present (Figure 15.39).

Figure 15.34. Red Revenge in progress (b).

Figure 15.35. Red Revenge in progress (c).

Figure 15.36. Red Revenge in progress (d).

Figure 15.37. Red Revenge in progress (e).

Figure 15.38. Red Revenge in progress (f).

Figure 15.39. Red Revenge, 2011, oil on canvas, 72" × 60".

Turmoil and freedom

A few thoughts after a soul-searching conflict around *Uncompromised Subtleties*. One day, I was working on a painting I was quite happy with. Like my other recent work, it was a large abstract painting with browns, soft greens, and blues. Finishing up, I told my mentor at the time I didn't see anything else I could do with it. "You may want to add an element of surprise," he said, suggesting I put some bright red in one of the shapes. I told him I thought the red would make the subtleties in the painting irrelevant. He argued that, on the contrary, the red would enhance the painting's subtleties.

Reluctantly, I followed his advice. Since he was acting as a mentor, I should open myself to his ideas. I photographed the painting so that I could study it later. The next week I looked at it again. It still didn't feel right! I sent the photo to other artist friends and colleagues, including my son, who said, "What is that red doing there? It doesn't belong!" Other people said it was interesting, but there was no conviction. A psychoanalytic colleague wrote that she wanted to know how the red ended up there—she was upfront with her doubts. When I sent the photo to my German dealer, I asked him what he thought of the red and he responded: "The painting would be better without it." "He knows me", I thought. "He knows my work and likes it." It was all I needed to make up my mind.

Last night, after dinner, I did it! Getting rid of the red wasn't easy, but everything is possible with oils. Why did I decide to write about this? Because of the great turmoil I felt debating whether to follow other people's suggestions or stick to my own conviction. When one talks about freedom, and especially artistic freedom, one has to deal with the anxiety of opposing others whom one respects and risk losing their love. To follow one's own beliefs is to exercise one's freedom!

Psychological and psychoanalytic perspectives

Surprised at the paucity of psychoanalytic writings on mistakes, I realised that several psychological writings exist. In a book entitled *The Imperfect Therapist* (1989), Kottler and Blau compile stories about mistakes and their resolutions from therapists with different orientations. They include James Bugenthal, a relational-oriented therapist; Richard Fish, a pioneer in problem-solving therapy; Albert Ellis, rational emotive therapist; Arnold Lazarus, who practises a multi-model therapy; and Clark Moustakas, chief proponent of the humanistic psychology movement. All are unified in their belief that refinements in technique and theory occur as much from their mistakes as from their triumphs. They all share a respect for their failures and are utterly frank in admitting their part in negative outcomes—when, for example, premature interruption of treatment is caused by factors related to the therapeutic process rather than by internal factors of the patient. They conclude that valuable self-analysis is possible after failure, something that supervision and peer supervision help accomplish within psychoanalysis.

According to these therapists, the most common and significant mistakes come from excessive self-disclosure, misdiagnosis, and the "initial drag", where, in the name of patience and acceptance, the therapist tolerates variations in the frame such as: lateness, skipped appointments, verbal assaults, delinquent payments, and continued drug abuse. And in a narrow sense, for Kottler and Blau, countertransference, the analyst's feelings in response to the patient, constitutes an error.

On the other hand, these authors assert that mistakes, errors, and misjudgements can initiate a turning point during treatment. Admitting a mistake can become a model of self-acceptance for the patient. Failure, too, is a reminder of our fallibility; it fosters a sense of modesty and counteracts the tendency towards narcissism that is prevalent in our profession (Kottler & Blau, 1989, p. 72). We can regard failure as an opportunity for expanding our repertory of options. According to Robert Langs, therapists should not only recognise their mistakes, but such analysis "must take precedence over all other therapeutic work, since it is essential to the restoration of a proper therapeutic alliance" (Langs, 1978, p. 153). With every negative result, Kottler and Blau purport that we expand our knowledge, develop our theories, increase our resolve, expand our tolerance for frustration, and improve our performance (1989).

In psychoanalytic literature, it has been difficult to find allusions to mistakes, even in the subject indexes of pertinent books. Exceptions are Winnicott's *Psycho-Analytic Explorations* (1989), the more recent *Learning From Our Mistakes* by Patrick Casement (2002), and an all-encompassing and beautiful paper by Salman Akhtar entitled "Tethers, orbits and invisible fences: Clinical, developmental, and technical aspects of optimal distance" (1992).

Winnicott presents the fear of breakdown as the fear of the original agony that caused the defensive organisation, which the patient displays as illness, and suggests that, as a reaction to the analyst's failures and mistakes, the patient may achieve ego integration through transference. As the patient develops dependency on the analyst, the analyst's mistakes and failures become new traumata, and, eventually, the analyst and his room need to survive the patient's cumulative anger.

According to Winnicott, no treatment of borderline cases can be free from suffering, for both patient and analyst. Indeed, many an analysis has failed because the analyst could not allow a delusional failure due to his personal need to prove the truth of psychoanalytic theory through the cure of the patient (1989, p. 446). On the contrary, success in analysis

must include the patient's reaction to the analyst as a failure; this paradox needs to be allowed. According to Winnicott, "… the analyst must
be able to accept this role of failing analyst as he accepts all other roles
that arise out of the patient's transference neuroses and psychoses"
(ibid. p. 216).

Based on the work of Balint and Margaret Mahler, Akhtar has developed
the notion of optimal distance to depict the ideal emotional range sought
by the analyst with patients in analysis. According to his view, mistakes
are the result of the analyst's behaviour, which, with his actions, misjudges
at any given moment this optimal distance from the patient. His paper has
a conceptual overlap between optimal distance and the use of "tact" in the
analytic situation, as discussed by Warren Poland (Akhtar, 1992).

It was disappointing to discover that although Casement's book is
about mistakes, its main thrust is exploring how not to make them!
However, in his chapter eight he details a case of a patient who, after
four years, returned for a second analysis. Casement writes that he
found himself making extraordinary mistakes, concerned as he was
with not letting this patient down. Yet the mistakes became a positive
developing point in the treatment. Casement shows how, as part of the
analytic process, patients may revisit key experiences of early failure by
their parents or other caregivers through their use of similar failures by
the analyst. Of his patient, Casement says, "It was through his using me
to represent the key failure(s) experienced with his mother that he had
found release. He now was able to move on from his life-long conviction
that no one would be able to bear the intensity of his anger and his upset"
(2002, p. 84). In this case, Casement's views coincide with Winnicott's
and with my own assessment of mistakes in my paintings and in my
psychoanalytic practice as opportunities for new developments.

Winnicott and Casement's conclusions find their counterparts in the
world of science, where significant advances require an open mind to
correct disasters. A keen sense of observation permits the practitioner
to turn defeat into dramatic success. Failure draws one's attention to
a result in need of an explanation. It is a call to creativity and further
experimentation.

There is a commonly held belief that art and psychoanalysis aspire to
be as mistake-free as possible. With this exposé of mistakes in art making I hope to have challenged that belief. Mistakes and accidents are an
essential part of both art and psychoanalysis, since they can often lead
to unexpected outcomes and superior results than those of an original
and perfect conception.

CHAPTER SIXTEEN

As in the flesh

As the nude model was moving very slowly to the Andantino of Shostakovich's *String Quartet No. 15*, a different quality of experience took hold and I began to draw on the wet paper with both hands, each with a different colour pencil. The combination of the somewhat controlled line from my right hand and the clumsy line from my left hand was immensely gratifying. The left hand added the ugly, nasty and destructive element that was missing in the other watercolours, which were at risk of becoming too pretty. At some point I didn't know whether the music was coming from the CD player, from her exquisite body, or from my hands and pencils.

This work with a model started after painting some large canvases for the 2002 Florence Biennale that involved vigorous physical work with the canvases on the floor. I wanted to move back to the less strenuous and more intimate work on paper done at a table. The first time Sara came, I wasn't sure what to ask her to do, but I knew I didn't want to pursue realism. After she undressed, she asked me if I would like her to move slowly. I didn't expect to be in such awe of her beautiful body moving mindfully in such an exquisite way. I began to draw with a watercolour pencil on wet paper that I was simultaneously coating

239

Figure 16.1. Floor painting with Sara.

with colour while also spilling paint, in order to create accidents and unexpected "events".

In one of our sessions, I had asked Sara if she would mind having one of Shostakovich's quartets in the background—up to that point she had been moving without any music. She asked me if she should move *to* the music. Of course I was delighted (Figure 16.1). In the first few paintings I freely superimposed her body, but one could still recognise four or five discreet bodies in the finished painting (Figure 16.2). In time, I decided I would simply depict the model's movements. I wasn't sure what I was pursuing at that point. We had a few two and a half hour sessions. The work was changing towards complete abstraction with a new absence of articulation that became very satisfying to me. I continued to experiment with her movements. With the attempts that didn't satisfy me, I used the existing drawings as a starting point for a transition and transformation into something else: elaborating the space, adding complexity, and forgetting what was there before. In the abstract paintings you can see that even Sara's movements are hidden from view and, in this case, the paintings took off in their own direction (Figures 16.3, 16.4, 16.5, 16.6 and 16.7).

Several years ago I created nine paintings to Pierre Boulez's music (see Chapters Three and Seven) but could not bring myself to do Shostakovich's quartets, perhaps because they are filled with shades

Figure 16.2. Five discreet bodies, mixed media on paper, 22″ × 30″.

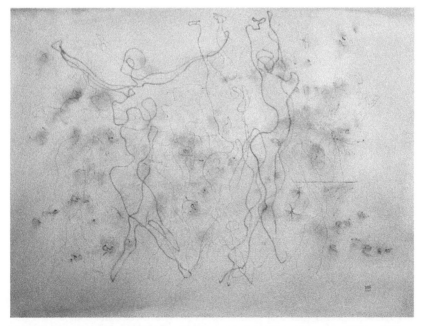

Figure 16.3. Hidden movements (a), mixed media on paper, 22″ × 30″.

Figure 16.4. Hidden movements (b), mixed media on paper, 22″ × 30″.

Figure 16.5. Hidden movements (c), mixed media on paper, 22″ × 30″.

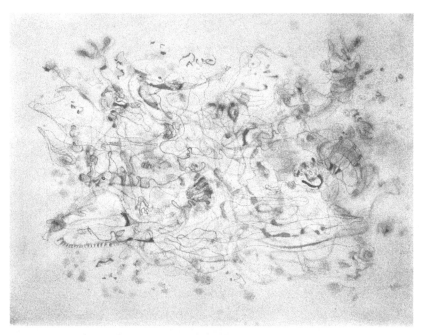

Figure 16.6. State of Grace, mixed media on paper, 22″ × 30″.

of despair and, at the time, I was fighting off despair. The week before the last session with Sara, I had a dream of a neglected garden with no flowers and was very upset as to how I had allowed this to happen. Then I saw some pots with plants, all dried for lack of water. I picked one up and saw that half the root was no longer attached to the plant, but to my amazement, there was a little sprout of light green leaves to the side of the main stem. I looked for my daughter Denise to show her this amazing thing—the plant had survived in spite of it all. The next morning, I was still filled with the dream image and told my husband, "I think I can now paint to Shostakovich's quartets." What I didn't anticipate was that I would be doing that through Sara's body.

Examining the process

For the artist, the work not only becomes a separate self or separate object, but also becomes a representation of what is internal. According to Hanna Segal, artists aim at establishing a truth about their inner reality and it is the contact with this truth that accounts for the experience of satisfaction for the artist and aesthetic pleasure for the viewer.

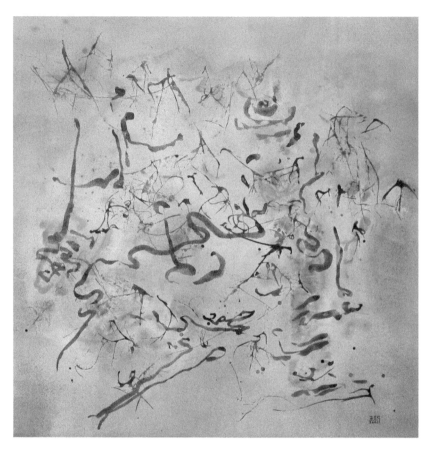

Figure 16.7. Brush painting—Roused to My Living Dream, 2002, acrylic on raw canvas, 48″ × 48″.

The viewer identifies with the work of art as a whole and with the internal world of the artist as represented by the work (Segal, 1991). I have used accidents in my ongoing work as well as dreams and now also my left hand to facilitate a contact with what is internal; with what I don't yet know and may not want to know.

One of the most consciously gratifying aspects of creative work for the artist is to confirm in the painting (the music, the piece of writing, etc.) a correspondence, a congruence with what is internal. The completed artwork, if gratifying, is a successful representation of what is true internally. Whatever personal conflicts the work has come out of, if it is to succeed as art, it objectifies these universal conflicts. Therefore, for some art critics, the artwork should explain itself and not require an exploration of the artist's life to understand it. Furthermore, as Richard Kuhns writes in his book *Psychoanalytic Theory of Art* (1983), "Art is not simply a working through of the artists' problems and conflicts; it is a representation of universal communal conflicts in which everyone is entangled" (p. 103). The artist's relationship to his or her art is a type of object relationship, imbued with reality and fantasy, comparable to that between patient and analyst. In my case, we have to add the role of the model, since I was so greatly touched by her beauty and her movements. If we consider my model as a muse, we can remember Plato, who writes in *Ion* about how the muse inspires and possesses the artist, empowering him or her to create. He writes, "… every poet has some Muse from whom he is suspended, and by whom he is said to be possessed, which is nearly the same thing; for he is taken hold of" (p. 536).

It is clear that during my experience of painting Sara she and I had become one. I was mixed up with my model and the feelings I encountered were primitive in origin. There was most likely a primitive empathy at work based on identification with my model's movements. As I drew, I felt this in both hands, and particularly in my fingers that held the pencils. From an object relation point of view, she was probably standing for my mother, the mother of infancy in all her perceived beauty (Meltzer, 1988). Whereas Plato has said that the artist is possessed by the muse, I would say that it is the artist who possesses the mother in the muse.

The inner process of the artist: the meaning of creativity

In *On Not Being Able to Paint*, Marion Milner made an independent discovery of Winnicott's transitional space, the sense of being separate and together. She worried that her wish to become more "mixed up" (1971, p. 10) with objects while she drew—an instance of regression—might work against her wish to be a separate person in the real world. Instead, she experienced her wish to become one with the object as a need to go back to look for something that would have value in her adult life if it was recovered. She quotes Cezanne, who beautifully describes the way in which both the artist and later the viewer (the art lover) can lose their grip on conscious activity: [A painting is] "an abyss in which the eye is lost, … All these tones circulate in the blood … One is revivified, born into the real world, one finds oneself, one becomes the painting. To love a painting, one must first have drunk deeply of it in long draughts. Lose consciousness. Descend with the painter into the dim tangled roots of things, and rise again from them in colors, be steeped in the light of them" (ibid., pp. 24–25).

While the artist is trying to get to the truth of the object, the model, he can't help but project aspects of himself into it. Figurative artist Lucien Freud's early portraits had all his models depicted with very big eyes. A fellow artist, who studied with him in London many years ago, told me that Lucien himself had amazingly big eyes and that those eyes in his early portraits were, in fact, his own. Another instance of this phenomenon occurred when I saw the figurative drawings an artist friend had been making of Sara, our model (*MY model!*). Sara's slim body seemed much heavier in her drawings. Smiling sheepishly in recognition, my friend said, "I guess I give my models my own body." While even trying to get a true representation of the model, the artist projects aspects of himself or herself into it. A few years ago, Ruth Weisberg, another talented artist friend, did a portrait of me, but the face she painted didn't quite resemble my face. After examining it carefully we decided that the problem was in the shape of my nose, which wasn't right. We scheduled another sitting for her to try to correct it and after trying and trying to change my nose in the portrait she exclaimed in disbelief, "You know what? I gave you my nose! That is *my* nose!"

All of these examples illustrate how the artist projects aspects of the self during the encounter with the model. While at work, the artist is in the intermediate area of experience Winnicott refers to when he writes about transitional phenomena and transitional objects. One may want to be truly objective and depict the truth of the object, but the object's truth and our own truth become indistinguishable. I have to think that something of myself has gone into these recent paintings, even though they are ostensibly about my model's movements. Likewise, if we enter a state of reverie with our patients and, as Bion has suggested, we abstain from memory and desire, we may be unwittingly projecting aspects of ourselves in the patient. But this need not worry us that we (analysts and therapists) will be losing our so-called objectivity. I believe that in our work with patients we experience similar states of fusion and separation to the ones involved during the creative process. Meltzer, for example, was not afraid of getting mixed up with his patients. In his book *Dream Life* (1983) he tells us that in his work with patients' dreams he projects himself into the dream to experience it as if it was his own dream. He can only then use his understanding of this dream, which has become his, and offer the patient an interpretation.

Within the Kleinian tradition, when it comes to creativity, the emphasis has been on the artist's unconscious phantasies towards the internal parents and in particular the destructive ones. According to Segal, the artist has to confront the effect that his or her aggression has had on the loved objects in internal reality (1991).

Creative activity instigates a reawakening of the internal anxieties and conflicts of the depressive position whereby the person experiences anxiety about the attacks on the internal objects, guilt for the damage done, and the wish to repair the object. For Segal, the act of creation is actually a *recreation* (1991). What is felt as a lost past and a lost or dead object (the product of rage and destructiveness) must be adequately mourned in order to be successfully re-created. Guilt and despair generated by these attacks drive artists to reparative activities. The actual process of creation is experienced as infusing dead objects with new life, rejuvenating them, reviving them, and restoring their lost, destroyed and depleted potency.

In my dream of the neglected garden, I must have become aware of my neglect towards my objects and confronted the devastation of my attacks on them. I was relieved to still find some life in all the destruction I had caused. In my wanting to paint Shostakovich's quartets and depict their despair, I was apparently willing to mourn my attacks and repair the damage by bringing new life to them. Perhaps by making clumsy "ugly" lines, my left hand was leaving traces of the earlier attacks on my parents, satisfying to me insofar as they represented my truth about these attacks. However, I experienced relief that these ugly markings on the paper were counteracted by the swift and harmonious lines of my right hand, which would carry out the parallel reparation. For Segal, creative work is a genital, bisexual activity based on adequate identification with a father who gives a mother a child and a mother who bears it. It is an identification with a restored parental couple in the internal world (Segal, 1991). This is perhaps why this series of paintings has been so deeply satisfying.

Bion

As far as what Bion (1962) would have to say regarding this work, we should remember that he saw the mind as extremely limited in its ability to comprehend reality. For him, our mind is unable to discern the underlying pattern of phenomena concealed in the formless infinite. He suggested that perhaps these underlying patterns can only be hinted at in art, music, and poetry. Bion considered the various psychoanalytic theories as surface manifestations of an underlying configuration and directed his attention to the universal restriction of thinking and how it blocks awareness of psychic truth.

Bion was profoundly concerned with what occurred in the consulting room, but he used this only as a window into the whole human phenomenon. He was committed to the view that there is an absolute truth, which can never be known directly. Bion called this absolute truth, the thing in itself, "O". We cannot know O itself, but only emanations from it, which are perceived as phenomena. What we know of O is our transformations of it. This is similar to Plato's ideal of which we only see the shadow on the wall of the cave. "In a slightly different way, transient experiences of becoming O can be felt as being 'allowed' to us by the object; this is the experience of being at one with O, no matter for how short a time and is an experience like incarnation, becoming of the same flesh" (Symington & Symington, 1996, p. 122).

My experience with my model Sara was precisely that, of being allowed to transform her body in movement into lines in my painting. This experiencing of O is, to me, related to the experience of fusion with the model that I have described. For Bion (1970), religious mystics and artists probably approximate most closely to the expression and experience of O. However, for him, the pathway by which such an experience becomes possible is through the close relationship with another, and this includes the relationship of the artist with the work in progress. Psychoanalysis investigates such a relationship and it is what I am attempting to do here by critically examining what went on in the creation of these paintings and in my relationship with my model.

Psychoanalysis and art: Matte Blanco

We can examine now how Ignacio Matte Blanco's ideas about thinking in the conscious mind and feeling in the unconscious mind help us understand what happened with these paintings (1998). According to Matte Blanco, the unconscious, viewed from the outside (the area of thinking), is composed of infinite sets, but we can only think about these infinite sets in terms of discrete elements. We cannot think and have the experience of the infinite at the same time. This seems to explain why I was so bothered initially by the discreet bodies of the model on the paper. Apparently, I wanted to go deeper into a symmetrical way of seeing, not only by fusing with my model, but by also having Sara's body fuse with herself or replicate herself many times over. I wanted to depict infinite movement and a continuous experience of Sara's body. Matte Blanco has explored in detail the dichotomy between thinking and feeling. From his perspective, what I am trying to do with this chapter is the opposite of what I was doing with my model. Whereas, when painting, I wanted to go deeper into feelings and to extract feeling from thinking; by trying to understand what I did and write about it I am extracting thinking from feeling.

Marion Milner and Ehrenzweig

The workings of conscious and unconscious activity in the arts continue to intrigue psychoanalysts. I have already mentioned Marion Milner, psychoanalyst and artist of the British middle school, who wrote sensitively about her own experiences, not only trying to free herself in her paintings but also in the pursuit of ineffable qualities of experience. Her book, *On Not Being Able to Paint* (1950), is a marvellous application of Kleinian theory to her own experience with painting. According to Ehrenzweig (1967), a psychoanalyst and art teacher, the artist experiences a genuine conflict between two kinds of sensibility: conscious intellect and unconscious intuition. His concerns parallel Winnicott's, Bion's, and Matte Blanco's. However, Ehrenzweig is, without a doubt, the most cogent writer about the conflicts of the artist with the work in progress and has written specifically about the problems of the contemporary artist trying to break through established patterns of seeing and doing. He writes about the differentiated surface functions of the conscious mind as opposed to the undifferentiated depth functions of the unconscious mind, another way of contrasting thinking and feeling, but this time applying these notions to the artist's struggle.

> The modern artist attacks his own rational sensibilities in order to make room for spontaneous growth. A vicious circle operates. The attacked surface faculties fight back in self-defense and overnight the spontaneous breakthrough from below is turned into another deliberate, manneristic device. This in turn stifles further

> spontaneity and has to be overthrown by another burst from
> the depth ...This total victory of the depth functions leads to an
> equally drastic defensive action on the part of the surface functions.
> (Ehrenzweig, 1967, p. 66)

Creativity is always linked with the happy moment when all conscious control can be forgotten. My provoked accidents with water and paint and my use of the clumsy left hand are my attempts to bring up elements from the depth of my unconscious mind. To me, when a painting is not satisfying because it looks contrived or too finished, I will use the existing structure as a starting point for a new attempt at a break-through, during which I hope to be surprised by what happens to it.

Ehrenzweig also writes about satisfying work:

> A truly fertile "motif"—in music or drama as well as in the visual
> arts—often has something incomplete and vague about its struc-
> ture. It bears the imprint of the undifferentiated vision which cre-
> ated it in the first place and which guides its use ... A fertile motif,
> through its undifferentiated structure, often refuses immediate aes-
> thetic satisfaction ... The gestalt law of "closure" ruling our surface
> vision will always strive to round it off and polish its structure pre-
> maturely and so may cut off its further development ... Fortunately,
> the creative thinker is at home in those deeper mental levels where
> the gestalt principle no longer holds sway. (1967, pp. 48–49)

Something like a true conversation takes place between the artist and his own work. Often times the medium, by frustrating the artist's purely conscious intentions, allows him to contact more submerged parts of his own personality and draw them for conscious contemplation. Taking back from the work on a conscious level what has been projected into it on an unconscious level is perhaps the most fruitful and painful result of creativity.

Creative regression in art and psychoanalysis

In presenting these ideas one needs to also recall the well-known notion Ernest Kris developed in 1952 of the artist being capable of regression in the service of the ego. For Kris, this process resembles childlike states or characteristics usually associated with madness, but they are under the artist's control. The artist has the capacity to make the transition back from these primitive states to others requiring observation, discipline, and criticism. The question as to what facilitates creative regression is pertinent to both the work of the psychoanalyst and the artist. In my experience as a painter, even though my attention is on my model, I am still discovering what I don't yet know and may not like to know about myself.

Psychoanalytic papers by Galler (1981), Loewald, (1981) and Tuttman (1979) recognise the hybrid quality of regression's potential for both pathological deterioration and reorganisation or integration. Artists have tried to capitalise on the potential for reorganisation of this regression, as they value and cultivate it. They try to go back to the world of the infant, imbued with a dynamic sense of physical and emotional involvement, where knowing and feeling are not yet differentiated and even inanimate objects are experienced as vital and alive. In the *Manifesto of Surrealism*, André Breton writes, "From childhood memories, and from a few others, there emanates a sentiment of being unintegrated, and then later of *having gone astray*, which I hold to be the most fertile that exists" (1969, p. 40). More recently, contemporary artist Willem de Kooning has followed in this tradition of promoting regression. In the book *de Kooning: An American Master*, he is stated as saying, "when I'm falling, I'm doing all right; when I'm slipping, I say, hey, this is interesting! It's when I'm standing upright that bothers me: I'm not doing so good; I'm stiff" (Stevens & Swan, 2004, p. 571). He facilitated his figure drawing by closing his eyes, concentrating inwardly, centring and intensifying his sensation. He also removed the eye from the hand's production so that the two senses would cease to operate in mutual support. As a managed loss of control, the method caused skill and chance to become indistinguishable. De Kooning's strategies succeeded in distancing him from proper proportion and conventional form and led him to a breakthrough in his powerful paintings of women.

In a more recent revision of the concept of regression in the service of the ego, Knafo (2002) wishes to update the term by expanding its use beyond ego psychology. She defines it as "the ability to maintain contact with early body and self states and with early forms of object relationships, as well as with different modes of thinking" (2002, p. 29). For Knafo, "Creative regression is facilitated by the artistic setting and relationship to one's craft, just as therapeutic regression is by the analytic frame and transference relationship" (ibid., p. 46). She clearly sees a parallel between the regression in art and the regression required of a patient in the consulting room.

What about the viewer's regression? Just as the analyst is called upon to regress temporarily along with his or her patients (Loewald, 1981; Blum, 1994), so too the art audience is invited to participate in regressive processes parallel to those the artist experiences during creation as well as the regression depicted in the artwork itself. These regressive forces ultimately belong to a dynamic two-way relationship between artist and viewer. Those who allow themselves to regress as part of their aesthetic response to artworks become not only art observers, but also co-creators.

Bion argued that an analyst has to approach the patient without memory and desire, which is precisely my attitude as I look at the model, allowing her to be the main thing and to guide me while my mind and hands are free from pre-existing ideas. My model is the external stimulus for what my hands will do. I focus on Sara's movements, which in a way means that I de-personify her, responding to the structure of the movement rather than to "Sara moving". This reminds me that the infant seems to respond to the abstract dimension whereby things that move together become an object, irrespective of the nature of the object that moves. Studies by Daniel N. Stern (1985) and others suggest that I may be trying to get back to an amodal perception characteristic of infants to take information received in one sensory modality and translate it into another sensory modality. The information seems to transcend mode or channel and exist in some unknown supra-model form. According to Stern, two separate studies found that infants recognise audiovisual correspondences. They can detect a correspondence between the configuration of a sound as heard and the configuration of the articulatory movements of the mouth that produce the sound. Moreover, researchers have found an innate correspondence between what infants see and what they do; newborn infants, age two days, know that specific configurations of the other face, as only seen, correspond to the same specific configurations in their own face as only felt proprioceptively—that is, through the babies' observations of their own faces. The amount of cross-modal fluency in terms of predesign is extraordinary, but it is not possible yet to know if this is a specific innate social releasing stimulus or a case of cross-modal correspondence.

Brain researchers have studied the basis of synaesthesia in adults. According to them, the brain is cross-activated so that one sensory experience (hearing, for example) triggers a totally different one (seeing). They suspect that cross wires in the brain's angular gyrus (where information from different senses converges) underlies synaesthesia. Not coincidentally, when this structure is damaged the person can't understand metaphors.

A distant parallel can be drawn from the infant's amodal perception and the adult's synaesthesia to the analytic situation. In our work, like with the model's movements, we listen to what the patient is saying and observe what he or she is doing, but we are *extracting* the transference from all those external manifestations. Unlike amodal perception or synaesthesia, which are automatic, we attempt to get at the phantasy about the analyst that underlies the manifest content of the patient's communications. The model's movements and the transference constitute our aim (or focus) and we need to somehow ignore the rest—my model's beautiful hair, her alabaster skin, the light on her body; or in the case of a patient, aspects of the patient's narrative and its details that don't seem that pertinent to the transference.

This brings us back to a consideration of the inherent truth we are all after, analysts and artists alike, and how, just like the transference, this inherent truth has to be "extracted" from what is in front of us. The outward appearance does not by itself constitute the truth. Likewise, Matisse seemed to hold the belief that an appearance does not constitute the truth. He has been quoted as saying that an inherent truth must be "disengaged" from the outward appearance of the object to be represented.

What about the relationship between psychic and external reality? When I moved from this work on paper to the large canvases on the floor, I found myself acting as an intermediary between what was already on the prepared surface and the movements I was extracting from my model. The canvas with the event depicted on it could be seen to represent my pre-existing psychic reality, while the model's movements represent the external reality. My experiencing of the movement is fluid and dynamic, but always linked to what is already on the canvas—my psychic reality. This means that the movement would be represented differently on two different canvases because the existing psychic reality is different. The implication seems to be that we experience external reality only through our psychic reality and that there is a degree of correspondence between the two. As Winnicott, Milner, Ehrenzweig and others have pointed out, there need not be a dichotomy between psychic reality and external reality. They have recognised the value of the intermediate form of experience in play, creativity, and psychoanalytic work. As I said earlier, the paper, the canvas, and the events already there constitute my pre-existing psychic reality, while the model's movement represents my external reality and I find what I am looking for between the two.

How is this played out in infancy? According to Meltzer (1986), the baby's lulling sounds in the mouth are somewhere in the middle between external play and internal thought. This suggests that verbalisation grows out of vocalisation. Both have intense communicative value and are meant for a listener ear.

Developments within psychoanalysis provide a favourable climate for a richer dialogue between art criticism and psychoanalysis. Analysts on the cutting edge of theory already talk in aesthetic terms, both about their ideas and their practice. In the early 1980s, Robert Michels, for example, spoke of psychoanalytic theories as being similar to works of art claiming that "they can be appreciated and evaluated aesthetically as well as scientifically" (1983, p. 129). Spence reversed the direction of the interdisciplinary dialogue by borrowing terms and notions from aesthetics, rather than applying psychoanalysis to issues pertaining to the aesthetic domain. Spence argued that analysts are "functioning as artists and storytellers in the analytic hour" and considered aesthetic finality an essential ingredient of an interpretation that hits the mark (1982, p. 23). He even claimed that a psychoanalytic "interpretation can be seen as a kind of artistic product, and as such, it becomes possible to consider its effect on the patient as a kind of aesthetic experience" (ibid., p. 37). On the same line, Loewald (1981) argued that if one takes an interdisciplinary perspective on symbolism, one might be tempted to define the aim of psychoanalysis as enabling patients to increase their capacity for symbolisation; as restoring their formerly crippled symbolic functioning and as bringing multiple connections back into consciousness and thus enriching their inner life with meaning. As I have expressed in several other chapters, I believe my work as a psychoanalyst is no different than my work as an artist. The pleasure of connecting with a patient is quite similar to that of finding a solution to a work in progress.

It was gratifying to finally be able to do a performance in Los Angeles in November 2013. This was part of an art festival sponsored by the Los Angeles County Psychological Association (LACPA) for psychologists and therapists who engage in artwork (Figures 16.8, 16.9, 16.10, 16.11, and 16.12). They provided me with a beautiful model, a dance instructor from the University of California, Los Angeles, but

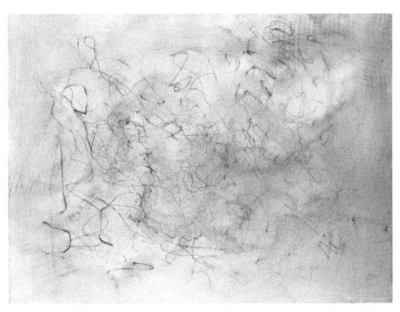

Figure 16.8. From Mirrors of the Mind 2, I, 2013, mixed media on paper, 22″ × 30″.

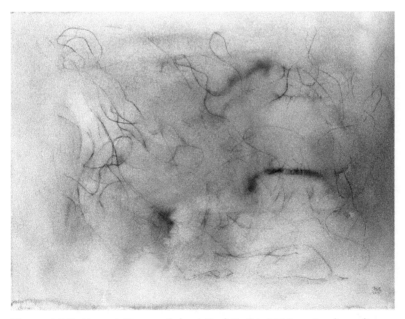

Figure 16.9. From Mirrors of the Mind 2, IV, 2013, mixed media on paper, 22″ × 30″.

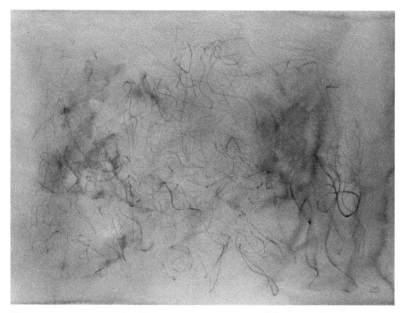

Figure 16.10. From Performance at Mirrors of the Mind 2, III, 2013, mixed media on paper, 22" x 30".

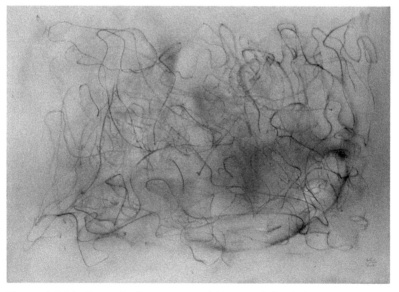

Figure 16.11. From Performance at Mirrors of the Mind 2, II, 2013, mixed media on paper, 22" x 30".

Figure 16.12. Los Angeles performance.

LACPA did not allow nudity in my performance (we were not in Paris!), so I had to buy the dancer a nude-colour body suit. On this occasion, they installed a large screen behind me to project my hands. The film-maker used two cameras to film the performance and my hands at work. In this way the audience could see the model moving slowly, me painting at my table, and the screen where the paintings were evolving. For the music this time, I selected *Beneath the Surface of a Sea of Silence* for string quartet by L.A. composer and dear friend Jane Brockman.

The transition between privately working in my studio to publicly sharing what I do in front of others has been quite rewarding. No longer am I alone in my studio, but in a public setting in front of a live audience. I get anxious when introducing myself, explaining what I will be doing. But once I place myself in front of the table with my materials ready, hear the music, and notice the expectant model across the stage, I lose all anxiety. I become completely caught up in translating on to paper the model's movements responding to the music. There is a special thrill when I feel that the audience is caught up with what I am doing. We are all experiencing the same response to the emergence of beauty through the music, the model, and the coloured lines on the wet paper. It is magic again! The same magic of a psychoanalytic session when an interpretation hits the mark; the patient feels understood in a profound way and the analyst is moved by the depth of feelings experienced in response to the patient.

As with all of my work, I have continued to try to find a place between chaos and organization, walking the fine line between complete break-down and rigidity. Somewhere between chaos and control, I discover a space where development can take place in such a way that I am nei-ther lost in the chaos nor strangled trying to operate within a fixed struc-ture. By engaging in a constant experimentation with my work, I allow a play of destructive and loving forces that permeates all of my paint-ings. I let myself uncover, reveal and open myself up to being surprised or dismayed by what happens in front of me while I paint, by what I bring forth. I would like to think that I work at a point of juncture where instinct and intelligence converge.

Encoded Abstractions

My physicist life partner leaves pieces of paper with his working equations everywhere in my house, evidence of his mind at work. In them, he is both a thinker and a draftsman. These equations, which I so love, inspire me to bring odd graphic elements and my own drawings into dialogue with them. My more recent *Encoded Abstractions* include music score segments, presents from my dear composer friends.

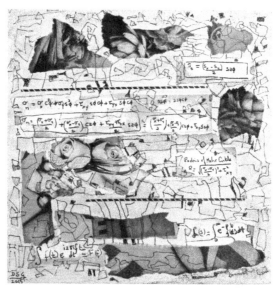

Encoded Abstractions V, 2015, watercolor, ink and collage on paper, 12″ × 12″.

Encoded Abstractions VII, 2015, watercolor, ink
and collage on paper, 12″ × 12″.

Encoded Abstractions XI, 2016, watercolor, ink
and collage on paper, 11″ × 8 1/2″.

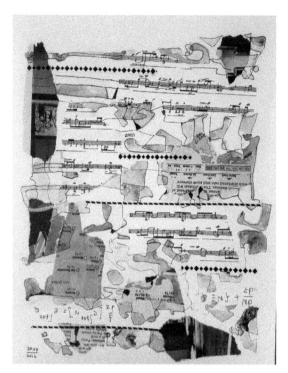

Encoded Abstractions XIII, 2016, watercolor, ink and collage on paper, 11″ × 8 1/2″.

REFERENCES

Aagesen, D., & Rabinow, R. (2012). *Matisse: In Search of True Painting*. New York: Metropolitan Museum of Art.

Akhtar, S. (1992). Tethers, orbits, and invisible fences: Clinical, developmental, socio-cultural, and technical aspects of optimal distance. In: S. Kramer & S. Akhtar (Eds.), *When the Body Speaks: Psychological Meanings in Kinetic Clues* (pp. 21–57). Northvale, NJ: Jason Aronson.

Bion, W. R. (1957). On arrogance. In: *Second Thoughts: Selected Papers on Psychoanalysis* (pp. 86–92). London: Heinemann, 1967.

Bion, W. R. (1959). Attacks on linking. In: *Second Thoughts: Selected Papers on Psychoanalysis* (pp. 93–109). London: Heinemann, 1967.

Bion, W. R. (1962). *Leaning from Experience*. London: Heinemann.

Bion, W. R. (1962). A theory of thinking. *International Journal of Psycho-Analysis*, 43: 306–314.

Bion, W. R. (1963). *Elements of Psycho-analysis*. London: Heinemann.

Bion, W. R. (1967). *Second Thoughts: Selected Papers on Psychoanalysis*. London: Heinemann.

Bion, W. R. (1970). *Attention and Interpretation*. London: Tavistock.

Bion, W. R. (1992). *Cogitations*, F. Bion (Ed.). London: Karnac.

Blatt, S. J., & Blatt, R. B. (1996). Relatedness and self-definition: A dialectical model of personality development. In: G. G. Noam & K. W. Fisher (Eds.), *Development and Vulnerabilities in Close Relationships* (pp. 309–338). Hillsdale, NJ: Erlbaum.

261

Block, J., & Kremen A. M. (2002). Absorption: Construct explication by q-sort assessments of personality. *Journal of Research in Personality, 36*: 252–259.

Blum, H. P. (1994). The conceptual development of regression. *Psychoanalytic Study of the Child, 49*: 60–79.

Brand-Claussen, B., Jádi, I., & Douglas, C. (1996). *Beyond Reason: Art and Psychosis: Work from the Prinzhorn Collection*. London: Hayward Gallery.

Breton, A. (1969). Manifesto of surrealism. In: R. Seaver & H. Lane (Trans.), *Manifestoes of Surrealism* (pp. 1–47). Ann Arbor, MI: University of Michigan Press.

Britton, R. (1998). Before and after the depressive position. In: E. Bott Spillius, *Belief and Imagination* (pp. 69–81). London: Routledge.

Bugental, J. F. T. (1976). *The Search for Existential Identity*. San Francisco: Jossey-Bass.

Carotenuto, A. (1980). *A Secret Symmetry: Sabina Spielrein between Jung and Freud*. A. Pomerans, J. Shepley and K. Winston (Trans.). New York: Pantheon.

Casement, P. (2002). *Learning From Our Mistakes: Beyond Dogma in Psychoanalysis and Psychotherapy*. New York: Guilford Press.

Chasseguet-Smirgel, J. (1985). *Creativity and Perversion*. New York: Norton.

Copland, A. (1952). *Music and Imagination*. Cambridge, MA: Harvard University Press.

Corigliano, J. (1993). Program notes, Los Angeles Philharmonic, Los Angeles.

Eagle, M. (1982). Interests as object relations. In: J. Masling (Ed.), *Empirical Studies in Analytic Theory* (pp. 159–188). Hillsdale, NJ: Erlbaum.

Eagle, M. (2015). Personal communication.

Ehrenzweig, A. (1967). *The Hidden Order of Art*. Berkeley, CA: University of California Press.

Eliot, T. S. (1943). East Coker. In: *Four Quartets*. New York: Harcourt.

Emerson, R. W. (1860/1968). *The Conduct of Life*. New York: AMS Press.

Erikson, E. H. (1950). Growth and crises of the healthy personality. In: *Identity and the Life Cycle*, pp. 50–100. New York: International University Press, 1959.

Fairbairn, W. R. D. (1938). Prolegomena to a psychology of art. *British Journal of Psychology, 28*: 297.

Fairbairn, W. R. D. (1952). *An Object Relations Theory of the Personality*. New York: Basic.

Freud, S. (1905d). *Three Essays on the Theory of Sexuality. S. E., 7*: 125–245. London: Hogarth.

Freud, S. (1910c). *Leonardo da Vinci and a Memory of his Childhood. S. E., 11*: 59–137. London: Hogarth.

Freud, S. (1912b). The dynamics of transference. *S. E., 12*: 97–108. London: Hogarth.

Freud, S. (1914b). The Moses of Michelangelo. *S. E., 13*: 211–238. London: Hogarth.

Freud, S. (1914c). On narcissism: An introduction. *S. E., 14*: 69–102. London: Hogarth.

Freud, S. (1917e). Mourning and melancholia. *S. E., 14*: 237–260. London: Hogarth.

Freud, S. (1920g). *Beyond the Pleasure Principle. S. E., 18*: 7–64. London: Hogarth.

Freud, S. (1930a). *Civilization and its Discontents. S. E., 21*: 64–145. London: Hogarth.

Galler, F. (1981). The two faces of regression. *Psychoanalytic Inquiry, 1*: 133–1516.

Gedo, J. (1983). *Portraits of the Artist: Psychoanalysis of Creativity and Its Vicissitudes.* New York: Guilford Press.

Gedo, M. M. (1980). *Picasso: Art as Autobiography.* Chicago: University of Chicago Press.

Gedo, M. M. (Ed.) (1985). *Psychoanalytic Perspectives on Art.* Vol 1. Hillsdale, NJ: Analytic Press.

Gedo, M. M. (Ed.) (1988). *Psychoanalytic Perspectives on Art.* Vol 3. Hillsdale, NJ: Analytic Press.

Gilot, F. (1997). Responses: A painter responds. In: J. D. Oremland, *The Origins and Psychodynamics of Creativity: A Psychoanalytic Perspective* (pp. 123–131). Madison, WI: International University Press.

Glaser, B. (1966). Questions to Stella and Judd. *ARTnews*, September: p. 58.

Goldwater, R., & Treves, M. (Eds.) (1945). *Artists on Art: From the XIV to the XX Century.* New York: Pantheon.

Green, A. (1985). *On Private Madness.* London: Hogarth.

Greenacre, P. (1957). The childhood of the artist—libidinal phase development and giftedness. *Psychoanalytic Study of the Child, 12*: 47–72.

Grotstein, J. (1981). *Splitting and Projective Identification.* New York: Aronson.

Herbert, R. L. (Ed.) (1964). *Modern Artists on Art: Ten Unabridged Essays.* Englewood Cliffs, NJ: Prentice-Hall.

Hickey, D. (1996). *Between Artists.* Los Angeles, CA: A. R. T. Press.

Hollander, K. (1993). Report from Queens: Art asylum (the Creedmoor Psychiatric Center's living museum). *Art in America, 81*: 50–54.

Janson, H. W. (1973). Chance images. In: Wiener, P. (Ed.), *The Dictionary of the History of Ideas,* Vol. I (pp. 340–353). New York: Charles Scribner & Sons.

Jaques, E. (1970). *Work, Creativity and Social Justice.* London: Heinemann.

Kandinsky, W. (1913). Reminiscences. In: Herbert, R. L. (Ed.), *Modern Artists on Art*. Englewood Cliffs, NJ: Prentice Hall.

Kavaler-Adler, S. (1993). *The Compulsion to Create*. London: Routledge.

Keats, J. (1899). *The Complete Poetical Works and Letters of John Keats*. Cambridge: Houghton Mifflin.

Kernberg, O. (1976). *Object Relations Theory and Clinical Psychoanalysis*. New York: Jason Aronson.

Kerr, J. (1993). *A Most Dangerous Method: The Story of Jung, Freud, and Sabina Spielrein*. New York: Knopf.

Klein, M. (1921). The development of the child. In: *The Writings of Melanie Klein* (pp. 1–53). London: Hogarth, 1975.

Klein, M. (1928). Early stages of the Oedipus conflict. In: *The Writings of Melanie Klein* (pp. 186–198). London: Hogarth, 1976.

Klein, M. (1929/1984). Infantile anxiety situations reflected in a work of art and in the creative impulse. In: *The Writings of Melanie Klein, 1*. London: Hogarth.

Klein, M. (1930). The importance of symbol-formation in the development of the ego. In: *The Writings of Melanie Klein* (pp. 219–232). London: Hogarth, 1975.

Klein, M. (1935). A contribution to the psychogenesis of manic-depressive states. *International Journal of Psycho-Analysis, 21*: 125–153.

Klein, M. (1946/1975). Notes on some schizoid mechanisms. In: *The Writings of Melanie Klein* (pp. 1–24). London: Hogarth.

Klein, M. (1961/1984). Narrative of a child analysis. In: *The Writings of Melanie Klein, 4*. London: Hogarth.

Knafo, D. (2002). Revisiting Ernst Kris's concept of regression in the service of the ego in art. *Psychoanalytic Psychology, 19*(1): 24–49.

Kottler, J., & Blau, D. S. (1989). *The Imperfect Therapist: Learning from Failure in Therapeutic Practice*. San Francisco, CA: Jossey-Bass.

Kris, E. (1952). *Psychoanalytic Explorations in Art*. New York: International Universities Press.

Krukowski, S. (1991). Drama and discontent in the work of Andy Nasisse. *Ceramics: Art and Perception, 5*: 18–22.

Kuhns, R. (1983). *Psychoanalytic Theory of Art: A Philosophy of Art on Developmental Principles*. New York: Columbia University Press.

Langer, S. K. (1953). *Feeling and Form*. New York: Scribner.

Langs, R. (1978). *Technique in Transition*. New York: Jason Aronson.

Letley, E. (2014). *Marion Milner: The Life*. London: Routledge.

Loewald, H. (1981). Regression: Some general considerations. *Psychoanalytic Quarterly, 50*: 22–43.

Lombardi, R. (2006). Being in space-time: On approaching the difference between life and death. Unpublished paper presented at the International Matte-Blanco Conference in Santiago, Chile.

Lord, J. (1965). *A Giacometti Portrait*. New York: Museum of Modern Art/ Doubleday.

Maconie, R. (2013). *Experiencing Stravinsky: A Listener's Companion*. Lanham, MD: Scarecrow Press.

Mailer, N. (2014). *Selected Letters of Norman Mailer*. M. Lennon (Ed.). New York: Random House.

Matte Blanco, I. (1998). *The Unconscious as Infinite Sets: An Essay in Bi-Logic*. London: Karnac.

Martin, A. (1992/2005). *Writings/Schriften*. D. Schwarz (Ed.). Ostfildern, Germany: Hatje Cantz.

Marton, J. (2002). *Journey of Hope: Artwork from the Living Museum: A Space for Art and Healing*. New York: Bristol-Meyers Squibb.

Mawson, C. (2015). On the clinical relevance of negative capability. Presented at the Regional Bion Conference in Los Angeles, April 2015.

Meltzer, D. (1978). *The Kleinian Development*, 3 Vols. Perthshire: Clunie Press.

Meltzer, D. (1983). *Dream Life*. Perthshire: Clunie Press.

Meltzer, D. (1986). *Studies in Extended Metapsychology: Clinical Applications of Bion's Ideas*. Perthshire: Clunie Press.

Meltzer, D., & Williams, M. H. (1988). *The Apprehension of Beauty: The Role of Aesthetic Conflict in Development, Art and Violence*. Perthshire: Clunie Press.

Meltzer, D. (1998). Personal communication.

Michels, R. (1983). The scientific and clinical functions of psychoanalytic theory. In: A. Goldberg (Ed.), *The Future of Psychoanalysis: Essays in Honor of Heinz Kohut* (pp. 125–135). New York: International Universities Press.

Milner, M. (1950/1971). *On Not Being Able to Paint*. London: Heinemann.

Milner, M. (1952). Aspects of symbolism in comprehension of the not-self. *International Journal of Psychoanalysis, 33*: 181–195.

Milner, M. (1987). *Eternity Sunrise: A Way of Keeping a Diary*. London: Virago.

Neubauer, P. B., Abrams, S., & Dowling, A. S. (Eds.) (1994). *The Psychoanalytic Study of the Child*, vol. 49 (pp. 60–76). New Haven, CT: Yale University Press.

Nunberg, H., & Federn, E. (Eds.) (1962). *Minutes of the Vienna Psychoanalytic Society*. Volume 2 (p. 335). New York: International Universities Press.

Oremland, J. (1981). Talent and creativity. Paper presentation given at LAISPS, 29 March, 1981.

Oremland, J. (1984). Empathy and its relation to the appreciation of art. In: J. D. Lichtenberg, M. Bornstein, & D. Silver (Eds.), *Empathy I (Psychology Revivals)* (pp. 239–265). London: Routledge.

Oremland, J. (1997). *The Origins and Psychodynamics of Creativity: A Psychoanalytic Perspective*. Madison, WI: International University Press.

Oremland, J. (2014). Conversation in Sausalito.

O'Shaughnessy, E. (1999). Relating to the superego. *International Journal of Psychoanalysis, 80*: 861.

Pater, W. (1893/1980). The school of Giorgione. In: D. Hill (Ed.), *The Renaissance: Studies in Art and Poetry* (p. 106). Berkeley, CA: University of California Press.

Plato. (380 B.C.E./1953). *Ion*. In: B. Jowett (Trans.), *The Dialogues of Plato, I*. Oxford: Clarendon.

Poland, W. S. (1975). Tact as a psychoanalytic function. *International Journal of Psycho-Analysis, 56*: 155.

Prinzhorn, H. (1922). *Artistry of the Mentally Ill: A Contribution to the Psychology and Psychopathology of Configuration*, von Brockdorff, E. (Trans.). Vienna: Springer [reprinted 1972].

Racker, H. (1957). The meanings and uses of counter transference. *Psychoanalytic Quarterly, 26*: 303–357.

Reiss, R. (1998). Desy Safán-Gerard. Unpublished essay for art catalogue.

Rickman, J. (1940). The nature of ugliness and the creative impulse. *International Journal of Psycho-Analysis, 21*: 294–313.

Rilke, R. M. (1969). *Letters of Rainer Maria Rilke 1910–1926*, J. B. Green & M. D. Herter (Trans.). New York: Norton.

Rilke, R. M. (1981). *An Unofficial Rilke*, M. Hamburger (Ed. & Trans.). London: Anvil Poetry.

Rilke, R. M. (1987). *The Selected Poetry of Rainer Maria Rilke*, S. Mitchel (Ed. & Trans.). London: Pan Books.

Rosenfeld, H. (1987). *Impasse and Interpretation*. London: Tavistock.

Rivière, J. (1958/1987). A character trait of Freud's. In: J. D. Sutherland (Ed.), *Psycho-Analysis and Contemporary Thought*. London: Hogarth.

Rose, G. (1980). *The Power of Form: A Psychoanalytic Approach to Aesthetic Form*. New York: International Universities Press.

Rosenfeld, H. A. (1965). *Psychotic States: A Psych-Analytical Approach*. New York: International Universities Press.

Safán-Gerard, D. (1978). Creativity as communication. *Psychology Today, 4*: 46–53.

Safán-Gerard, D. (1978). How to unblock II. *Psychology Today*, January, 78–86.

Safán-Gerard, D. (1978). On *not knowing*. Paper presented at the 27th Annual Meeting of the American Academy of Psychoanalysis, New York.

Safán-Gerard, D. (1982). The role of the accident in the creative process. Creativity and Madness Conference. Maui, Hawaii.

Safán-Gerard, D. (1983). The evolution of a painting. 27th Annual Meeting of the American Academy of Psychoanalysis. New York.

Safán-Gerard, D. (1984). Chaos et contrôle dans le processus créateur. *Psychoanalyse à l' Université*, 9(35): 483–490.

Safán-Gerard, D. (1985). Chaos and control in the creative process. *Journal of the American Academy of Psychoanalysis*, 13: 129–138.

Safán-Gerard, D. (1990). Creativity at risk in the patient/analyst dialogue. Southern California Chapter of Division 39, Los Angeles, CA.

Safán-Gerard, D. (1991). From A to B and back to A: Emotional development in groups. *Group*, 15(4): 213–218.

Safán-Gerard, D. (1996). A Kleinian approach to group psychotherapy. *International Journal of Group Psychotherapy*, 46(2): 177–191.

Safán-Gerard, D. (1999). Destructiveness and reparation in the creative process: A retrospective. International Psychoanalytical Association (IPA) 41st Congress. Santiago, Chile.

Safán-Gerard, D. (2002). On not knowing: Discerning the mental and emotional requirements of creative work. Bion International Conference. Los Angeles, CA.

Sandler, P. C. (2011). *A Clinical Application of Bion's Concepts Volume 2: Analytical Function and the Function of the Analyst*. London: Karnac.

Searles, H. (1975). The patient as therapist to his analyst. In: R. Langs (Ed.), *Classics in Psychoanalytic Technique* (pp. 103–138). New York: Jason Aronson.

Segal, H. (1952). A psycho-analytical approach to aesthetics. *International Journal of Psychoanalysis*, 33: 196–207.

Segal, H. (1957). Notes on symbol formation. In: *The Work of Hanna Segal* (pp. 349–367). New York: Jason Aronson, 1981.

Segal, H. (1981). The function of dreams. In: *The Work of Hanna Segal* (pp. 89–97). New York: Jason Aronson.

Segal, H. (1981). *The Work of Hanna Segal: A Kleinian Approach to Clinical Practice*. New York: Aronson.

Segal, H. (1991). *Dream, Phantasy and Art*. London: Tavistock/Routledge.

Segal, H. (1997). Some implications of Melanie Klein's work: Emergence from narcissism. In: J. Steiner (Ed.), *Psychoanalysis, Literature and War* (pp. 75–85). London: Routledge.

Segal, H. (1998). Personal communication.

Sharpe, E. (1930). Certain aspects of sublimation and delusion. *International Review of Psycho-Analysis*, 11: 12–23.

Shimada, S. (1961). Concerning the I-p'in style of painting. In: *Oriental Art*, 7, pp. 3–11.

Sobel, E. F. (1982). A psychoanalytic approach to understanding form in abstract expressionist and minimalist painting. *International Review of Psycho-Analysis*, 9: 167–177.

Spence, D. P. (1982). *Narrative Truth and Historical Truth: Meaning and Interpretation in Psychoanalysis.* New York: W. W. Norton.

Spielrein, S. (1912/1994). Destruction as the cause of coming into being. K. McCormick (Trans.), *Journal of Analytical Psychology, 39*: 155–186.

Spillius, E. B. (1983). Some developments from the work of Melanie Klein. *International Journal of Psychoanalysis, 64*: 321–332.

Spitz, E. H. (1985). *Art and Psyche.* New Haven, CT: Yale University Press.

Steiner, J. (1990). The retreat from truth to omnipotence in Sophocles' Oedipus at Colonus. *International Journal of Psychoanalysis, 17*: 227–237.

Steiner, J. (1993). *Psychic Retreats.* London: Routledge.

Stern, D. N. (1985). *The Interpersonal World of the Infant: A View from Psychoanalysis and Developmental Psychology.* New York: Basic.

Stevens, M., & Swan, A. (2004). *de Kooning: An American Master.* New York: Alfred A. Knopf.

Stokes, A. (1965). *The Invitation in Art.* New York: Chilmark.

Stokes, A. (1972). *The Image in Form: Selected Writings of Adrian Stokes.* R. Wolheim (Ed.). Baltimore, MD: Penguin.

Storr, A. (1991). *The Dynamics of Creation.* London: Penguin.

Sylvester, D. (1975/1980). *Interviews with Francis Bacon: 1962–1979.* London: Thames and Hudson.

Symington, N. (2000). Personal communication.

Symington, N., & Symington, J. (1996). *The Clinical Thinking of Wilfred Bion.* London: Routledge.

Taylor, D. (2006). The role of psychoanalytic psychotherapy in the treatment of chronic and refractory depression. Paper presented at the Psychoanalytic Center of California, Santa Monica, CA.

Tellegen, A. (1992). Note on the structure and meaning of the MPQ absorption scale. Unpublished manuscript, University of Minnesota.

Thorner, H. (1991). Notes on the desire for knowledge. *International Journal of Psychoanalysis, 62*: 73–80.

Tuchman, M., & Eliel, C. (Eds.) (1992). *Parallel Visions: Modern Artists and Outsider Art.* Los Angeles, CA: Los Angeles County Museum of Art.

Tuttman, S. (1979). Regression: Is it necessary or desirable? *Journal of the American Academy of Psychoanalysis, 7*: 221–230.

Weiss, J. (2010). Matisse: Radical invention, 1913–1917. *ArtForum, 48*: 201–211.

Wilhelm, R., & Jung, C. G. (1931/1962). *The Secret of the Golden Flower: A Chinese Book of Life*, C. F. Baynes (Trans.). Chicago, IL: Mariner.

Winnicott, D. W. (1965). *The Maturational Processes and the Facilitating Environment.* New York: International Universities Press.

Winnicott, D. W. (1971). *Playing & Reality*. London: Tavistock.

Winnicott, D. W. (1975). Transitional objects and transitional phenomena. In: *Through Pediatrics to Psycho-Analysis* (pp. 229–242). London: Hogarth.

Winnicott, D. W. (1989). *Psycho-Analytic Explorations*. London: Karnac.

Wordsworth, W. (1995). *Wordsworth: Poems*. New York: Knopf.

INDEX

www.ingramcontent.com/pod-product-compliance
Ingram Content Group UK Ltd.
Pitfield, Milton Keynes, MK11 3LW, UK
UKHW020347010325
455677UK00020B/330